D1098028

MURDERERS' ENGLAND

Robert Christiansen Jr.
TRUE CRIME

By the same author

HORROR IN THE CINEMA
RELIGION IN THE CINEMA
THE CINEMA OF ROMAN POLANSKI
THE MAKING OF FEATURE FILMS—A GUIDE
TO ENCOURAGE THE ART OF THE FILM
CINEMA IN BRITAIN
THE 100 BEST PLAYS FOR AMATEURS
THE WAR FILM—A STUDY
MURDERERS' LONDON

Murderers' England

Ivan Butler

ROBERT HALE · LONDON

ISBN 0 7091 4054 1

Robert Hale & Company
63 Old Brompton Road
London SW7

Printed in Great Britain by
Clarke, Doble & Brendon Ltd
Plymouth

CONTENTS

ILLUSTRATIONS

PICTURE CREDITS

The above pictures are reproduced by permission of the following: Mrs Gerald Richardson and the *West Lancashire Evening Gazette* (number 9); Mr Francis Beuttler (18, 19, 24, 26, 32); the Press Association (12, 34); *Radio Times* Hulton Picture Library (1, 2, 6, 7, 21, 23, 25, 27, 28, 29, 31); Syndication International (3, 4, 5, 8, 10, 11, 13, 14, 15, 16, 17, 22, 30, 33).

FIGURES IN THE TEXT

ACKNOWLEDGEMENTS

In the course of preparing this book I have received unstinting and courteous help from the reference and local history departments of the following libraries, particularly in providing copies of contemporary accounts and maps of the earlier crimes: Bath Public Library, Birmingham Public Libraries, Carlisle Public Libraries, Cheshire County Libraries, Derbyshire County Library, Dorset County Library, East Sussex County Library, Essex County Library, Godalming Public Library, Harrogate Public Library, Hereford County Libraries, Hertfordshire County Library, Hillingdon Public Libraries, Kent County Library, Leeds City Libraries, Leicestershire County Library, Liverpool City Libraries, Norfolk County Library, Oxfordshire County Library, Peterborough Central Library, Poole Public Libraries, Sheffield City Library, Staffordshire County Library, Surrey County Library, West Riding County Library, Wiltshire County Library. My thanks also to the Derby County Constabulary, the Hertfordshire Constabulary and the Suffolk Constabulary for details of specific cases; to the *News of the World* in respect of the Nottingham murderer Herbert Leonard Mills; and to the Buckinghamshire and Surrey Record Offices.

I am indebted to Mr David T. Chapman of Byfleet for information regarding the Blue Anchor inn; to Mr W. Parker of Monmouth Street, Bath, in connection with the tragic case of William Bartlett; to Mr Geoffrey F. Hadrill of Denham concerning the massacre at Marshall's cottage; to Mr. Patrick Strong of Eton for details about Salt Hill; to Miss Grace Reynolds for information about bygone Nottingham; and to Mr S. C. Chinery and Mr S. V. Yorke for help in trying to trace the elusive Kingswood 'Rectory' and Reigate 'Cricketers' Arms'.

I am most grateful to the owners for permission to photograph a number of houses that are included in the illustrations.

Lastly my thanks to my wife and son, who spent much time travelling with me to various sites, taking photographs, making invaluable comments, and resigning themselves without undue impatience to driving round and round in search of some particularly elusive scene of the crime.

I.B.

INTRODUCTION

The journeys undertaken in the following pages to over 200 murder cases pass through every county in England with the exception of Westmorland and Rutland. Regretfully this does not necessarily mean that the inhabitants of those two delightful districts are more law-abiding or less inclined to settle their differences by extreme action than their neighbours: it may merely indicate that they are more adept at covering their traces—at committing the 'perfect murder' which is never recognized as such.

With limitations of space to be considered, famous crimes which, though perhaps long and complicated, have been written about in detail elsewhere—such as the Moors Murders, Constance Kent, the A6 Murder—are discussed only briefly here, with suggestions given for further reading. If Hertfordshire and Middlesex appear to be less fully represented in proportion to other counties, this is because several of the noted cases that occurred within their boundaries have been recounted in my book *Murderers' London*.

The cases selected (unhappily only a tiny proportion of those available) range from the personal drama of Stella Maris in Whitstable or the pathetic "Chocolate Box" in Bath, to the organized robbery that went wrong: from the grim comedy of the farm labourer who climbed a wall with a full-length sword thrust down his trousers and flung a parsimonious parson into his own mash-tub, to the bucolic tragedy of two lovers whose quarrel after milking the cows led to violence and death.

Though many recent murders are included, a fair proportion of those discussed took place from 50 to 150 years ago. There is without doubt an aura about 'old murders' such as surrounds old wars. Those who committed them, those who directly or indirectly suffered through them, are alike gone. The passion and the pain are stilled. Their stories can be related without fear of reawakening past unhappiness. As in the case of battles (in reading about which, incidently, some people who regard the study of murder as morbid, happily indulge), Wordsworth might have written, of

> . . . old, unhappy, far-off things:
> and murders long ago.

AUTHOR'S NOTE

This book recalls a number of murder cases in which a charge of murder was brought against someone. In a few of these the accused was acquitted or convicted of a lesser crime, or had the sentence reduced on the ground of diminished responsibility.

To Veronica and
Oliver Gilbert

1

THEY DIED OF A FEVER
The North East: Northumberland, Durham, Yorkshire

There must have been more than a few occasions when some poor, obscure private soldier in the Roman Legions—lonely and shivering as he peered across the damp misty moorland from his outpost on the 73-mile Wall, smarting from some unjust reprimand from his superior officer, dreaming frustratedly of his girl miles away under the Mediterranean sunshine, embroiled in some quarrel over the coarse local doxies—gave vent to his overcharged feelings and stained the ancient Northumberland soil with the blood of his companions. Such bygone crimes, however, have long faded from account, and for our first case we move forward in time nearly eighteen hundred years, and northward from Hadrian's Wall about 14 miles towards Morpeth. As with our London survey,* we start our travels, appropriately, with a railway murder—the sixth to be recorded.

John Nisbet was a book-keeper and cashier employed by the Stobswood Colliery Company—a small, plump man, 44 years of age. He lived at 180 Heaton Road, Newcastle-upon-Tyne, and every Friday would leave by the 10.27 train from that city to travel north some 35 miles to Widdrington with money for the wages of the men who worked at the pits. On 18th March 1910 he set off with about £370 in a black leather bag which he locked, putting the key in his pocket. The money was all in coin—gold, silver and copper—and thus easily disposable. At Newcastle station he was seen with an acquaintance, a man named John Alexander Dickman, who lived at 1 Lily Avenue, Jesmond, and who was known to be in financial difficulties, caused mainly by

* *Murderers' London* (Robert Hale, 1973).

losses incurred at the races. From the combined statements of two witnesses, one of whom knew Dickman but not Nisbet, the other Nisbet but not Dickman, it seems certain that both men got into the same compartment at the front of the train. The journey was a slow one, lasting well over an hour. Widdrington was four stations short of Alnmouth, the terminus, and there were nearly a dozen in between. Those that concern us are Heaton, a suburb of Newcastle and the first stop; Stannington, six stations further on; and Morpeth, a six-minute ride from Stannington.

At Heaton, according to her pleasant wifely custom, Mrs Nisbet waited on the platform for a brief word with her husband. She was surprised to find him seated near the engine as he generally preferred the rear of the train; the run along the platform must have irritatingly curtailed what was to be their last conversation in this world. Mrs Nisbet noticed another man in the compartment, sitting in a corner with his coat collar turned up as if to hide his face. At Stannington station two travellers who knew Nisbet alighted, and both noticed him as they left the platform: the other man was still in the compartment. At Morpeth, the next stop, Dickman got out and gave the collector (who did not know him) a ticket to Stannington plus 2½d—in those happier days the modest excess fare for the six miles on. At the same station a platelayer noticed that the compartment was, apparently, empty. The train then went on past Widdrington to Alnwick, where a porter checking the carriages found Mr Nisbet. He had been shot five times (with two different revolvers), and his body stuffed under the seat. Dickman, reported to have been with the dead man, was brought in for questioning, and eventually arrested.

His story was a moderately convincing one. Two roads lead south from Morpeth. One, to the west of the railway (now the A1), goes through Catchburn, past a track to Dovecot House, on to Stannington. Dickman stated that he meant to get out at Stannington, went on to Morpeth by mistake, then walked back along this westerly road towards Dovecot House in order to look over some sinking operations at the colliery near by—he had at one time worked as secretary to a colliery syndicate. On the way there he was suddenly, inexplicably, and most inconveniently taken ill with diarrhoea. He rested a while by the side of the road then returned to Morpeth, failing to keep his appointment at the colliery, and took a train home. The man with whom he said he had made this appointment, however, denied all knowledge of it. No money was found on Dickman, nor was any weapon—though he was known to have owned a revolver.

Later the police found Nisbet's leather bag, slit open and

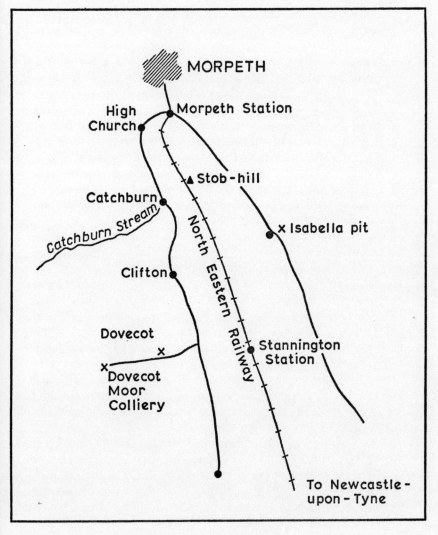

The Murder of John Nisbet

emptied, down a disused shaft at the Isabella Pit. This old shaft was situated along the *easterly* road from Morpeth (now the A192), about the same distance, in fact, as Dovecot House on the westerly road. It was obvious that Dickman could have taken the easterly road instead, and still have been seen (as he was) catching his train home from Morpeth. Though some doubts were expressed as to the conclusiveness of the circumstantial evidence, Dickman was convicted, and executed at Newcastle-upon-Tyne on 10th August 1910. He never admitted his guilt.

Otterburn, about 30 miles north-west of Newcastle (on the A696), is probably best known as the site of the border battle of Chevy Chase in 1388 at which James, second Earl of Douglas and Mar, lost his life in a struggle that ended in a victory for the Scots and the capture of Harry Hotspur. Close at hand, at Steng Cross by Elsdon, stands Winter's Stob, an isolated gibbet marking the spot where, in 1791, was hung in chains the body of one Willie Winter, executed at Newcastle for the murder of an old woman whose name is lost to posterity. A wooden head is attached to the gruesome relic: it was replaced from time to time as it rotted away.

The neighbourhood of Otterburn was also the scene of an unsolved tragedy much nearer our time. Late on 6th January 1931 a bus was returning to the garage of the proprietor, Mr Foster, when the driver saw a car smouldering some yards from the road at a desolate moorland spot known as Wolf's Neck. Lying by the car was the garage proprietor's daughter, 27-year-old Evelyn Foster, terribly burned (all the lower part of her clothing had been completely destroyed) and badly frost-bitten. She was still alive and moaning for water, but died very shortly afterwards. She managed, however, to tell of a man who had stopped her at Elishaw Bridge, two miles from Otterburn, and asked her for a lift to Ponteland where he could pick up a bus for Newcastle. On reaching Belsay Hall, about seventeen miles on the way and six from Ponteland, he suddenly ordered her to return to Otterburn. When she asked him why, he hit her in the face, rendering her unconscious, and drove the car back as far as Wolf's Neck, then turned onto the moor. He set fire to the car while Miss Foster was still inside it, and drove away, after a whispered consultation, with a man in another car that had arrived at that moment. Her story, gasped out in great agony, was vague and confused, and not altogether borne out by the facts. No trace of bruising, for instance, was found on her face. Nor were there any signs of the attempted sexual assault which, in answer to questions, she had seemed to suggest. Her handbag had not been rifled, and there seemed no comprehensible motive for the crime. At the inquest the possibility was raised that she might herself have set fire to the car for some unknown reason, and been caught by the flames while doing so, but this appeared equally improbable. The verdict was murder by some person or persons unknown, and the secret of her agonizing death has never been discovered.

Nearly one hundred years previously, in Newcastle itself, Mr Millie, assistant head clerk of the Newcastle Savings Bank, was found dead in an office on the premises. His skull was fractured, and his pockets were filled with lumps of coal. The date was 7th November 1839. The crime was discovered after an alarm had been raised that the building was on fire. In an adjoining room Mr Bolam, the manager, was lying unconscious with wounds in his throat. On recovering he said that a man with a black face had attacked them both, murdered the clerk, attempted to murder Bolam himself, then escaped with all the money in the till. He added that he had already received a number of anonymous threatening letters which he had, unfortunately, burnt. It was noticed, however, that the blood from the wounds in his throat (which were superficial) had run down his coat in such a way as to suggest that he had made them himself while sitting on the floor, and then lain down. Sums of money, together with some account books, were found in his house and he was sent for trial, convicted of manslaughter, and sentenced to transportation for life. It was considered possible that, despite the ominous evidence, the immediate cause of Millie's death might have been a blow struck during a sudden quarrel. Bolam's remaining years being veiled in darkness, we cannot tell whether or not he had cause to consider himself lucky on receiving the lesser sentence.

On Saturday 25th May 1968, 4-year-old Martin Brown, of St Margaret's Road, Newcastle-upon-Tyne, was found lying dead from asphyxia on the first floor of a derelict house in the same street, number 85. On 31st July, the body of Brian Howe, aged 3½, was discovered on some waste ground off Scotswood Road,

which runs more or less parallel to St Margaret's Road, across
a railway line. He had been strangled, and light cuts or scratches
had been made across his stomach. Their killer was a girl 11 years
of age, Mary—or May—Bell, who had already been in trouble
for attacks on children. At her trial, which took place in the
Moothall, Newcastle, in December 1968, she showed a skill in
lying, elaborating, and creating deliberate confusion, which
many an accused adult might have envied, together with a total
lack of feeling or remorse. She even tried to lay the blame on
a totally innocent boy of eight, for whom, fortunately, an
unbreakable alibi was proved. One of her remarks, when asked
if she realized how a strangled person might suffer before dying,
was a macabre echo of the words spoken by George Joseph Smith
after the death of one of his 'brides'—"Why, if you are dead,
you're dead."* She was found guilty of "manslaughter because
of diminished responsibility" on both counts, and sentenced to
detention for life. A girl who was charged with her, and had
been present at any rate part of the time in the case of Brian
Howe, was acquitted: though some two years older than Mary
Bell, she had obviously been very much under her influence. In
June 1970 Mary Bell accused a 35-year-old master at her place
of detention in Newton-Le-Willows, Lancashire, of indecent
assault. The charge was found to be totally false. Though Mary
Bell's life appeared to have been a somewhat erratic one, it was
certainly no more so than that of many other children—and just
as certainly she never lacked affection from many people around
her. The dreadful events of 1968 in Newcastle must surely raise
uncomfortable and fundamental questions concerning modern
and 'enlightened' assumptions as to the nature and cause of
'wickedness'.

In March 1875 Elizabeth Pearson, 28, killed her uncle-by-
marriage by dosing him with a mixture of strychnine, prussian
blue and flour known as "Battle's Vermin Killer". The 75-year-
old widower, who lived at Gainford, on the road between Dar-
lington and Barnard Castle (now the A67), suffered from severe
lung trouble, and Elizabeth had come with her husband and
baby to look after him. The old man later arranged to go to his

---

* After Alice Burnham's death in Blackpool, Smith ordered the cheapest
coffin he could get. When his landlord, Mr Crossley, said he would not
bury his wife like that, even if he had not a penny in the world, Smith
replied: "When they are dead they are done with."

son at Barnard Castle, but died—suddenly—before he could make the move. It was clear that Elizabeth was after what she could get (when the son arrived after the death he found the place stripped of everything except the bed on which the body lay), and enquiries inevitably followed. The purchase of "Battle's Vermin Killer" was clumsy and secretive, involving the collaboration of her own mother-in-law, who afterwards appeared as a witness for the prosecution. Elizabeth Pearson was executed at Durham in August of the same year. It is difficult to see how she expected to get away with it.

Compared to Mary Ann Cotton, County Durham's most prolific poisoner, Elizabeth Pearson seems a modest practitioner. Mary Ann was born in 1832, of strict Wesleyan parents, in East Rainton, one of a series of Rainton villages ('the home of Regna's people'), a few miles north of Durham. After working for a short while as a dressmaker she married her first husband, a miner named William Mowbray, in Newcastle-upon-Tyne. The couple went south to Cornwall, where Mowbray worked as a navvy. Five children were born to them, of whom four—all boys —died suddenly of "gastric fever". The youngest child, a girl, returned with her parents to Durham, but very shortly she died too—of "gastric fever". They then went to live at Heaton, a district of Sunderland close to the sea, where Mowbray got a job as a ship's stoker. There a sixth child was born, dying one year later (of "gastric fever"). Four months later Mowbray himself died, while enjoying a brief holiday following an accident to his foot. He had recently insured his life. The cause of his decease broke the pattern a little, being given as "diarrhoea". After the death of one more baby ("gastric fever"), Mary Ann went to Seaham Harbour, forged a reference as a nurse, and married one of her patients, George Ward. She had previously had a little nursing experience looking after her mother, who had died—poor woman—under her daughter's care. George Ward followed her shortly afterwards—"gastric fever". Bravely struggling on, Mary Ann then married a widower, James Robinson, who worked in a shipyard. He already had five children and was advertising for a housekeeper. Alas, "gastric fever" struck again, and all five young ones speedily passed on. So did all Robinson's savings —for Mary Ann disappeared from the district, taking them with her. She moved, in fact, a little south, obtaining a post (with a forged reference in the name of Mowbray) as housekeeper to

a doctor in Spennymoor. Here, however, she failed to give satisfaction and soon received her notice. The next move was over
the county border to Walbottle, on Hadrian's Vallum. Here,
while staying with a friend, she met the man under whose name
she was to achieve the recognition her actions undoubtedly deserved. Frederick Cotton asked her to stay with his ailing wife
and her sister—and also his children, the number of whom is
uncertain. Mrs Cotton soon died (astonishingly, it was from
tuberculosis) and was apparently soon followed by her sister,
cause unknown. Frederick and Mary Ann were 'married' (Robinson, of course, was still alive) at St Andrew's, Newcastle, and
three months later she bore his child. The family, now consisting of Frederick, Mary Ann and three children, moved south
again to West Auckland, near Bishop Auckland. The chief
reason for this uprooting was Mary Ann's remarkable unpopularity with her neighbours, whose pigs kept dying in suspicious
circumstances—Mary Ann trying things out? Frederick did not
long survive the move. Neither did one of Mary Ann's stepsons,
nor her own baby. "Gastric fever" every time. A lodger who
had willed all his belongings to Mary Ann, and probably became
her lover, followed along the same well-beaten path. All this most
unfortunate woman now had left was one stepson, Charles
Edward Cotton, 7 or 8 years of age. Understandably lonely,
Mary Ann became attached to a customs official named Mann,
and it now appeared that Charles Edward, a poor little specimen
of humanity, weak-brained and scrofulous, was an obstacle to her
progress. Most incautiously (for her) she remarked that he was
likely soon to join his brother. When he did so, pat, suspicions
were (somewhat belatedly, one might think) aroused. Mary Ann
was arrested, the last four of her victims were exhumed, and
arsenic was discovered inside them. At her trial, which was for
the murder of Charles Edward, a defence was put forward that
the child might have contracted arsenical poisoning by inhaling
it from some green wallpaper in his bedroom. Mary Ann was
executed at Durham in March 1873, at the age of 41. The nearest
she got to a confession was to say that she *might* have administered the poison, but only by a most unfortunate mistake.

Pickering is a small market town on the fringe of the North
Yorkshire moors (on the A170), noted for the remains of a
moated Norman castle wherein for a time the unhappy King
Richard II was confined. The building also suffered damage dur-

ing the Civil War. After these far-off events nothing very much seems to have disturbed the tranquillity of the little place until, on 5th November 1949, an old man with the same name as the town itself, Thomas Pickering, was found lying on the floor of his cottage, 10 Willowgate, with his head severely beaten. Some time beforehand a young Irish labourer, Anthony O'Rourke, had been lodging in the old man's house with his wife and several children, before moving to an even humbler dwelling in Castlegate. At midday on the 5th he was seen to enter the house in Willowgate, and, an hour later, to leave it. The old man was discovered by neighbours and rushed to hospital. For a while it seemed that he might survive, but his condition suddenly worsened, and on 15th December he died. Before this, however, he was able vaguely to recollect O'Rourke's calling to see him. "We talked together and then something went wrong and something went bang in my head", he said.

O'Rourke disappeared immediately after the crime, going to Scarborough and Stockton-on-Tees, but he returned four days later and was already under arrest at the time of Pickering's death. While in Scarborough he had cashed Pickering's old-age-pensioner's tobacco coupon, a fact that did not help his defence. His story was that there had been a quarrel and the old man had insulted Florrie, O'Rourke's mistress. In righteous indignation—and in self-defence—O'Rourke had then struck him with unintentional force. Ably defended by John Parris, he was acquitted of both murder and manslaughter.

In an interval between leaving old Pickering's house and settling in Castlegate, O'Rourke had lodged briefly with Miss Rose Harper, a woman of 55, at 129 Westgate. At 9 p.m. on 4th June 1951 neighbours found the house apparently empty and in a state of complete chaos. Miss Harper was nowhere to be seen at first, but early the following morning O'Rourke went to the police and confessed to having killed her. A further search resulted in the discovery of her body under a table and covered with a rug. She had been strangled with a black stocking. Taken to Armley prison, O'Rourke asked to be defended by the same counsel who had represented him previously. Mr Parris, who had had a difficult enough task the first time, told him: "This is getting somewhat monotonous." The defence this time was that he went to see Miss Harper who suggested that they should have intercourse. When he declined, she followed old Pickering's example by insulting Florrie, then attacked him where no lady should. During the resulting struggle, "in great pain", he killed her. He was found guilty of manslaughter, and sentenced to ten years' imprisonment. O'Rourke, described by Mr Parris as a meek-looking little man with a quiet manner, already had convictions for bigamy, theft and cruelty to children. After earning full remission in prison (during which time his wife divorced him) he married Florrie immediately on release. As Parris emphasizes in his detailed account*, the tragedies were played out in circumstances of desperate poverty.

It is difficult to see why Eugene Aram should have had such appeal to the imagination of poets, playwrights and novelists (undoubtedly he owes his lasting fame to Thomas Hood's famous "Dream"), for in truth he was a cold, cruel, callous murderer and liar, notable only for the assiduity—and success—with which he pursued his ambitions in academic self-education. The son of a gardener, he was born in 1704 at Ramsgill ('grove of wild garlic'), a village in Nidderdale a few miles north-west of Pateley Bridge, and was baptized at Middlesmoor. He went to school at nearby Skelton, and seems to have inherited a love of learning in general, and poetry in particular, from his father, who worked for over twenty years for Sir Edward Blackett in Newby. On leaving school Eugene became a schoolmaster at his birthplace, Ramsgill, and there married a girl named Anna Spence, who bore him several children. Three years later he moved to Knaresborough (on the B6165), the town with which he is principally linked. There he opened his own school, and stayed for ten years. Before long, it seems, he began to feel that his wife, who was of humble origins, was a burden and a drag on a man of his intellectual ability. To give vent to his frustration he tormented her in various mean and ingenious ways. For instance he dressed a pretty-faced boy in girl's clothes and pretended to flirt with 'her' in Anna's presence—a curiously circuitous method of arousing jealousy. He also engaged in extra-curricular activities of a less edifying nature than schoolmastering. A poor man with no intention of remaining so, he took up petty thieving, receiving stolen goods and other minor crimes. One of his chief associates was Richard Houseman, another was Francis Iles—a name to become familiar by adoption to any,

* *Most of my Murders*, by John Parris (Muller, 1960).

connoisseur of detective stories. A third partner was Daniel Clarke—a cordwainer or shoemaker, a wealthy, well-read man whose reason for participation in minor swindles is a mystery. Younger than Eugene, weak, pockmarked and with a noticeable stammer, he was probably very much under the learned schoolmaster's influence. He paid for his co-operation with his life, for on 7th February 1744 Houseman and Aram murdered him for some £200 he was known to be carrying, and put his corpse under a rock in St Robert's Cave.

A few days later Aram was arrested for debt and secured his release by paying up in full, though he was believed to own very little money. Shortly afterwards he disappeared, and for the next twelve or thirteen years lived a wandering life, first briefly in Nottingham then in London and the south. In 1758 he went to King's Lynn, Norfolk, teaching at the local grammar school and building up an excellent reputation. When a chance visitor from Knaresborough accosted him he denied his identity. Meanwhile a skeleton had been found in St Robert's Cave: Houseman was questioned, and confessed. Eugene's whereabouts were disclosed by the Knaresborough traveller, and he was brought back to the town—greeting his wife, after 14 years, with noticeable lack of enthusiasm. With Houseman turned King's Evidence, Aram was found guilty despite the fact that, as he himself said, there was no proof now that the skeleton was that of Clarke. Just before his execution he admitted the crime but said that the reason was he suspected Clarke of having an affair with his wife Anna—a totally unfounded and despicable suggestion. Aram's body was hung in chains just outside Knaresborough, after he had twice tried to anticipate justice by cutting his wrists.

Though not very easy to find, St Robert's Cave still exists, in a field off Abbey Road, Knaresborough.

York and Leeds were the principal areas of operation of Mary Bateman, known as the Yorkshire Witch. Born just outside Thirsk, she tried earning her living as a servant in both towns, but was soon sacked in each case for stealing. She then married John Bateman, a wheelwright, and added fortune-telling to her other dubious practices. Bateman became a soldier, moving about the country, and she was thus able to extend her sphere of activities. In 1806 she began swindling a family by the name of Perigo, using an imaginary 'wise woman' who was supposed to live in

Scarborough. Battening on Rebecca Perigo's superstitious beliefs in witchcraft, Mary Bateman—through her own particular 'Mrs 'Arris'—deprived the foolish family of a large proportion of their money and possessions. One day she persuaded them to partake of a special pudding prepared by the non-existent Wise Woman. It made them both ill, and Mrs Perigo died. For a while the widower continued to be duped but eventually (surely not before time) he began to be a little suspicious of his extraordinarily helpful friend, caught her out in a minor piece of petty trickery, and denounced her to the authorities. She was convicted of the murder of Mrs Perigo and sentenced to death, arriving for her execution with a baby in her arms. A gruesome sequel was the stripping of the skin from her body, the pieces being sold as lucky charms.

Rape and subsequent murder of a 75-year-old woman occurred in York in 1953, when on 10th March the body of Flora Gilligan was found lying naked in the yard of her home, 30 Diamond Street, having apparently been thrown from a window. Nothing, it appeared, had been stolen from the premises. Military camps in the district were investigated and, led by the print of a newly repaired shoe, the police apprehended Philip Henry, a coloured soldier in the King's Own Yorkshire Light Infantry. An alibi that he was in camp during the night of the murder was disproved, his fingerprints matched those found at the scene, and he had recently washed his clothing. He had been due to go overseas in a few days. The official theory was that he had first tried unsuccessfully to force an entry into an adjoining house, broken into Miss Gilligan's, assaulted and killed her, and then tried to make the murder look like a suicide. Henry was convicted and executed.

At 7 Railway Place, Hunslet—now a district of southern Leeds, there lived in 1925 a watchman named Arthur (Arty) Calvert. He had recently engaged a new housekeeper, a tiny, thin, black-eyed, toothless woman of 33 whom he knew as Louie (or Louise or Louisa) Jackson, a widow of 28. She had a small boy with her, and a girl who lived with her sister in Dewsbury. After a while, housekeeping having progressed to activities more intimate, she told him (untruthfully) that she was pregnant. Anxious to do the right thing by her, the innocent Calvert married her at the local Register Office and settled down happily to await the arrival of his child. After a surprisingly long delay,

Louie showed him a pencilled letter inviting her to go to her sister's home for her confinement. She left on 8th March, and three weeks later returned home with a baby girl. The following morning a suitcase appeared in the house containing, she told him, the baby's clothes. That very evening the police called on Mrs Calvert, and very shortly afterwards the unfortunate Arty must have been the most bewildered man in Britain. Louie Calvert, known to the police as a prostitute by the name of Louisa Gomersal, was revealed to him as a liar, schemer, thief, and finally murderer. Those three missing weeks had been some of the fullest, and most incredible, of her life. To confess that her supposed pregnancy had been merely a trap to ensnare a husband was far too straightforward a course for devious Louie. Despite the risks involved, she determined to provide herself with a real baby by hook or crook. She embarked on a fantastically complicated, and stupid, course. Having gone to Dewsbury and telegraphed her husband of her arrival, she returned at once to Leeds and found a room in the house of Mrs Lily Waterhouse, a 40-year-old spiritualist who lived in Amberley Road, only a couple of miles away from her own home at Railway Place. She advertised in a local paper and a few days later met the mother of a 17-year-old girl from Wrangford who had given birth to an illegitimate baby in Leeds. It was arranged that Louie should take over the child on 31st March. During the waiting period Mrs Waterhouse noticed that some of her few possessions were mysteriously vanishing and suspected her lodger. Louie's vile and vicious temper was so formidable, however, that the woman was afraid to accuse her directly. Instead, she went to the police to take out a summons. The day before this was due to come up, Louie collected the baby and returned to her home. At five o'clock the following morning, while Arty and the child were peacefully sleeping, she went back to Amberley Street and picked up the mysterious suitcase. Later that day the police called on Mrs Waterhouse to find out why she had not appeared in connection with the summons and found her lying dead. She had been strangled and then beaten with the utmost violence. They also found the letter which was supposed to have come from Louie's sister, and called at Railway Place. She admitted them, looking grotesque in Mrs Waterhouse's boots which were several sizes too large for her. The suitcase was found to contain —not clothes for the new baby—but odd pieces of crockery and

cutlery stolen from the dead woman. She was tried at Leeds
Assizes and found guilty. A second plea of pregnancy was found
to be as false as the first.

While awaiting execution, Louie Calvert confessed to an
earlier murder, that of John Frobisher, to whom she had acted
as housekeeper in Mercy Street, Wellington Lane, Leeds. His
body was discovered on 12th July 1922 in the canal at Water
Hall, nearly a mile from Wellington Bridge, which was the
nearest spot the waterway approached to his home. If true, it
meant that this tiny woman, strengthened by her titanic temper, killed a man far stronger than herself and lugged his body
two hundred yards from his house to the canal at the Bridge.
His boots were never found—whether his murderess clumped
around in them as she did in those of Mrs Waterhouse is not
recorded. After her conviction, she violently abused her husband,
saying he was the cause of all her misdeeds, to which that poor
bewildered man merely replied, "Well, lass, it can't be helped".
Among the names this appalling, foul-mouthed miniature virago
chose for herself was that of Edith Thompson, executed a couple
of years previously; and among the more incongruous of her
activities was that of attending Salvation Army meetings (for
what she could get out of them), wearing a stolen bonnet.

In 1856 Armley, now a district of western Leeds on the A647,
was a separate community providing its own amusements.
Among these, in September of that year, was a modest theatrical
company that travelled around the West Riding towns. Principal
dancer of the troupe was a girl named Jane Banham. She was
married, but for some time had been separated from her husband
and living with a tailor named John Hannah who worked in
Manchester. They had two children and for some years, despite
the absences presumably necessitated by her profession, seem to
have enjoyed a reasonably happy relationship. At Christmas
1855, however, she took the children and went to live with her
father, refusing Hannah's desperate pleas that she should return
to him. When he discovered that she was performing at Armley
he went to the Malt Hill Inn, meeting her there with her father.
Once more he begged her to come back. When she still remained
adamant he dragged her into another room and closed the door.
People heard cries, and rushed in to find the distracted man
grabbing her by the neck. "What do you mean, you rascal?",
one of them cried. "I mean murder", Hannah answered and,

in front of them all, cut Jane's throat. A defence of manslaughter was rejected, and he was executed at York.

The Malt Hill Inn, which first appears in local directories of 1826, was renamed the Royal Hotel in 1871: as such it still stands at 60 Town Street. The present house incorporates parts of a much older building, including an ancient well in the cellar. The case of John Hannah and Jane Banham was a tragic one, for he was obviously devoted to his mistress and children. We have no clue now to the motives that lay behind Jane's fatal decision—no inkling of her thoughts as she danced with her little company around the Yorkshire towns over a hundred years ago.

North-east of Leeds towards Tadcaster (on the A162) is Towton, a village remembered for Edward IV's great victory in the Wars of the Roses in 1461. In 1933 a grim drama of smaller proportions was played out at Saxton Grange, a lonely farmhouse near by. Ernest Brown, a groom employed by a wealthy cattleman named Frederick Morton, had for some time taken as his mistress his employer's wife. In June of that year he left his job in a temper because he was asked to mow the lawn, a chore he evidently regarded as beneath the dignity of one in his privileged position. Later he sought Mrs Morton's help to return to work. Though apparently long tired of the alliance, Mrs Morton agreed to try, but succeeded only in restoring him to the humbler post of odd-job man. Rage, frustration and humiliation boiled up—and over—in Brown. On 5th September, while Mr Morton was away, he had a violent scene with Mrs Morton, who had been out swimming with another man, and knocked her down. That evening, when she was alone in the isolated place except for her baby and a young help, Ann Houseman, Brown embarked on a campaign of terror—firing shotgun pellets at the windows, cutting the telephone wires and prowling around the outside of the house. At 3.30 a.m. there was a loud explosion and the terrified women saw the garage ablaze. They rushed out of the house to Towton in order to give the alarm, while Brown let loose the cattle and horses from the adjoining buildings. In the burnt-out garage next morning was found the blackened body of Mr Morton who, it appeared, had been shot before he could get out of the car. The prosecution's case against Brown, who was charged with murder, was that he had killed Morton at 9.30, then cut the wires, frightened the women to keep them in the house, and set fire to the garage and cars with petrol. Brown's story was that his employer had come home at 11.30 with a few drinks inside him, and had then accidentally set fire to the car himself as he sat smoking inside it after Brown had gone to bed. This tale was—not surprisingly—disbelieved, and the ex-groom was executed at Armley Road prison.

Moving south, we come to Mirfield (the 'pleasant, or merry, meadow'), about 2½ miles from Dewsbury on the A644. Here are to be found a set of old stone stocks, an ancient cross (or, more accurately, column) known as the Dumb Steeple, and the house, Roe Head, where Charlotte Brontë attended school under Miss Wooler's management. At about the time she was there a couple named Mr and Mrs Wraith inhabited a nearby farm. A few years later, in 1847, a nephew called on his relatives—now getting on in years—and was surprised to find the place locked up and apparently deserted. With the help of neighbours he broke in, to find them both lying dead, their throats cut and their heads beaten in. An Irish tinker, Michael McCabe, was interrogated by the police and said he had called at the farm but could get no reply. Following tinker custom, he rattled his pots and pans to attract attention, whereupon a young man opened the door and told him to clear off. McCabe heard groans and saw blood on the man, but thought he had been killing fowls—or so he said. A few days later another hawker, Patrick Reid, was questioned, and later arrested. His clothes were blood-stained, and a key to the house together with a soldering iron belonging to his father, were found in a well on the farm grounds. McCabe identified Reid as the young man. New evidence came from a third hawker (door-to-door salesmanship seeming as prevalent a nuisance then as now), and a little girl who had seen both McCabe and Reid leaving the farm; and the two tinkers were tried together. Reid confessed, adding that he alone was responsible. He was executed at York in January 1848, McCabe receiving a sentence of penal servitude.

A black year in the annals of Huddersfield gaol must surely be 1840. Andrew M'Laghlin Smith was a Scotch gardener who worked around Halifax and Elland and was feared for his violent temper. On 28th April he was in Huddersfield bargaining over the price of a plant. He became even more excitable than most gardeners about the excellence of his produce, and finished up in the charge of Police Officer Dawson. When locked up he grew so obstreperous that three officers, their names sounding like a firm of solicitors—Dalton, Dawson and Duke—went to reprimand him. Duke opened the door and asked what he meant by such behaviour. Smith's reply was to rush out with a pruning-knife and attack Dawson and Duke. It throws a strange light on the security precautions of the time that he should still have such a weapon in his possession. Duke died twenty minutes later. When asked by the coroner if he had any questions to put, Smith shouted, "Me ask any questions? Are you satisfied with what you have got? Then be doing!" The authorities followed his advice and found him guilty—but insane. On being convicted, Smith remarked that he thought no more of killing men who behaved to him as the police had, than of slaughtering bullocks.

Todmorden today is a manufacturing town just inside the Yorkshire border, on the A646 between Burnley and Halifax. One hundred years ago it was a village, and its rector, the Reverend Mr Plow, lived with his wife in Parsonage House attached to the parish church. Also in the village dwelt Miles Weatherill, a weaver, who had fallen for one of the parson's four servants. The stern rector sent the girl back to her home on discovering this, and the frustrated lover vowed vengeance, becoming so menacing that a night watchman was engaged. On 2nd March 1868 the rector heard a banging at his back door and went to investigate. Miles, waiting outside, fired at him, missed, then hit him with an axe. The servants ran for help. Miles grabbed one girl, nearly severed her hand from the wrist, then shot her, killing her instantly. Then he rushed up to the bedroom where Mrs Plow was sleeping, fired at her, missed, and struck her with a poker. By this time help had arrived, but the Reverend Plow died from his injuries. On apprehension, Miles said, "I've done all I wanted to do. I'm only sorry the pistols didn't go off better." He was executed at New Bailey Prison, Salford, before over 20,000 spectators. Calcraft, the hangman, was moved to remark that he had never in his long experience witnessed such nerve and unfaltering resolution as that which Weatherill displayed on the scaffold. What the surviving members of the household, or indeed the exiled girl, thought of his resolution is not recorded.

The case of Alec Wilkinson, who murdered his mother-in-law at Wombwell (about four miles from Barnsley on the A633) on

30th April 1955, is movingly told by John Parris, who defended him. A pleasant, quiet young man, he married Maureen Farrell when he was 21 and they lived at 21 Mitchell's Terrace, also called Bradbury Back Walk. Next door but one was Maureen's mother, Mrs Farrell, a woman once known as the "Green Linnet". She was, though Wilkinson was not aware of this, an erstwhile prostitute. To begin with things went well with the young couple, and as they were both working Mrs Farrell used to help with the household chores. She was a disgustingly coarse-mouthed and aggressive woman, however, and in time relations between them began to deteriorate. Unfortunately for the marriage, Maureen seems to have been very much under her mother's influence, and at length Alec Wilkinson was more or less turned out of his own house, and went to stay with his parents. Maureen moved back to her mother, refusing all his pleas that they should make a fresh start. On one occasion he broke down and sobbed to a neighbour, "It's Mrs Farrell—we'd be all right if it weren't for her".

On the evening of 30th April, after doing some shopping and changing his library books in Barnsley, he had a few drinks and went round to Mrs Farrell's house. His object was to see Maureen who, he had heard, was leaving her job, but Mrs Farrell was in the house alone. When he asked her how Maureen was to live if she stopped working Mrs Farrell told him, in filthy language, that his wife could go on the streets before she would return to him. Whether or not she meant this seriously, it was obviously the most insulting thing she could say to him. She then rushed at him with a carving knife, whereupon, as he put it, he "saw red" and knocked her down. The next thing he remembered was standing in a bedroom which was in flames. In his first statement to the police, made in a state of great excitement at four o'clock in the morning, he had declared that he banged her head on the floor and kicked her, then set fire to the house. Just as he was going out Maureen entered, and he got hold of her and hit her head on the floor also. Whatever the details, there is little doubt that Wilkinson had been under the direst provocation and was in a frenzy of misery and frustration, and Parris fought to get the charge reduced to one of manslaughter. The verdict, however, was guilty of murder; an appeal failed and Wilkinson was hanged at Armley prison.

A particularly brutal child murder, in which in-laws played

a very different role, occurred in Doncaster in 1947. Like many
other couples at that time, Iris and Edwin Dacey, faced with
the impossibility of finding a home of their own, lived with her
parents in Arbitration Street. With them was their son Alan,
a baby just under a year old. They had been married about two
years when Dacey, who had served in the Eighth Army and
was now training to become a miner, began to drink heavily and
to reveal a vile temper. He both threatened and used violence on
his wife. In July her father, returning from work to find Iris
with bruises on her face, turned his son-in-law out of the house,
saying that she had stood enough from him. Dacey took a room
at Edlington, a village about 6 miles south of Doncaster and
near the pit where he worked. On the morning of 25th August
he accosted Iris in Doncaster as she was taking Alan to the day
nursery, grabbed the baby, hit his wife in the face, and ran
off. When the police made enquiries he told a story of handing
Alan to some strangers who had agreed to pass him on to his
parents. Early on 29th August the child's body was found hidden
in a sack under some bushes by the bank of the river Don. The
spot was not far from the Cecil Hotel, Warmsworth, between
Doncaster and Edlington, where Dacey professed to have met
the mysterious and obliging strangers. The baby's skull was
fractured and there were several knife wounds in his body. To
the surprise of the Court, Dacey pleaded guilty, writing a full
and frank confession to the police and stating his motives. Despite a plea of insanity (against Dacey's own wishes), he was convicted of murder. On the day fixed for his execution, however,
he was taken instead to St James's Hospital, Leeds, for an
appendicitis operation, and was later—after his appeal had been
dismissed—reprieved. The grounds were not revealed but, as
Mr Parris remarks, "in these enlightened days, it is very convenient to arrange to have appendicitis on the day you are due
to be hanged".

Finally, before leaving Yorkshire, we glance at one of its
most famous—if deplorable—sons, Charles Peace. He was born
at Angel Court, Sheffield, in 1832, youngest of a family of four.
His father, at that time a shoemaker, had once been known for
his efficiency as a wild-animal tamer—a somewhat ironical
occupation in view of the son he begot. Peace's abilities as poet
and violinist were grossly exaggerated in the years of his infamy,
but he could read and write to some extent and had a certain

c

mechanical ability that was to serve him well in his more
nefarious pursuits. In 1859 he married Hannah Ward, a widow
with one son. She bore him a son of his own, who died in in-
fancy, and later a daughter. After some years in and out of prison
for various crimes in Manchester, he moved with his family to
Darnall, a suburb to the east of Sheffield, where he took up
residence in 40 Victoria Place, Britannia Road. An official description issued around this time portrayed him as "thin and
slightly built, 55–60 years of age"—he was, in fact, 43—"five
feet four inches high, grey, nearly white hair, beard and
whiskers". He also, said the report, had one or more fingers missing from his left hand, walked with his legs wide apart, spoke
as though his tongue was too large for his mouth, and was a
great boaster. Among his aliases were George Parker, Alexander
Mann and—with becoming modesty—Paganini. It was shortly
after the above description that he began to wear his notorious
false fore-arm with a hook at the end.

Next door but one in Britannia Road lived Mr Arthur Dyson,
a civil engineer, with his wife and small son. Very soon the
attractive Mr Peace began to pay attentions to Mrs Dyson, a
lively Irishwoman some twenty years younger than her husband.
Dyson resented these familiarities to the extent of dropping a
note over Peace's wall requesting him "not to interfere with my
family". Charles retaliated by assaulting him in the street and
later waving a revolver at Mrs Dyson and threatening to blow
out both her and her husband's brains. After these neighbourly
exchanges the Dysons decided to move, despite the fact that
Peace himself had gone to Hull to open an eating-house. He
might at any time return to plague them anew. They therefore
went to Banner Cross Terrace, Eccleshall Road, about six miles
from Darnall on the other side of Sheffield. They were not,
however, to escape so easily. The move was watched by a somewhat mysterious figure named Bolsover, Peace's son-in-law; and
even before the Dysons were able to install themselves, while
their goods were still being taken off the wagon, Mrs Dyson saw
Peace himself actually coming out of the house they were going
into. "You see, I am here to annoy you, wherever you go," was his
hospitable welcome. Then off he went with Bolsover, leaving the
unfortunate Dysons with fears that may well be imagined.

This incident took place at the end of October 1876. Four
weeks later, shortly after eight o'clock on 29th November, Mrs

Dyson came into her yard and passed the back of the adjoining house (inhabited by a Mr Gregory) to pay a visit to the communal privy, with a lantern in her hand and clogs on her feet. As she came out she saw Peace standing by the door with a revolver. Rather oddly, he said, "Speak or I'll fire". Mrs Dyson screamed and wisely shut herself back in the privy. She heard her husband come into the yard, and then emerged again in time to see Peace shoot him, run across Eccleshall Road and climb

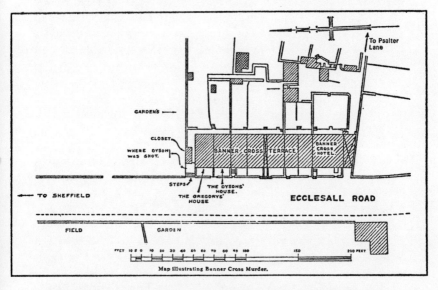

Map Illustrating Banner Cross Murder.

The Murder of Arthur Dyson from *Notable British Trials* series
(William Hodge)

over a wall into the garden beyond. She screamed for help, but Peace disappeared.

He was not seen again in the North for two years—until his apprehension on a charge of attempted murder at Blackheath and the realization by the police that at last they had the killer of Mr Dyson in their hands. The story of his sojourn in Peckham is told in my book *Murderers' London*. Peace made a dramatic but unsuccessful escape attempt on the journey north, leaping out of the carriage as the train was running at speed.

Exhibiting throughout his historic trial a mixture of whining and bravado (and an undeniable sense of humour), he was convicted and sentenced to death. While awaiting execution he confessed to another murder that had taken place at Whalley Range, described as "one of the most respectable suburbs of Manchester". On the night of 1st–2nd August 1876 Peace was prowling around the district when he became aware that a policeman, P.C. Nicholas Cock, was following him. He pulled out a revolver and fired. The constable continued to advance so Peace fired again, then ran off across the neighbouring gardens and fields. Cock died an hour later, and the following day two brothers named Habron, aged 23 and 18, were arrested. They were known to harbour a grudge against P.C. Cock, who had summoned them for being drunk and disorderly. The elder brother was acquitted, the younger imprisoned. The death sentence was remitted on account of his youth. As soon as the authorities were satisfied as to the reliability of Peace's statement Habron was released and given £800 indemnity.

The Whalley Range murder took place at the junction of Upper Chorlton Road, Seymour Grove and the Chorlton-cum-Hardy Road—now Manchester Road. Though the locality is of course altered almost beyond recognition the triangular meeting-place of the roads still remains. The house in Banner Cross Terrace where Dyson was killed still stands at the time of writing, but the area is due for development, and it may well have disappeared before this book appears in print.

Peace was hanged at Armley prison, keeping up his reputation as a 'character' to the end. On his last morning he mingled pious sentiments with complaints about the quality of the bacon served him. When called to order for spending too long in the lavatory he exclaimed, "You're in a hell of a hurry. Are you going to be hanged or am I?" He even wrote his own funeral card commemorating his execution on Tuesday, 25th February 1879 "for that I don but never intended".

2

INSCRUTABLE ORIENTALS
The North West:
Cumberland, Lancashire

It was probably the incongruity of a murder committed by a Chinese law student on his Mandarin-class wife in the middle of the most beautiful part of the English Lake District that aroused so much interest in the crime of Chung Yo Miao in 1928, for in itself it was a commonplace, stupid and sordid story, puzzling only in its lack of apparent motive.

On 18th June 1928 Chung Yo Miao, 28, and his wife Wai Sheung Siu, a few months older, arrived at the Borrowdale Gates Hotel, south of Lake Derwentwater. She was the daughter of a wealthy merchant prince and, though physically plain, a woman of great intelligence, culture and charm. They met in New York in 1927, married (both were Christian by religion) in May the following year, and were now on a European tour before returning to China. The hotel is just north of the beautiful little village of Grange, close to where the hills advance together to form the Jaws of Borrowdale before opening out into the valley beyond. After spending one night there the couple went out after lunch the following afternoon. At four o'clock Chung returned alone, telling a maid his wife was shopping in Keswick. This rather unlikely story seems to have aroused little interest even when she had not returned by dinner time. It was not, in fact, until ten o'clock that the newly-wed husband asked the maid whether he ought to do something about it—maybe tell the police? Having asked that question, all he did "do about it" was retire to bed. Meanwhile, however, the body of Mrs Chung (as she was called) had been discovered. About a mile south of Grange is a little wood with the oddly sinister name of Cumma

Catta. It lies to the left of the Borrowdale Road (B5289), and just below it is a small pool known as Kidham Dub, on the edge of Holm Crag Wood. Beside this pool a farmer saw a woman lying beneath a parasol. It was a sunny evening and he thought she was asleep, but by chance he mentioned the fact to a detective constable named Pendlebury who was on holiday in Grange. He happened to have seen Chung alone by the pool that afternoon and his curiosity was aroused. He went along to Kidham Dub and realized at once that here was a case of murder. Mrs Chung had been strangled by a white cord. She was lying on her back, her knees drawn up and apart, and her underclothing torn. There was no sign of sexual assault, but every sign of an attempt to suggest one. Rings had evidently been wrenched from the third finger of her left hand, but an expensive watch was still on her wrist. When questioned, Chung, though full of horror, seemed to know more details than the police had yet revealed to him. The missing rings were found in a roll of camera film in the hotel bedroom, he went to great trouble to account for bloodstains on his coat when in fact none had been discovered. Both his behaviour and a number of remarks he made struck the authorities as peculiar even allowing for his situation in a foreign country. He offered a vague and totally unsubstantiated story of two sinister Orientals he had seen tracking himself and his wife, presumably after the jewellery she liked to display—or even, perhaps, members of some secret society bent on mysterious revenge. Not surprisingly, these suggestions were treated with a certain doubt. Chung, found guilty of murder, was executed at Strangeways prison, Manchester. It was a case of incontrovertible circumstantial evidence, for there seemed no reason for the crime. No-one had noticed any signs of discord between husband and wife. There were, however, hints that Mrs Chung may have been sterile and this perhaps had some bearing on the tragic outcome of what, by all outward appearances, should have been a happy and lasting marriage.

An earlier Lakeland murder, less exotic in its details, occurred in 1855 near Ennerdale, the 'lonely lake'. Isaac Turner, aged 58, was 'overlooker' in charge of Kelton iron pit near Lamplugh. Every week he set out from Cleator, the village close to Whitehaven where he lived, carrying money to pay the men's wages. On the day in question he collected two £5 notes from his employer—this being sufficient in those days to satisfy the whole company. His way led along the narrow lane south of Cleator Moor and its ancient stone circle, to Ennerdale Bridge. He changed one of the notes at a shop in the tiny village, then crossed to a pub to change the other. He was last seen passing Hunter How on his way to Kelton Fell. A very short time later a hedge-trimmer found him lying dead in a field near by. His body was still warm, and there were signs of a violent struggle. He was gashed about the head and all the money had been torn from his pockets. Beside him was a razor broken in two pieces. A youth of 18, Thomas Munroe, who had earlier been loitering around, was seen to hurry from the field. It transpired that he had absented himself from work that morning and, when questioned, was unable to account for his whereabouts at the time of the murder. The following morning he returned to the spot, overheard someone saying that the police were looking for a youth with long hair, and went immediately to a blacksmith in the district and asked him for a short back and sides. The smith presumably concealed his astonishment at such a request, but remembered it later in court. When asked to produce his razor, known to be similar to that found by the body, Munroe was unable to do so. A puzzling feature of the case was that Turner was a huge and powerful man and Munroe very slightly built and boyish. Though a fearful struggle had obviously taken place not a single cry or other sound was heard by men working near. Despite this, and despite the fact that no money was found on him, Munroe was convicted of murder and executed in due course.

On the morning of 12th April 1861 William Horsley, a young man of 23, was found lying dead on a wooden settle in the kitchen of a small inn, the Packhorse, Water Street, Carlisle. He had been strangled with his own tie. Almost immediately afterwards Jane Davidson, a woman in her forties who kept the inn, was taken seriously ill. After much vomiting she died, and arsenic was found in her body. William Horsley had been married to her daughter, who had herself died shortly before these events. Jane Davidson had then become infatuated with her son-in-law, who often spent the night at the Packhorse sleeping on the settle. Recently it had been rumoured that he had begun paying attentions to a young girl and Mrs Davidson became desperate. She visited a fortune-teller named Clubby who informed her that her husband would soon die and she would then marry a much younger man. Mrs Davidson next asked a neighbour to go to a druggist and buy on her behalf some "dragon's blood". This, she believed, if burnt on a fire would act as a charm to keep Horsley away from his new girl. It was clear that Jane Davidson, evidently losing her faith in magic spells, had killed her son-in-law from jealousy and then committed suicide, and a verdict was returned to this effect. Mr Davidson appears to have been regarded throughout as a mere cypher: what he thought of the proceedings, including the prophecy of his imminent death, is not recorded.

Though Water Street may still be found in Carlisle the Packhorse Inn did not long survive the crime committed within it. By 1880 it had disappeared from the register.

Bukhtyar Rustomji Ratanji Hakim will probably be long remembered in the town of Lancaster—though the name may not be readily recognized. During 1930 a Parsee doctor set up in practice at 2 Dalton Square in the central part of the city close to the County Cinema. There he resided with a Scots mistress who passed as his wife, his children and, in 1935, a young nursemaid named Mary Rogerson. He was known as Buck Ruxton, and his supposed wife's real name was Isabella Van Ess. She had left her Dutch husband in 1928. Though they appeared fond enough of each other there were frequent quarrels between the doctor and Isabella, often on account of his jealousy over her supposed (but totally non-existent) affairs with other men. On 14th September 1935 Isabella went off to Blackpool in the doctor's car to see the famous illuminations with her sister. She certainly returned home again because her car was in the garage next morning. The doctor, however, called on his charwoman, Mrs Oxley, very early that Sunday and told her not to bother to come to the house as both his wife and Mary the nursemaid had gone off on a holiday to Edinburgh. Later he took his children to a friend asking that they be looked after during his wife's absence, and also asked a patient, Mrs Hampshire, to come and help him scrub down the stairs in preparation for the decorators who were expected the next day. He had pulled up the carpets in readiness but could not do any more as he had cut his hand. One thing to be said for Dr Ruxton is that he appears to have had the most obliging friends and neighbours. The cut on his hand (caused, he said, by a tin-opener) must have been a very severe one, for Mrs Hampshire noticed that blood had stained not only a shirt but towels, his suit and even the stair-carpets to a considerable extent. He generously presented her with both the carpets and the suit, but called to take the latter back the next day, explaining that he wanted to have it cleaned and that it was undignified for one man to wear another man's suit. During the following days he was engaged in a certain amount of travelling, and was involved in a minor collision in Kendal. The charwoman noticed a lot of bloodstains about the house, and also a very nasty smell. The latter Dr Ruxton counteracted by spraying the place with eau-de-cologne.

On 29th September the gruesome portions of two human bodies were found near a bridge at Gardenholm Linn, about two miles north of Moffat on the Carlisle–Edinburgh road. The pieces had been made into bundles and thrown down by a deep ravine that empties itself into the River Annan. It was, of course, a long way (almost exactly one hundred miles) from Lancaster and the remains were at first thought to be those of a man and a woman : on reading the details from the newspaper to Mrs Oxley, Ruxton remarked, "You see—it is not our two". It was an odd—not to say injudicious—observation. Mrs Oxley replied reasonably, "I do hope not"—but it was the sort of thing one remembers. Indeed, fears were growing as to what had become of both Isabella and Mary Rogerson. On 9th October Mary's relations told the police that she was missing, and the following day the doctor said he would like some enquiries made about his wife.

Now the net began to close. Clothing found with the remains were identified as belonging to the Ruxtons' children and to Mary Rogerson. After further investigation Ruxton was charged with the murder of Mary Rogerson and three weeks later with that of Isabella. The putting together and identification of the bodies (only parts of which were ever found) was brilliantly achieved by Professor James Brash of Edinburgh University— the full details recounted in the *Notable British Trials* series make engrossing if grim reading—and the result sealed the fate of the Parsee doctor. The prosecution's case was that he attacked his mistress in a blind fury of jealousy, hitting her in the face and strangling her on the landing above the stairs; Mary Rogerson witnessed this and so had to be killed also—probably with a knife, which would account for the bloodstains. The bodies were then dismembered and drained of blood, made up into bundles with household linen and clothing, and taken by car to the spot where they were discovered. Ruxton described the charge as "absolute bunkum", but was nevertheless executed at Strangeways prison, Manchester, on 12th May 1936.

Seaside holiday resorts feature to a fairly large extent in the story of murder. They were a favourite haunt of George Joseph ('Brides in the Bath') Smith. When his only lawful wife, Caroline Beatrice Thornhill (they were married as Mr and Mrs Love) was taking places as a domestic servant in order to steal for him, their working ground was South Coast resorts such as Brighton, Hastings and Hove. He picked up Alice Reavil in Bournemouth (she was lucky to escape with no more than the loss of all her personal possessions). He met other victims at Southsea (Alice Burnham) and Weston-super-Mare (the fatal reunion with Beatrice Mundy—he had previously 'married' and deserted her in Weymouth), and bought a house at Southend (22 Glenmore Street). Lastly, he committed two of his three 'bath' murders at Herne Bay and Blackpool respectively.

It was on 10th December 1913 that he arrived in the last-named town with Alice Burnham, whom he had 'married' at Portsmouth Register Office on 4th November. They went first to 35 Adelaide Street but the absence of a bath rendered the rooms unsuitable for Smith's purpose so they tried again for lodgings at 16 Regents Road. Their landlady here was Mrs Crossley, a sharp, perceptive, ungullible woman who was to play a considerable part in his undoing. A day or so previously Alice had obligingly made a will in her 'husband's' favour (he had already succeeded in estranging her from her family), and on the evening they arrived in Blackpool she equally obligingly went to a doctor and complained of feeling unwell. The following day she asked Mrs Crossley (prompted, no doubt by Smith) for a hot bath.* While she was still in it, he left the house to buy "something for supper". (This was his usual custom. He always went out to buy "something for supper" after drowning his victims —fish for Miss Mundy, eggs for Miss Burnham, tomatoes for Miss Lofty.) Meantime Mrs Crossley was horrified to see water pouring through her kitchen ceiling. Smith returned with his groceries, ran upstairs and said, "My wife does not answer me".

---

* Alice Burnham was the second of Smith's brides in the bath. For the first, at Herne Bay, Kent, see page 146; for the third and last, that of Margaret Lofty in Highgate, see *Murderers' London*. A full-length account of his complicated career is in the relevant volume of the *Notable British Trials* series.

The doctor who had seen Alice the previous day was fetched, and she was found dead, submerged in the bath water. Mrs Crossley liked her lodger's manner so little that she refused to let him sleep in the house: after he had left Blackpool she wrote on a card he had given her, "Wife died in bath. We shall see him again." And indeed she did—in the dock.

Still in Blackpool, we move on to 1953, when Mrs Sarah Ricketts, a woman of 79, well under five feet in height with a sharp tongue and a sharper temper, lived alone in a bungalow called "Homestead" in Devonshire Road. At the beginning of the year she advertised for a housekeeper-companion and from a large number of replies selected—very foolishly as it turned out—Louisa Merrifield, 46, and her 74-year-old (and third) husband. They moved in on 12th March. On 31st March Mrs Ricketts made a new will in favour of her employee. On 14th April she died. According to Mrs Merrifield, she found the old lady at about three o'clock in the morning lying on the floor of her bedroom, and put her back between the sheets. "She said she was thankful to me. Those were the last words she spoke." Mrs Merrifield pressed for an immediate cremation, but a post-mortem was considered necessary. She was also anxious to have the Salvation Army Band along to play "Abide With Me" in the street—a touch reminiscent of G. J. Smith's playing "Nearer my God to Thee" on the harmonium in Highgate as his wife lay dead in her bath. The post-mortem revealed that the cause of death was yellow phosphorus, an ingredient of some forms of rat poison. The evidence linking Mrs Merrifield to the poison was rather tenuous and much disputed. Medical experts also disagreed (as they have before and no doubt will again) as to the cause of death itself. It was probably Mrs Merrifield's character and behaviour more than anything that brought her to justice. She was foul-mouthed, boastful, coarse, a heavy drinker whenever possible, and it seemed beyond human power ever, by any means, to stop her talking. Even before Mrs. Ricketts' death she was chattering about the fine house she had been left. "We're landed," she told one woman. "I went to live with an old lady and she died and left me £4,000." On another occasion she remarked, "She's not dead yet, but she soon will be". She habitually referred to her recently wed husband as the old bastard, and told a complete stranger that she'd found him in bed with Mrs Ricketts and would poison them both if it went on. After her

arrest the stream of lies, evasions, contradictions, cheap senti-
mentality and coarse boasting poured out unabated. She was,
in fact, as stupid as she was maddening, and did her best to ensure her own execution. After her arrest Mr Merrifield went to
visit her and was promptly arrested on his own account and
charged together with his wife. The jury failed to agree, the
prosecution declared their intention of taking no further steps,
and the bewildered old man was released. The main mystery in
the case of Mrs Merrifield is how Mrs Ricketts, who may have
been old and ill-tempered but seemed to have most of her wits
about her, could ever have admitted so appalling a woman into
her house, let alone draw up the will that proved to be her death
warrant. Mrs Merrifield was executed on 18th September 1953.

On 23rd August 1971 five men, Frederick Sewell, John Spry,
Charles Haynes, Dennis Bond and Thomas Flannigan attempted
to carry out an armed robbery on Preston's, a jeweller's shop in
the Strand, Blackpool, a narrow one-way street by Queen Square.
The plan was thwarted, partly because, unknown to them, the
manager was able to ring the alarm bell—partly through the
chance arrival of Ronald Gale, whom the thieves, misled by his
fireman's uniform, mistook for a policeman. The gang broke
away, grabbing whatever they could, and made for the first of
their two getaway cars. A window-cleaner, Malcolm Sarjantson,
hurled a brush at them as they struggled into the car. In the
ensuing chase, through Springfield Road, Lord Street, Dickson
Road, Clevedon Road, Clifford Road and Egerton Road, two
policeman, Carl Walker and Ian Hampson, were shot at and
wounded. Sewell was cornered in an alley across Sherbourne
Road by Superintendent Gerald Richardson and threatened the
officer with his gun. Richardson said, "Don't be silly, lad" and
took hold of him, whereupon Sewell thrust the weapon into
his captor's stomach and fired twice. He then ordered two men
out of a van that was coming along the alley and drove off.
      Superintendent Richardson died in hospital later that morn-
ing. After a nation-wide search Sewell was run to earth at Bir-
nam Road, Holloway, on 7th October. He was sentenced to life
imprisonment, with a recommendation that he should serve not
less than thirty years. The other members of the gang, all of
whom were caught, received lesser sentences. Superintendent
Richardson, a married man of 38, was said to be the highest-

ranking officer ever to be killed on duty—he had already received three recommendations for bravery and, in the words of William Palfrey, Chief Constable of Lancashire, had "a great future in the police". Messages of sympathy poured into the police offices and to Mrs Richardson, the Superintendent's widow, who announced her intention of devoting her life to securing proper protection for those fighting crime, by the restoration of the death penalty in specified circumstances. In November 1972 Superintendent Richardson was posthumously awarded the George Cross.

The murder sent a wave of horror and indignation through the country comparable to that caused by the murder of three police officers at Shepherd's Bush in 1966 and the Gutteridge case in 1927—but such waves are apt to spend themselves, and it is a disturbing reflection on present-day society that every few years apparently a man must be killed in the course of his duty in order to awaken a sense of responsibility towards those to whom it looks for its protection.

About five miles south of Blackpool is St Anne's-on-Sea, now generally conjoined as Lytham-St Anne's. Early on Christmas Eve 1919 the body of a young girl was found lying half buried at a spot known as the Sandhills. She had been shot three times. The night before the discovery had been a particularly wild one of wind and rain, which may have accounted for the covering of sand that lay over her. She was identified as Kitty Breaks, a young married woman living apart from her husband. For some eighteen months she had been the mistress of Frederick (generally called Eric) Holt, a Lancashire man who had been invalided out of the army during the war, worked for a while with a company in Malaya, and then returned to England to live a light-hearted and socially energetic life in the prosperous middle-class circles of his native county. His relationship with Kitty Breaks, formed very soon after his return, showed every outward sign of mutual happiness. On Christmas Eve 1919 they were travelling by train from Bradford. For some reason he alighted a station or two before Blackpool; she went on to complete the journey, dined alone in the resort, then walked to the Sandhills. There was little doubt that Holt was responsible for her death. He was seen taking a tram late that evening near the spot where she was found, and a desperate attempt to prove an alibi failed. A second line of defence was insanity—two of his relatives were known to have been mentally unstable. Holt's counsel was Marshall Hall, who put every ounce of his great emotional powers into his defence, reading love-letters between the accused and the dead girl with such pathos as to reduce most of the court, including himself, to tears. Only Holt remained stoically silent throughout. Hall submitted that the killing could only have been done in a frenzy by a man whose mind, already delicately balanced, had been finally overthrown by his war experiences. There was, however, another side to the picture. Holt had tried earlier that year to insure Kitty's life for £10,000 (she had no money of her own), but the company said this could not be arranged unless he was married to her. She then insured her own life for £5,000 and left what little else she possessed in addition, to her lover. After being convicted and sentenced to death Holt remarked, "Well, that's over. I hope my tea won't be late."

Clitheroe ('hill of the song-thrush') is on the A59 road between Preston and Skipton. Close to the east of it is Pendle Hill, famed as the haunt of the Lancashire witches. Just west of it is the village of Bashall Eaves. On 19th March 1934 John Dawson, farmer, spent an evening playing dominoes at the Edisford Bridge Hotel. At about nine o'clock he laid down a final double-six and returned to his home at Bashall Farm. There he ate some food and went to bed. The following morning he asked his sister to have a look at his back, which felt a bit stiff. To her horror she saw that it was covered in blood, and that this had come from a gaping wound. A doctor was called—against Dawson's wish—but was not permitted to make a very thorough examination. When gangrene set in Dawson refused an operation. He told the police, who had been called in, that as he was entering the farmyard he heard a click and felt a gentle blow on his back. Presuming that someone had flung a small stone at him in joke, he ignored it, but during the night felt some pain, and his left arm grew stiff. Two days later, Dawson died from the effects of blood poisoning. An examination was now possible, and a bullet was extracted from his body, close to the liver. Enquiries were at once opened, but with little success. In the opinion of Robert Churchill, the gunsmith expert, the weapon used might not have been a true gun at all but an 'air cane', the bullet being propelled by compressed air. This would account for there having been no sound of an explosion. Suggestions were also made that a catapult was used. The mystery was never solved. Dawson was apparently a popular man with no known enemies, and the tightly-knit little community under the shadow of witch-haunted Pendle Hill closed its ranks against all probing questions. Asked at the inquest if it were true that the people of the district went in for "full-blooded jokes" a police constable replied, curtly, firmly, and perhaps from rueful experience, "Yes".

It will be long before the town of Blackburn forgets the name of Peter Griffiths. At about midnight on 14th May 1948 the 22-year-old ex-Irish Guardman, of Birley Street, after an evening of heavy drinking, took a taxi to the Queen's Park Hospital (where he had earlier been a patient for two years), removed his shoes, broke into Ward CH3, picked up the sleeping Joan Anne Devaney from her cot, carried her out to an adjoining field that belonged to the hospital, raped her, and dashed her head against a stone wall. She was four years old. He collected his shoes and went home, arriving about 1 a.m. The discovery of the little girl's body, and subsequently of a set of fingerprints on a Winchester bottle by the cot and marks of stockinged feet in the ward, led to one of the most laborious investigations yet known. Collections and examinations of fingerprints were undertaken in a series of increasingly wide circles: first those of everyone who might have been in the ward during the past two years, then of everyone who might have been on the premises for any reason, finally—when these brought no result—of every male person over 16 known to have been in Blackburn on the night of the murder. Over nine million comparisons were made—without result. Eventually a number of hitherto unobtained prints were secured as a result of comparing the lists of names already obtained against those compiled for the issuing of ration cards. At last, three months after the crime, one of the searchers cried, "I've got him!"

Griffiths, still in the town, was arrested—and promptly confessed. Fibres from his clothing matched those found on the body and on the stocking marks in the ward. A plea of insanity was put forward, but Peter Griffiths was found guilty of murder and hanged at Walton prison, Liverpool. He stated in his confession that he had banged the little girl's head against the wall because she would not stop crying.

In 1949 the people of Rawtenstall, a manufacturing town set in the old Forest of Rossendale (on the A56 south of Burnley), demonstrated in no uncertain fashion their disapproval of murder. Only 152 out of some 26,000 inhabitants signed a petition for the reprieve of Margaret Allen, convicted of killing a 68-year-old woman by beating in her head with a hammer. Margaret Allen, a 42-year-old ex-bus conductress, was an aggressive Lesbian, wearing male clothes, close-cropped hair, calling herself "Bill", claiming she had once worked as a labourer and had had a sex operation. She indulged in frequent moods of violence and ill-temper, and her only close friend (though she is reported to have been both capable and popular on the buses) was a Mrs Annie Cook, who seems throughout to have treated her with the utmost kindness and sympathy. Miss Allen lived in a very small, very ill-kept stone house, 137 Bacup Road, near the turning into Fallbarn Close. For this she paid a rent of 6s. 4d. per week. On the early morning of 29th August the battered body of old Mrs Chadwick, a somewhat eccentric widow who worked as a housekeeper near by, was found lying in Bacup Road almost outside the stone cottage. Margaret Allen watched the subsequent search for the murder weapon, and herself pointed out Mrs Chadwick's handbag floating in the River Irwell behind her home. The bag was empty, though Mrs Chadwick, like many unwise old women, was known to carry a lot of money around with her. Miss Allen's volubility and exaggerated interest in police proceedings eventually aroused suspicion and she was questioned closely. At first she protested she knew nothing of the murder but later, after bloodstains were found on the walls of the house, she changed her mind and confessed. Mrs Chadwick, like Margaret Allen herself, had a habit of wandernig about the Rawtenstall streets. On this particular Saturday morning she turned up on the doorstep of the house in Bacup Road and asked if she could come in. Margaret Allen told her (not surprisingly, in view of the condition in which she kept the place) to make it some other time. Mrs Chadwick, however, "seemed to insist on coming in. I happened to look round and saw a hammer in the kitchen. . . ." Then, she said, she hit old Mrs Chadwick with it several times "on the spur of the moment", pulled the body into the coalhouse, and placed it in the road after dark. She planned to throw it into the river, but it was too heavy. A plea of insanity was rejected, and the jury saw no

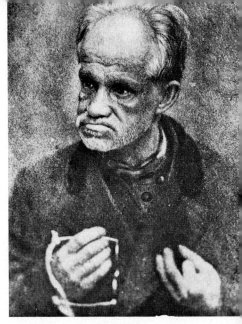

(*above left*) Eugene Aram and Richard Houseman hiding the murdered body of Mr Clarke in St Robert's Cave, near Knaresborough. (*right*) Charles Peace at the time of his trial. (*below*) The house in Dalton Square, Lancaster, where Dr Buck Ruxton murdered his mistress and nursemaid.

(*above left*) Louisa Merrifield, the Blackpool murderess. (*right*) Margaret Allen, ex-bus conductress and murderess.

(*below*) Florence and James Maybrick.

reason to add any recommendations to mercy to their verdict of guilty arrived at in a bare fifteen minutes.

Margaret Allen was obviously a frustrated unhappy and probably lonely woman, "deeply and desperately conscious", as Spencer Shew puts it, "of her sexual abnormality".* Even if one discounts a partial motive of robbery, however, her violent attack was clearly out of all proportion to any provocation she may have received, as she vented all her ill-feeling and habitual bad temper on one feeble, if somewhat irritating, old woman. "I didn't actually do it for the money", she is stated to have said, "I was in one of my funny moods".

Pendleton, now long absorbed into the Salford area of western Manchester, was in 1817 a pleasant, field-surrounded village on the outskirts. In that year a Mr Thomas Littlewood owned a house there on the west side of the Lancaster–Manchester road, near a spot known as the Three-nooked Field. Immediately behind the house was a burial ground and chapel, and almost opposite stood the 2-mile stone to Manchester. In the house with Littlewood, who owned a grocer's shop in Salford, lived his wife, an old lady of 75, named Mrs Marsden, and a 20-year-old girl Hannah Partington. Mr and Mrs. Littlewood used to visit the shop every market-day, leaving what seems—on this particular day at any rate—a dangerously large sum of money in the house, about £160. While they were away a friend of Hannah's called Harriet Towel called to see her at about four o'clock. Unable to get any reply to her knocking she peered through the partly shuttered kitchen window and saw old Mrs Marsden sitting motionless with bowed head, and blood sprinkled over the dresser. Displaying a singular lack of curiosity, she went away and did not return for three hours. Then, finding the old woman still in the same position (and the bloodstains still on the dresser), she came to the conclusion something a little odd might have happened, and gave the alarm. At this moment Mr Littlewood returned, found his own front door locked against him, went in through a window and found both Hannah and Mrs Marsden dead in the kitchen. They had been attacked with a poker and a cleaver and the house had been ransacked. All the money and certain articles of clothing were gone. Five men, James Ashcroft, 53, David Ashcroft, 48, James Ashcroft, 32, William Holden, 47, and John Robinson, 53, were charged with murder and robbery.

* *A Second Companion to Murder* (Cassell, 1961).

D

They had been seen together in the Crown and Anchor Inn, Hilton Street (which still runs parallel to Bury New Road in the nearby Broughton district), where they sat whispering together as if plotting some wickedness. On the day of the murder the four first named were noticed hovering about near the house, and later on they were displaying bundles of banknotes and handfuls of gold at two other neighbouring public houses, the Black Horse and the Horseshoe. They were all strangers to the Littlewoods and their household. The jury took no more than two minutes to find all guilty save Robinson, who was acquitted. All were weavers by trade, but known to the authorities as gamblers and thieves. They were hanged together on 8th September 1817, protesting their innocence to the end. As the final preparations began they started to sing a hymn, and continued until the drop fell. The elder James Ashcroft had been brought up a strict Methodist. His belief in the power of faith was such that he declared his hand could not be consumed by fire if he willed it otherwise. One day he undertook to demonstrate this, and was severely burned.

Probably the most discussed case of central Manchester was that of Walter Graham Rowland, who was convicted in December 1946 of the murder of Olive Balchin. She was a prostitute aged about 40, and her body was found the previous October on a bombed-out site in Cumberland Street, off Deansgate, by two children on their way home from church. She had been savagely hit about the head, and a hammer of the type used for leather-beating was lying close to her side with its wrapping paper near by. Their investigations led the police to question a 35-year-old labourer, Walter Rowland, who lived at a neighbouring hostel. He was a morose and unsociable man whose lonely wanderings about the city streets at night had already provoked comment. As soon as the police approached him he exclaimed, "You don't want me for the murder of that woman, do you?" He admitted knowing Olive Balchin well enough to call her by a nickname, Lil, but that was all. After further evidence came to light Rowland was charged, tried, found guilty and sentenced to death. Before his appeal was heard a man named David John Ware, 38, who was in prison at Walton, Liverpool, for theft, declared that he was the murderer of Olive Balchin, and went round the district with the police, describing what had happened. On 22nd February he retracted everything, saying his confession was made "out of swank—but I had a feeling all along I wouldn't get very far with them. I wanted to see myself in the headlines."

On 27th February 1947 Rowland was executed at Strangeways. In 1951 Ware walked into Bristol police station announcing that he had killed a woman. "I keep on having an urge to hit women on the head." He was charged with attempted murder (the woman, Mrs Adelaine Fuidge, survived), found guilty but insane, and committed to Broadmoor. The case of Rowland has been put forward as an argument against capital punishment. The evidence against him, however, was exceedingly strong. In his trouser turn-ups were found samples of brick-dust and soil similar to that on the bombed site, a bloodstain on his shoe was of the same group as Olive Balchin's, hairs on his jacket were identical with her own, it was proved that he was the purchaser of the hammer. None of these points applied in any way to Ware, and his account of the killing did not match that of the pathologist. In addition, years previously Rowland had been accused of murdering his young daughter. In this case also he had been found guilty, but was later reprieved.

There would be no difficulty in choosing the two most famous cases in Liverpool's history. They are, without any doubt, those of Mrs Maybrick and William Herbert Wallace. So large a volume of literature already exists about each that we shall only glance at them briefly here.

In 1881, when she was 18, Florence Elizabeth Chandler, daughter of an American banker, married James Maybrick, 41, whom she met when he was on a business trip to the United States. They took up residence in Battlecrease House, Riversdale Road, Aigburth, Liverpool, an imposing dwelling that still stands, though no longer known by its former unusual name. He was a wealthy cotton broker and they lived, outwardly at least, in circumstances of material comfort, pleasant social activity and domestic tranquillity, with a large house, servants, and two children. Beneath the surface, however, all was not so unruffled. Maybrick was an irritable, at times violent hypochondriac. Florence sought solace in an extra-marital love affair with a man named Brierley. In March 1889 she spent three days with him in Flatman's Hotel, London. The following afternoon she went with her husband to the Grand National at Aintree, where they met Brierley by chance. Shortly after their return she was seen to sport a black eye. Things were, seemingly, patched up on this occasion, but in April Maybrick was taken ill. He spent the next few weeks getting alternatively better and worse, but on 11th May he died. Mrs Maybrick was arrested on 14th May, and on 6th June charged with murder by arsenic. Much of the evidence against her rested on the alleged purchase and subsequent use of flypapers. An unpleasant picture is conjured up, as one reads the trial, of a wretched woman surrounded by suspicious relatives and spying servants. She was found guilty and sentenced to death, but as a result of widespread agitation the sentence was commuted to penal servitude for life. She served 15 years at Woking and Aylesbury, and on her release in 1904 left to spend what remained of her life in a small, three-room dwelling in South Kent, Connecticut.

It is difficult to avoid the impression that Mrs Maybrick was tried for adultery (of which she was guilty) as much as for murder (of which she may well have been innocent). Mr Maybrick's hypochondria led him to indulge in an astonishing amount of patent, not to say quack, self-medication. In his body were found, apart from arsenic, traces of strychnine, jaborandi, cascara, henbane, morphia, prussic acid, papawi, iridin, *et al.* Well might a writer questioning the justice of the verdict in a letter to *The Times* describe James Maybrick's stomach as a "druggist's wastepipe".

William Herbert Wallace's trial for the murder of his wife Julia has probably had more words devoted to it than any other case—largely because of the well-known fact that almost every element in it can be equally strongly interpreted as a pointer to either his innocence or his guilt. The full-length books generally appear in a regular alternating for/against sequence, and the susceptible reader is torn this way and that by each in turn. At the moment, following two excellent studies by Jonathan Goodman (*The Killing of Julia Wallace*) and, interestingly, an American writer, Robert F. Hussey (*Murderer Scot-Free*) the odds are strongly on the side of innocence – until the next study comes along.

The Wallaces lived at 29 Wolverton Street, a totally unremarkable Liverpool side road. They were, in fact, a totally unremarkable pair – to all appearances. He was a 52-year-old insurance salesman, she a fragile, retiring, faded, genteel woman with vague musical aspirations long faded like herself. On 20th January 1931 she was found brutally murdered in the little-used parlour of their small house – found by her husband on his return from a hunt for a mythical address to which he had been summoned, through a telephone call, by an equally mythical prospective client calling himself Qualtrough. The call was received at the City Café, North John Street (where Wallace went regularly as a member of a chess club), and had been put through from a kiosk close to his home. Wallace was asked to call at 25 Menlove Gardens East the following evening. Accordingly, as the time for the appointment approached, Wallace left his house, took trams from West Derby Road to Lodge Lane, along Southdown Road to Penny Lane, and thence to the Menlove district. He trudged around Menlove Avenue, to Menlove Gardens North, South and West (taking care to ask his way on several occasions), but found no Menlove Gardens East for the simple reason that it does not exist. He then returned home to tragedy and horror. The answer to the whole mystery is contained in the identity of the telephone caller – the evidence as to Wallace's guilt rested mainly on whether he could have had time to murder his wife and conceal the fact of his having done so, between the moment when *she* was last seen alive and the moment when *he* was seen (and he seemed anxious to make sure he *was* seen) on his journey.

Wallace was, in fact, found guilty, despite lack of apparent motive and a very favourable summing-up by the judge, Mr Justice Wright, but the verdict was quashed on appeal. After his release he returned to Wolverton Street but met with such hostility and persecution that he moved to live in seclusion in a bungalow called The Summer House, at Meadowville Road, Bromborough, Cheshire. He died, from liver trouble, on 26th February 1933. He may have been a very fortunate man, or a much maligned man: he certainly was not, in the few years between Julia's death and his own, a happy one.

In 1913 Miss Christie Bradfield was manageress of her brother's shop selling tarpaulin, sacking and similar goods, in Old Hall Road, close to the Liverpool docks area. On 10th December, a very windy night, a ship's steward named Walter Eaves was waiting for his girl in the street when a shutter from Miss Bradfield's window fell right on top of him. Fortunately he was wearing a bowler hat, which took the force of the blow but itself suffered a couple of nasty dents in the crown. A young man hurried out of the shop to replace the shutter, and when Walter Eaves pointed to his damaged hat he went back to fetch a slightly older man. The latter apologized profusely and immediately paid out two shillings in compensation. A little later, as Eaves still waited for his dilatory girl, both men emerged from the shop with a tarpaulin-covered cart and went off towards Lock Fields, an open space by the Leeds–Liverpool canal. The following morning Miss Bradfield was not to be found, the only persons in the shop being her two employees, George Ball (known at work, for some reason, as George Sumner) and Sam Eltoft, a youth of 18. They made various excuses to account for her absence, but before very long it was only too fully explained, for her body was found in the canal, tied in a sack and weighed down with bits of iron and other oddments. Eltoft was arrested at once, but George Ball managed to disappear and was not apprehended until a week later when, wearing a vague attempt at disguise, he was spotted leaving a football match at Goodison Park. Both were tried for murder, there being also some evidence of attempted rape. Ball was hanged at Walton prison in February 1914; the younger man received four years' imprisonment. Ball had been recognized after his photograph was shown on cinema screens throughout Liverpool, one of the earliest examples of such a method being used.

The triviality of motive in many cases of murder is a constant source of astonishment, but the apparent reason for the final act is often, in all probability, merely the last small straw – or the tip of an iceberg of resentment, frustration, unreasoning rage, the hidden depths of which may never be revealed and may have little connection with the act itself. In March 1849 a man named John Wilson wished to rent a room in a house in Leveson Street, Liverpool (now Grenville Street South, between Kent Street and Great George Street), which was owned by a Mrs Henrichson. Her husband, a sea captain, was away at the time on a voyage. Mrs Henrichson asked her prospective lodger either to furnish a reference or to pay a week in advance. He was unwilling, or unable, to do either, and was presumably told that he could not have the room. Mrs Henrichson then went out shopping. When a delivery boy called a little later it was Wilson who opened the door, his face covered with blood. Mrs Henrichson was last seen by the same delivery boy as he went back to his shop. With that extraordinary lack of curiosity sometimes found surrounding cases of murder, the boy said nothing at all, as he passed her, about the bloodstained face that had looked out from her front door. Mrs Henrichson went home. Some time later Wilson was seen leaving the house. When the neighbours, becoming anxious, forced their way in, they found Mrs Henrichson and her servant in the front room with their heads bludgeoned, and the former's two small boys, aged 4 and 6, in the kitchen with their throats cut. The maid was still alive, and was able to identify Wilson as the killer before she died. It seems a drastic revenge to take for being refused a lodging.

The sight of money pouring into the box-office during the golden days of the cinema has proved an irresistible temptation to the petty criminal on more than one occasion. As the last film programme got under way on the evening of 19th March 1949 at the Cameo Cinema, Webster Road, Liverpool, the manager, Leonard Thomas, and his assistant, John Catterall, were going through the night's takings in the office when a masked man forced his way in brandishing a revolver. A moment later several shots were heard by the box-office cashier and the man ran out, still waving the gun, threatened her and the doorman, and escaped down an emergency staircase. Both manager and assistant were fatally wounded, and died without being able to help the police by giving any description of their attacker. Six months passed before any progress was made. Then, as the result of an anonymous letter, two small-time thieves named George Kelly, 27, and Charles Connolly, 26, were charged with murder. Connolly's share was said to be that of keeping watch outside the cinema. The jury at the first trial failed to agree. At a second the men were tried separately and Kelly was sentenced to death. No evidence was offered against Connolly on the murder charge; he pleaded guilty to robbery and conspiracy (with Kelly and persons unknown, possibly the writer of the anonymous letter), and was sentenced to imprisonment. Kelly was executed at Walton prison in March 1950.

The Cameo closed its doors as a cinema in the mid-fifties. On the night of the murder there was a full audience watching the week's attraction in happy ignorance of the real-life drama being enacted within a few yards of them.

3

SUFFER LITTLE CHILDREN
The North Midlands: Cheshire, Derbyshire, Shropshire, Staffordshire

One of the most debated mysteries of the early nineteen-hundreds took place in 1909 just within the borders of Cheshire's north-western tip, near the manufacturing town of Dukinfield. In a large and dignified house known as Gorse Hall lived George Henry Storrs, an affluent mill-owner and builder, with his wife, her niece Marion Lindley, a cook and a housemaid. A coachman and his wife lived over the stables. George Storrs, 49, healthy and vigorous, was a generous and kindly man, popular both socially and among his employees. His household was regarded as an example of harmonious, solid Edwardian comfort. Suddenly, on 10th September, all this pleasant edifice collapsed. As Storrs, his wife and Miss Lindley were sitting at dinner a shot was fired through the long windows. Storrs leapt up in time to see a dark figure disappearing among the bushes in the extensive grounds. He said later, rather hesitantly, that he did not know the man. The police were informed and precautions taken, including the installation of an alarm bell on the roof. On the last Saturday in October this bell rang, but the police were greeted by an apologetic Storrs who said he had rung it himself as a test. On 1st November the family were again gathered in the dining-room. As the maid, Mary Evans, went past the scullery she saw to her surprise that the gas was lit and the window broken. At the same moment a man came from behind the door with a revolver. Mary ran screaming through the house with the man at her heels. Storrs came out of the dining-room. Seeing him, the man shouted, "I've got you at last", and rushed at him.

Instead of firing the revolver, however, he attacked Storrs with a knife, stabbing him fifteen times. He then escaped through the scullery window. Meanwhile Mrs Storrs had frantically rung the alarm bell and Miss Lindley had run to summon help from the Stalybridge Central Club near by. Storrs died without speaking.

Following descriptions from the two women, the police arrested a man named Cornelius Howard, a cousin of the deceased, who lodged some twenty miles away across the moors in Huddersfield. He was a shabby and apparently somewhat shady young man who worked as a butcher and had little contact with the leisurely life at Gorse Hall. In fact, neither Mrs Storrs nor Miss Lindley had ever met him, but when confronted with him both identified him as the murderer – as also did Mary Evans and the cook. There was blood on his clothing and a knife in his pocket, though these facts meant little in themselves as he was not arrested until 17th November. He said at first that he had fallen on some glass in his room, but later admitted having cut himself while breaking into a building in Stalybridge. His defence was an alibi: this proved unassailable and he was acquitted. Later another man, Mark Wilde, was arrested – and he also was identified by all the occupants of the house. The cook said he was even more like the murderer than the other one. Wilde lived at Stalybridge, and had blood on his clothing. He said he had been in a fight. At one point during his trial both men were placed side by side so that their resemblance to each other could be judged. Mark Wilde, who had no apparent connection at all with the family, was acquitted. Though it seems clear that Storrs was apprehensive that he was in some sort of danger, nothing further ever came to light. Gorse Hall remained in private hands, but was demolished in 1948.

Four full-length books have already appeared on the Moor Murderers, Ian Brady and Myra Hindley, and we shall only summarize the details here.* Brady was born in Glasgow in 1938. On 16th January 1961, while working as a clerk with a chemical supply firm in the West Gorton district of Manchester, he met Myra Hindley, a typist living in Bannock Street – now

* *The Moor Murders* by David Marchbanks (Leslie Frewin, 1966); *The Monsters of the Moors* by John Deane Potter (Elek, 1966); *On Iniquity* by Pamela Hansford Johnson (Macmillan, 1967); *Beyond Belief* by Emlyn Williams (Hamish Hamilton, 1967).

demolished. Their friendship, founded mainly on a mutual interest (born in Brady and fostered by him in Hindley) in Nazi Germany and the works of De Sade, grew apace after a slow beginning. When the Bannock Street house was condemned and Myra, together with her aged grandmother with whom she lived, were moved to a council house at 16 Wardle Brook Avenue in the 'spill-over' estate at Hattersley in Cheshire, Brady joined them permanently. There, between November 1963 and December 1964, they murdered 12-year-old John Kilbride and 10-year-old Lesley Ann Downey, after subjecting the little girl at any rate to the most revolting and obscene treatment, and buried their bodies on the moors. On 6th October 1965 they killed a 17-year-old engineer named Edward Evans, Brady hacking him to pieces with an axe. This murder was committed in the presence of David Smith, 17-year-old husband of Myra's younger sister Maureen. As soon as he dared escape from the house, Smith rang the police – hiding with Maureen near the telephone kiosk until they arrived – and Superintendent Robert Talbot, head of Stalybridge police, called at 16 Wardle Brook Avenue early that same morning. As a result of discoveries made when a suitcase of Brady's was withdrawn from Manchester Central Station (the left-luggage ticket had been hidden in the spine of Myra Hindley's confirmation prayer-book), a massive search was set up for the bodies of the missing children. On 16th October Lesley Ann Downey was found buried three feet underground at a spot known as Hollin Brown Knoll, a small ridge off the A635 some 2½ miles from the village of Greenfield on Saddlemoor. Five days later John Kilbride was found in a shallow grave some four hundred yards away. Brady and Hindley were tried at Chester in April 1966 and sentenced to long terms of imprisonment. While torturing Lesley Ann Downey they had made tape recordings of her screams and pleas for mercy – these were played at the trial, and there can have been no more horrifying moment in any courtroom than when, after a few moments of muffled movements, the silence was rent by her first piercing shriek. In the Foreword to his book, Emlyn Williams quotes Superintendent Talbot as saying to him, "I keep reminding myself that this isn't a tale. . . . Even as a hardened copper, you just rub your eyes." The horrors enacted by Brady and Hindley in that bright, dull little council house on the new estate may seem to us incredible – Emlyn Williams entitles his brilliant study *Beyond Belief* – but the Moor Murders *have* to be believed because, in the year 1966 of our permissive welfare society, they happened.

Crossing the Mersey to that part of Cheshire known as the Wirral Peninsula (named after the bog myrtle or 'wir') we arrive in Birkenhead – as, on 25th September 1902, did the famous Protestant leader John Kensit. His purpose was to hold a meeting at the Claughton Music Hall. As might be expected in a district so strongly Irish and Catholic, the gathering was a notably turbulent one. After it was over Kensit, escorted by his followers, set off for Hamilton Square station on his way to Liverpool; but so menacing were the crowds that they changed their route and made for the Woodside Ferry. In this decision, however, they were anticipated, and were met by a yelling and abusive crowd. As Kensit tried to make his way through the mob he was struck over the eye by a heavy iron file and fell to the ground, seriously wounded. He was taken to Liverpool Infirmary and died there from septic pneumonia and meningitis a few days later. An 18-year-old Irish labourer, John McKeever, was charged with murder but acquitted – partly on evidence that Kensit, as he fell, called out, "Oh, *she* has blinded me". The verdict was greeted with wild enthusiasm by the Liverpool Irish.

Birkenhead's other well-known case, that of Lock Ah Tam in 1925, strikes a note of pathos if not of tragedy. Starting life as a ship's steward, Lock Ah Tam eventually became European representative of a Hong Kong organization of Chinese sailors, in addition to holding various other posts which included, at one time, that of secret agent to the Emperor Sun Yat Sen himself. Generous, dignified and kindly, he was equally welcome among poor children and wealthy socialites, and regarded almost with reverence by his own countrymen in the district. To them, indeed, he acted as a sort of modern Solomon, settling disputes and dispensing both justice and advice. He had, however, suffered two misfortunes. In 1918 a drunken sailor struck him a blow on the head, wounding him severely; and in 1924 he made a large financial loss in one of his enterprises, resulting in bankruptcy. Since the latter disaster, his Welsh wife Catherine was to say later, he would sometimes fly into terrible rages, seeming to become almost insane, and afterwards bursting into uncontrollable tears. He also started to drink heavily. Even so the police, many of whom knew him well, were astounded when, early on the morning of 1st December 1925, after giving a party for his son's twentieth birthday, he telephoned from his house at 122 Price Street and announced that he had shot his wife and children. They arrived to find Catherine and two daughters, aged 18 and 20, lying dead. His son, worried by his father's violent and un-reasoning behaviour after the party, had gone out to look for a policeman before the murders occurred.

Lock Ah Tam was tried at Chester Assizes. He was defended by Marshall Hall who, deeply affected by the case, made a pas-sionate plea that the killings had taken place while the accused was in a state of "epileptic automatism". However, the jury re-turned a verdict of guilty after only twelve minutes. The judge, Mr Justice Mackinnon, was clearly distressed as he pronounced sentence of death: the emotion displayed by both counsel and judged formed a strange contrast to the oriental stoicism of the accused man before them.

In the matter of murder the moors and mineworks of Derby-shire and Yorkshire are probably the silent holders of more dark secrets than will ever come to light. One that was kept for three years, and would probably never have been revealed but for the commission of a further crime, occurred in 1920 on Simmondley Moor, a little south of Glossop. In that year a cunning but oafish farm labourer called Albert Edward Burrows, nearly 60 years of age, found himself in the unenviable position of having to support both a wife who was applying for a maintenance order and a mistress who was applying for a bastardy order – with no money available for either. At the time, it was his mistress who was living with him in his house in Glossop, his wife having walked out as she walked in. He solved his tricky problem in finance by murdering the mistress, Hannah Calladine, together with the small son she had given him, and throwing the bodies down the Dinting Airshaft, part of a disused mine. The prob-ability was that he strangled them, though by the time the bodies were found, three years later, it was impossible to con-firm this. The following morning he killed a 3-year-old girl whom Hannah had by a former lover, and disposed of her in the same way. He made up various stories to account for the disappear-ances and a mollified Mrs Burrows returned home. Though they contradicted one another, his stories appear to have been generally accepted, even when they were backed up by some wildly improbable 'evidence' – including sending Hannah's mother a photograph of a small boy and declaring it to be her grandson whereas in reality it was of a complete stranger (a child named Williamson), and the picture had been stolen from, of all people, his own wife.

In all likelihood nothing more would have been heard of the matter but for the fact that, three years later, when a small boy of four years old disappeared, Burrows himself unaccountably came forward with the information that he had been with the child on the moors shortly beforehand. The body, criminally assaulted, was found in the Dinting shaft, and this inevitably led to the uncovering of Hannah and her babies. Burrows was charged, with overwhelming evidence against him, of murdering Hannah Calladine. He was convicted at Derby Assizes and executed in due course – a murderer in whom impudence, cunning and stupidity were mixed in almost equal proportions.

A little further south, on the A624, is Little Hayfield, a village forming part of Hayfield itself. At the New Inn (today known as the Lantern Pike), the wife of the licensee, Mrs Amy Collinson, was murdered on 11th October 1927 by George Hayward, a commercial traveller whose home, the White House, was nearby. It appeared that he had called at the Inn during the morning at an hour when she might be expected to be alone, battered her head with a home-made bludgeon of lead piping and wood (the piping sawn from the outlet of his own kitchen sink), and then cut her throat. The motive was robbery. Hayward was in serious financial difficulties, including a debt he had incurred by not forwarding to his firm cash he had collected from customers. After ransacking the Inn for money he drew his dole from New Mill, about three miles away, then went on to Manchester, where he purchased a £4 money order to pay off some of his more pressing debts. The rest of the money was found hidden in his bedroom chimney, and the wood found in the piping matched pieces found at the White House of a particular type of cane used for cleaning out waste pipes. Hayward's haul from the crime that sent him to his death was a little under £40.

Baslow is a village on the junction of the A623 and A619, at the edge of Chatsworth Park and about eight miles west of Chesterfield with its famous twisted church spire. Leading from it is an isolated road in the moors known as Clod Hill Lane. Here on 13th June 1960 was found the body of 60-year-old William Elliott of Haddon Road, Bakewell. His small 'bubble' car had been discovered the previous morning against a lamp-post in Park Road, Chesterfield. His skull had been fractured and he had obviously been left in the lane, the murderer making off with his car. It was learned that a week before this discovery a man named William Atkinson had been attacked in Boythorpe Road, Chesterfield, which runs close by Park Road. Both men frequented the same pub, the Spread Eagle, and Atkinson later declared that he thought he had been assaulted in mistake for Elliott. Several months later, on 29th March 1961, George Stobbs, a 48-year-old research chemist of Mansfield Road, Chesterfield, was found dead near Wingerworth, just south of Chesterfield and only a few miles from the spot where Elliott's body had been discovered. His car also was found in Park Road, and he too frequented the Spread Eagle. The crimes, inevitably, became known as the Carbon Copy Murders.

Among those the police interviewed was 63-year-old Arthur Jenkinson: the following day he was found gassed in the flat where he lived alone. A verdict of suicide was returned, though a suggestion was made that he might have been murdered by being overpowered and having his head forced into the gas oven. The cases looked like remaining unsolved but three years later a former regular soldier named Michael Copeland, 26, whose address at St Augustine's Crescent, Chesterfield, was close to the spot where both cars had been abandoned, was arrested and accused of both crimes. In addition he was accused of murdering Guenther Helmbrecht, a young German soldier, in Verden, Germany, in November 1960. Copeland confessed, saying he killed the men because "it was something I hated". (Both Elliott and Stobbs were homosexuals.) At his trial he retracted, declaring he made his statement in order to act the part of a murderer, and because he was worried at being suspected by the police. He was found guilty of all three crimes and sentenced to death. It was suggested, however, that he had recently been under mental stress, and he was later reprieved and the sentence altered to one of life imprisonment.

On the junction of the B5023 and B5035 some four miles south of Matlock is the old town of Wirksworth. Near by, set well back from the road to Whatstandwell (B5035) is Wigwell

Grange. In 1862 it was known as Wigwell Hall, owned by 82-year-old Captain Goodwin and destined to become the scene of a famous Victorian *crime passionel*. As housekeeper the Captain made use of a relative, Bessie Caroline Goodwin, 21, daughter of an affluent civil engineer. Bessie had been engaged since she was eighteen to a young man named George Townley. He was a clerk in a mercantile firm and son of a merchant who lived in Hendham Vale, Smedley – a district now swallowed up in Manchester. Townley was not looked on with any great favour by Bessie's family as a match, and it was probably with a view to terminating the engagement that Bessie was despatched to Wigwell Hall and the ageing Captain. The relationship, however, though broken off once, was renewed in an apparently somewhat desultory way. Then, at Wigwell Hall, she met a young parson – much better, thought the relatives. So, it seems, did Bessie, for she asked Townley in a letter to cancel their renewed engagement. On 21st August 1862 the desperate young man went to see Bessie at the Hall, asked her once again to marry him, and when she refused cut her throat with a knife he had brought along with him. The Captain, it appears, with admirable *sang-froid*, offered him a cup of tea, keeping him calm by its soothing influence until arrangements could be made for his arrest. Townley was condemned to death, but the sentence was later altered as a result of mental examinations, and he was imprisoned at Pentonville. He committed suicide there in February 1865 by jumping over a parapet to the stone floor beneath.

Finally in Derbyshire we visit Butterley Hall, only about half-a-dozen miles from Wigwell Grange. Over one hundred years before the tragic slaying of Bessie Goodwin by the unhappy Townley a much nastier gentleman was found guilty of murder. He was William Andrew Horne, eldest son of Squire Horne who owned Butterley Hall and was described as probably the best classical scholar in the country. William Andrew was that particularly unpleasant combination—a man both dissipated and miserly. Most of the female servants had been dishonoured by his attentions and when such normal pleasures palled he turned to incest—apparently with the willing co-operation of his sisters. Eventually one of them, Anne, presented him with the usual result. The arrival of a son and heir, however, brought the incestuous parents little joy. In those no-nonsense days incest was a hanging offence. He asked his brother Charles what to do, and the latter obligingly fell in with a little plot. The following morning a child was found dead in a field near Annesley, some five miles away.

There is now an interval—of 35 years. During the course of it the old Squire died (aged 102), and in 1747 William Andrew succeeded to the Butterley throne. He immediately proceeded to treat his brother Charles less than kindly, even to the extent of turning him from the house. This was a foolish, not to say an imbecilic, thing to do. Seething with anger and a new-born feeling for justice, Charles began to talk about certain dark events of the past. No-one, strangely enough, wanted to know. So William Andrew helped himself a step further towards well-deserved destruction by having a row with a Mr Roe who had accused him of being "an incestuous dog". William Andrew actually prosecuted the unfortunate truthteller, and won his case. Talk began to spread, but such was the strength of squire-power in those days that it was still a long time before any steps were taken. At last, however, the authorities were forced to act: in 1759 William Andrew Horne was brought to trial and the story came out. He said he had no intention of killing his ill-begotten child, but thought he would give it as a present to a Mr Chaworth of Annesley. What Mr Chaworth would have thought of such an unexpected gift is not recorded. William Andrew put the small mortal in a bag lined with wool and took it along to the Chaworth garden. Barking dogs, however, discouraged him from approaching the house, so he left his bundle under a haystack to be found (and presumably cared for) by farm workers. Not unexpectedly, the child did not live through the night.

Charles, it now appeared, had told his father all about this escapade and had been ordered to keep his mouth shut and not mention such matters again. Anne's feelings about all this were not, it seems, considered. After a series of postponements, the hanging of William Andrew took place on 30th November 1759, his seventy-fourth birthday. He was driven to the Gallows Hill from Derby by his own coachman. As the gloomy procession went along the Mansfield road, according to an account written in the middle of the last century (when they knew how to be colourful about such events)—"the withered locks of the hoary sinner streamed mournfully in the wind".

(*above*) The Blackpool Jewel Raid: (*left*) Frederick Joseph Sewell and (*right*) Superintendent Gerald Richardson.

(*below left*) Walter Graham Rowland, murderer of Olive Balchin. (*right*) Peter Griffiths, the Blackburn child-killer.

The Moors Murders:
(*left*) the house in
Wardle Brook Avenue,
Hattersley; (*below*)
police carrying away
the body of John
Kilbride.

Butterley Hall still stands on a coach-road leading off the A61 about half a mile from Ripley and two miles from Alfreton. With pleasant irony, it now houses the headquarters of the Derbyshire County and Borough Constabulary.

In the early nineteenth century, according to the records, a "dreadfully depraved set of people" lived around the now doubtless wholly respectable town of Market Drayton, Shropshire (or Salop). They were a closely-knit gang of some fifty or sixty villains—able to recruit as many more as they needed owing —as the writer stingingly concludes—"to the general depravity of the neighbourhood". Their activities included sheep stealing, potato pilfering, and general rural robbery and mayhem. Among the worst of the bunch, their names secure in infamy, were Ann Harris, John Cox the elder and the younger, Robert Cox and James Pugh. In 1827 one of the mob, a man named Ellson, was tried for stealing a sheep, and James Harrison, an intermittent member, gave evidence against him. The five people mentioned above determined to revenge their colleague. After trying in vain to buy arsenic from "a man going to Newcastle" (why such a journey should be supposed to make him a likely poison provider is not disclosed), they decided on more direct means. Ann Harris—who happened to be Ellson's mother—and John Cox senior each subscribed 50 shillings to hire the latter's two sons and James Pugh to kill Harrison—an early example, perhaps, of Murder Inc. In due course Pugh and John Cox junior strangled Harrison in Pugh's father's house, where he was lodging. While they were doing so Robert Cox was busy digging the victim's grave near by. For a time nothing untoward was suspected, it being supposed that Harrison was away at Ellson's trial. Ellson was acquitted and returned home. Later, unable to keep his hands off other people's livestock, he was arrested again for stealing fowls. He was now faced with possible transportation. In order to avoid this, he showed his gratitude to his mother and her associates for their act of revenge on his behalf by telling the whole tale to the authorities. Harrison's body was dug up, and all five concerned in his murder were sentenced to death— though old Cox and Ann Harris were later reprieved and transported. Thus the 150-year-old rural preview of Chicago gangsterism came to an end.

At the north-eastern tip of Wenlock Edge is Much Wenlock,

E

on the A458 between Shrewsbury and Bridgnorth. Just over
one hundred years ago the belief in witches and their powers
was strong in the district. Ann Evans, an old countrywoman
with a reputation for magic and spells, was feared and hated
by everyone around. It was said that by casting the evil eye she
affected the well-being of their sheep and pigs, their crops, and
their personal lives. In fact, she tyrannized the population.
Though nearly seventy she was a strong and muscular figure,
and when her husband died she brought William Davies, 35, to
live in her cottage. It was considered that he must have been
drawn there by an attraction he was powerless to resist, and
that he tried in vain to break from her influence. On 12th
September 1857 he returned home and was berated by her for
spending too long doing the shopping in the village. A small
boy saw a scuffle going on in the cottage, and later the old
woman was found on the floor, dead from stab wounds. William
Davies was found guilty, but it was decided that there were so
many extenuating circumstances that his life was spared. He
was, in fact, considered to have rid the neighbourhood of a
pestilential presence, rather than deprived a septuagenarian
woman of her remaining years.

Moving into Staffordshire, we come to Barlaston, a village just
off the A34, south of Arnold Bennett's Five Towns. In 1952 Mr
Cuthbert Wiltshaw, a pottery manufacturer, lived in a large
house named Estoril, Station Road. Among the servants he employed was 29-year-old Leslie Green. At one time he had worked
as a chauffeur, but following his unauthorized use of a car
for private purposes he had been dismissed. At the beginning
of July, his wife said, he had disappeared from his home. On
16th July Mr Wiltshaw returned to Estoril to find his wife, aged
62, lying dead in the hallway and her jewellery missing. On the
19th Green went to the police (who had been trying to locate
him), saying he wanted to clear himself. He had been staying
in Leeds with a young woman to whom, posing as a single man,
he had proposed marriage. On 17th July he gave her an engagement ring and a wedding ring. The following day she received
a letter from her sister informing her that the police were looking for a man named Leslie Green. Having an uncomfortable
feeling that the rings may have had some connection with the
murder of Mrs Wiltshaw, she returned them to Green. When,

on the following day, he admitted that he had once worked for the family, she told him he must go to the police.

Green put forward an alibi that he was at the Station Hotel, Stafford, on his way to Leeds, during the time of the murder. The police, however, worked out that between a number of occasions on which he was seen in Stafford he could have gone over to Barlaston, murdered and robbed Mrs Wiltshaw, and returned in time to catch the Leeds train. Among other points of evidence against him, the observant manager at the Station hotel noticed that at 6.30 p.m. (after the time of the murder) Green had an overcoat with his luggage that had not been there when he first arrived at the hotel. Later, the rings (proved to have belonged to Mrs Wiltshaw) were found hidden in the coalhouse of a block of flats in Leeds where he had been staying. Green, who had once worked as a page-boy in a luxury hotel and had a criminal record of theft, was found guilty, and executed on 23rd December 1952, at Winson Green, Birmingham.

In the little village of Ranton, six miles west of Stafford, on 16th December 1833, Mary Evans, a young woman of 20, daughter of the Parish Clerk and described as "possessing considerable personal attractions", was found by a wagoner lying in a ditch. She had been murdered. Her face was badly lacerated, her bonnet crushed, and there were signs that she had struggled for her life. The spot was only 200 yards from an inhabited house. Suspicion fell on a young man named Richard Tomlinson who had been keeping company with her. Within two hours he had been arrested and had confessed to the crime. The previous day, he said, they had set out together to call on her sister at Knightley, some five miles away. After spending the night there they had started out again, this time for High Ercall, a good 15 miles' walk, in order to consult a 'conjurer' about some possessions that Mary had lost. On the way Tomlinson was taken ill so they turned back to Ranton. As they neared it a fierce quarrel sprang up. Mary accused him of stealing her things and being afraid to visit the conjurer because he would be found out. He in turn accused her of stealing his watch and some sovereigns. Mary retaliated with a full salvo, declaring that his father had been poisoned and his mother had died in gaol. He said that if she repeated these words he would kill her. The foolish girl did repeat them, so he knocked her into the ditch. She shouted,

"You've murdered me!", to which he replied, "If I have not, I will do it". He then jumped on her as she lay in the ditch. She scrambled up to the bank, and there he left her. He said her wounds were caused by the heel of his boot when he jumped on her, but a bloodstained stone was found lying close by. Whatever the details, the young man paid with his life for this tragic end to a lovers' tiff.

Staffordshire's most famous case is, without doubt, that of William Palmer, druggist, abortionist, gambler and multiple poisoner. He was born in Rugeley, son of a sawmill proprietor, acquired a knowledge of drugs, and worked for a Doctor Tylecote at Hayward, Cheshire. His interests soon turned to betting on horses, and he also oddly combined the seemingly contradictory activities of prolific breeder of illegitimate children with abortionist. Had he combined the two, one cannot help thinking, it would have considerably lessened his future difficulties. The number of people he poisoned has never been established, but among them, almost certainly, were creditors, relatives, and various of his children, legitimate and otherwise. His dosage was strychnine, one of the most vicious and agonizing of all poisonous methods. He was finally arrested for the murder, at the Talbot Arms, Rugeley, of a gambling crony named John Parsons Cook, and executed at Stafford. The Talbot Arms, renamed the Shrewsbury Arms, can still be found in the Market Street.

Palmer came of a wealthy family: his father, who died when William was 13, left £70,000, of which his son received £7,000. This was soon swallowed up by gambling and amorous pursuits. Directly or indirectly, the motive for almost all his crimes was the obtaining of funds to pay his expenses. He was adept at concealing his infamous activities and the local worthies were astonished when the truth came out. "Mr Palmer a murderer?" exclaimed one. "Why, he used to make the responses in church louder than anyone else!"

A 'lodger' crime was committed in the village of Burntwood Green, some three miles west of Lichfield, when Sarah Westwood, 42, murdered her husband John, 40, by poisoning him with arsenic in November 1843. The bone of contention was Samuel Phillips, who had been staying in the house for about six years (together with Sarah's five children), and with whom she had been carrying on an affair. Phillips' mother, a 'wise woman' at Walsall, said in court that Sarah had asked her for a prescription to "cure the itch"—which is at least a change from the usual 'killing rats' excuse. Together they bought various ingredients from a chemist who mixed them together in his shop. Later, however, Sarah returned to the shop alone and persuaded him to sell her one of the ingredients—arsenic—by itself. Shortly afterwards John Westwood died, after the usual symptoms of violent vomiting and stomach pains. Large quantities of arsenic were found in his body—no-one in the cottage had the 'itch'. After a claim that she was pregnant had been disproved, Sarah was executed at Stafford in January 1844.

Moving south to Wolverhampton, we come to the scene of a crime which Marshall Hall, according to his biographer Edward Marjoribanks, regarded as his greatest victory as defender in a murder trial. It occurred on the evening of 29th December 1908 when Edward Lawrence, a rich wine-and-spirit merchant who lived at 2 George Street (later converted into offices) called on a Dr Galbraith and stammered out that he had killed a woman. Lawrence was known to be a violent and dissipated man, fully upholding a family reputation for hard drinking. His wife had recently started divorce proceedings on account of his adultery with a barmaid, Ruth Hadley, though she had sufficient remaining affection for him to hesitate from completing the break, and the *decree nisi* had never been made absolute. When Dr Galbraith arrived at the George Street house he found Ruth Hadley lying in the dining-room in her outdoor clothes, shot through the head. A meal for two, almost untouched, was on the table. Lawrence later denied that he had shot her, claiming it was suicide. Marshall Hall, with everything seemingly against him, managed to build up, piece by piece, a picture in Lawrence's favour, showing that Ruth Hadley also was often drunk and violent and had more than once threatened to shoot her lover. Lawrence again revised his story, telling now of a fierce quarrel during which he produced a revolver merely to frighten her, but in a struggle it went off. It was a defence produced with monotonous regularity in such circumstances, but after a dramatic re-enactment of the scene in court Marshall Hall proved that the gun, which had a defective mechanism, could in fact have gone off accidently. Lawrence was acquitted. Three days later he was arrested for a vicious attack on a man in a public house.

In February 1936 the body of Mrs Eliza Jane Worton was discovered in the Birmingham Canal at Coseley. She had apparently been bludgeoned with a heavy spanner and then, still living, flung from a bridge over the water. Frederick William Oakley, a 37-year-old lorry driver known to have been friendly with her and to have given her lifts, was charged with her murder. He admitted at his trial that he had seen her twice on the day she was killed but swore that both occasions were several hours before she met her death. Against this was the evidence of two boys who declared they had seen the lorry on the bridge late that evening. Oakley's family said that he was at home at that time, and blood on his clothing was accounted for as occurring in the normal course of his loading work. It was during this trial that Norman Birkett, who defended, made his famous remark that his client could draw upon his good character as a man with a credit balance at the bank. Oakley's past record was a spotless one—he was acquitted.

The same cannot be said of Stanley Hobday, who in August 1933 slew Charles Fox in a house in Moor Street, West Bromwich. Fox, a metal worker, was also collector for a clothing firm. Hobday broke into his house during the night and, when Fox went down to see what was going on, stabbed him with a bowie knife, grabbed what cash he could (Mrs Fox was by this time screaming for help from the window) and ran off. His haul was 14 shillings. He then entered a butcher's shop in Bromford Lane, a continuation of Moor Street, stole several pounds, shaved himself, poured himself a drink of milk and mended a tear in his coat. He then stole a car from a garage in the Lane and drove north. In passing through Cheshire he turned the car over in a somersault and continued on foot. Meanwhile he had been identified by fingerprints on the milk bottle (he had a previous record), and his description was broadcast by the B.B.C., the first occasion on which an arrest was made as a direct result of such a means. A farmer near Carlisle recognized him and he was arrested, picking blackberries, at Rockcliffe—a small town some five miles north of the city. He was executed at Winson Green Prison, Birmingham, in December 1933.

In the early evening of 22nd August 1967 the body of little Christine Darby, aged 7, was found by the foot of a tree in Cannock Chase, the extended wooded area now designated as an Area of Outstanding Natural Beauty some twelve miles north of Wolverhampton. She had been sexually assaulted with savage brutality. The discovery ended an intensive search lasting just over three days. On the 19th she had been playing with two friends in Camden Street, Walsall, where she lived. A car turned in from the adjoining Corporation Street and the driver asked the way to Caldmore Green—pronouncing the word Caldmore in a local way, as 'Karmer'. He asked Christine to get into the car and show him. She did so and, to the astonishment of the watching children, the man drove off in the opposite direction from the Green, which was in fact just round the corner. Her parents immediately informed the police, and one of the children was able to describe the car fairly accurately. Before Christine's body was discovered underclothing and a plimsoll had been found in a lane between Penkridge and Rugeley, a few hundred yards from the busy A34, and afterwards tyre marks near the body indicated that the car might have been an Austin A60. Later a man stated that he had seen a grey A55 or A60 parked in a 'fire ride'—an open channel cut in the woods to check forest fires—close to the spot. Despite unceasing and heartbreaking efforts by the police, however, little further of significance turned up and hope of solving the crime began to fade. Then on Guy Fawkes night 1968, over a year later, Margaret Aulton, a girl of 10, happened to be left alone for a few moments at a bonfire built on the corner of Bridgeman Street and Queen Street. A man drew up in a car and tried to entice her into it by saying that he had some fireworks for her. Margaret broke away and the man drove off. The incident had been witnessed by a young woman, Mrs Wendy Lane, who happened to be standing near by, and with commendable sense she noted the registration number of the car—a green Corsair with a white top. In this way the authorities were led to Raymond Leslie Morris, 39, a local man working as foreman engineer in an Oldbury firm. He lived with his second wife at Flat 20, Regent House, Green Lane, Walsall. From June 1966 until August 1968 he had owned a grey Austin A55 and on this account had been interviewed already during routine enquiries. He had then provided an alibi for the day of Christine's Darby disappearance. He was now questioned regarding the bonfire incident and put on an identification parade, but neither Mrs Lane nor Margaret Aulton were able to pick him out.

Following more intensive enquiries, Morris was arrested on 15th November and charged with the murder of Christine Darby.

During the subsequent investigations it was discovered that in August 1968, a year after the murder, Morris, unknown to his wife who was actually in the flat at the time, had taken obscene photographs of a 5-year-old girl who was staying with them, in positions very similar to that in which Christine's body had been lying. It was as if he was trying to recreate the circumstances of the murder. Other indications of perverted tastes were found in the flat, hidden from Mrs Morris—and eventually she stated that his alibi, which depended on her confirmation, was false. In fact, he had had ample time in which to commit the murder.

The trial of Raymond Morris opened on 10th Febuary 1969, the judge ruling that all three charges—the killing of Christine Darby, the attempted abduction of Margaret Aulton, the indecent assault on the little girl—should be admitted. Morris pleaded guilty to the third charge, and was convicted on all three. He was sentenced to life imprisonment.

Christine Darby was not the only child victim of that period in the district. On 8th September 1965 Margaret Reynolds, 6, of Clifton Road, Aston, disappeared on her way to school after lunch. By 3rd December she was still missing. On that day Diane Tift, 5, of Hollemeadow Avenue, Blakenal Heath, Bloxwich, just north of Walsall, also disappeared, after leaving her grandmother's house in Chapel Street half a mile away. On 12th and 13th January 1966 the bodies of both little girls were discovered together in a ditch by Mansty Gully, a lane branching off the Penkridge–Rugeley Road about six miles from the spot where Christine Darby would be found. Diane Tift had been suffocated by her pixie hood—it was impossible to tell how Margaret Reynolds had met her death. At the conclusion of the trial of Raymond Morris the judge, Mr Justice Ashworth, said to Detective-Superintendent Ian Forbes who had worked so long and arduously on the case, "There must be many mothers in Walsall and the district whose hearts will beat more lightly as a result of this verdict. . . . There will be many who are truly grateful to you and to those who have served under you."*

* For a full account of the case of Raymond Leslie Morris, and of the painstaking, unremitting police work it involved, see the excellent study by Harry Hawkes, *Murder on the A34* (John Long, 1970).

4

ON THE SCENT

The East Midlands: Nottinghamshire, Leicestershire, Northamptonshire, Huntingdonshire, Cambridgeshire, Bedfordshire

The name of Frederick Nodder ranks high in any list of the least pleasant murderers. A drunken, dishonest, mean and squalid man of disgusting personal habits, he was to stand trial twice in connection with his revolting crime. In January 1937, when he was in his early forties, he was charged by the Chief Constable of Newark with abducting 10-year-old Mona Lilian Tinsley, tried at the Victoria Courts, Birmingham, found guilty and sentenced to seven years' penal servitude. The girl was still missing and the certainty that a much greater crime had in fact been committed hung like a dark cloud over the courtroom as Mr Justice Swift, in passing sentence, added the often quoted words, "What you did with that little girl, what became of her, only you know. It may be that time will reveal the dreadful secret you carry in your breast."

In 1934 Nodder, a married man who had deserted his wife, had gone to live in Sheffield with a Mr and Mrs Grimes. He was then using the name Hudson and calling himself a motor mechanic. He was also seeking to evade a bastardy warrant. About a year later he moved to Newark and stayed with Mrs Grimes's sister, Mrs Tinsley. The family lived at 11 Thoresby Avenue. The children became friendly with him and called him Uncle Fred. He remained there only a short while, however, then went off on his own to a semi-detached house, with the unsuitable name of Peacehaven, near Hayton, a village about three

miles north of East Retford on the B1403. It was in a very isolated
spot, an unlit lane running from Tiln, a tiny hamlet by the river
Idle, to Clarborough. A tributary of the river known as the
Bolham Shuttle ran near the house. Once Nodder had left the
Tinsleys he did not see them again, though Mrs Grimes appears
to have been a regular visitor to him. In the late afternoon of
5th January 1937 Mona Tinsley left the Wesleyan School in
Guildhall Street, Newark, and was seen with Nodder at the
bus station by the Robin Hood Hotel. He said later that she had
asked him to take her to see her aunt and baby cousin who were
paying him a visit at Hayton. Accordingly he brought her from
Newark to his house, where she spent the night. The following day, her aunt's visit being postponed, he took her on a bus
from East Retford to Worksop and left her to travel the rest of
the way to Sheffield herself, a journey of over an hour. He then
had a drink in East Retford and returned to Peacehaven, where
the police were already waiting for him. Mona Tinsley never
arrived in Sheffield and no trace was seen of her again. At first
Nodder had said he had never set eyes on her since he left the
Tinsleys, but later gave the story as above.

He had served only three months of his sentence, during which
time an unceasing search was kept up, when her body was seen
by a boating party in the river Idle below Bawtry. She had been
strangled, but owing to decomposition it was impossible to ascer-
tain whether she had also been sexually assaulted. Nodder was
brought to trial again, repeating in the witness-box the statement he had made to the police. They spent the night in the
house together, he stated, the little girl in the bedroom, he himself downstairs. Without difficulty Nodder was found guilty.
His appeal was dismissed and he was hanged on 30th December
at Lincoln.

In 1930 the roads leading from Ollerton ('the village among
the alders') through Edwinstowe and Chipstone in the district
known as the Dukeries were still very much country lanes. At
about midnight on 24th September a police constable named
Holland was walking his lonely beat from the crossroads beyond
Chipstone downhill towards Warsop. Seeing a stationary car
drawn up to one side with no lights on, he went to investigate.
Inside was a man who had been shot dead. He was identified
as Samuel Fell Wilson, a young provision merchant of Warsop
who, in a modest way of business, used to drive his car through

the mining and agricultural district taking money and collecting orders. Two men said they had heard a shot at about 9.15 p.m. while chatting together outside a caravan belonging to one of them which stood in a field close to the lane, but had taken little notice as such sounds were not uncommon in this poacher-ridden district. The car was less than two miles from Wilson's home and he had evidently been returning there with the day's takings. Part—but oddly enough not the whole—of the day's takings were missing. Several people who knew him had seen him driving along the road and all agreed that he had been alone—yet he was found seated in a car which had been carefully parked by the roadside. Death had been caused by two fully-charged ·12 bore shotgun cartridges: to the police this ruled out poachers, who were in the habit of 'doctoring' sporting gun cartridges by extracting half the pellets and reloading old cases in order not to damage birds so extensively that they became unsaleable. The theory finally accepted was that he gave a lift to someone he knew: a quarrel developed in the course of which the car ran onto the grass verge: the man then backed out, keeping the door open, fired at Wilson, grabbed the notes and ran off—but who this remarkably invisible acquaintance was has never been discovered.

In 1844 there was a footpath running across a spinney between Carlton (on the A612) and Colwick that was famous for its beauty and views across the countryside just east of Nottingham. On a summer day in that year a gruesome discovery stained its quiet loveliness, when Mrs Ann Saville and her three small children were found lying by it with their throats cut. Her husband was accused of the terrible crime. He was aged 29 and was employed as a framework knitter in Radford. For some time, it transpired, he had been "paying addresses" to a Miss Tait of that town, and eventually proposed marriage. When she told him she was under the impression he already had a wife he replied, "She's not my wife. She has never troubled you and never will. She is safe, and the children provided for." For the previous three months, in fact, his unfortunate family had been "provided for" by Nottingham workhouse; but a week before the murder Mrs Saville had taken her children and gone out in search of her husband. Unluckily for her—she found him, and apparently agreed to an outing in the beautiful countryside. After death a razor had been placed in her hand—Saville's razor

was missing and there was blood on his trousers. He was convicted, and executed in front of Nottingham County Hall in a
street called High Pavement. As the drop fell a "party of
ruffians" started pushing among the crowd gathered to witness
the event. Panic ensued. People were crushed and hurled head-
long down Garner's Hill, women were stripped and smothered
against one another. Scores were seriously injured, and twelve
deaths were added to that of the murderer.

In 1935 a 36-year-old ex-factory worker calling herself Nurse
Dorothea Waddingham (she had no qualification to the title and
her real name was Leech) was running a self-styled 'nursing-
home' at 32 Devon Drive, Nottingham, together with her lover,
39-year-old Ronald Sullivan. They had only one patient, a Mrs
Kemp, and were probably pleased to receive a visit from the
County Nursing Association (which seems to have accepted very
trustingly 'Nurse' Waddingham's non-existent status) asking
them to take in Mrs Baguley and her daughter Ada. Mrs Baguley,
described by her family as a "delightful old lady", was 89, her
daughter 50. Ada suffered from disseminated sclerosis and was
an enormously heavy woman, unable to walk, barely able to
use her arms. Their joint payment was only £3 a week—but
Dorothea Waddingham agreed to this and was capable of realizing the work involved in caring for them. Soon after their arrival
on 12th January, Mrs Kemp died. In May, strongly against her
solicitor's advice, Ada made a will leaving everything to 'Nurse'
Waddingham, who was to look after both herself and her
mother during the rest of their lives. On 12th May Mrs Baguley
died; on 11th September, shortly after a visit from a friend who
found her cheerful and lively, Ada followed her mother. Waddingham lost no time in getting to work. She produced a letter,
signed by Ada but written by Sullivan, addressed to the Nottingham Officer of Health and requesting that she should be
cremated forthwith. The letter also asked "as my last wish" that
none of her relatives should know of her death. Not surprisingly,
this astonishing missive aroused considerable suspicion. A post-
mortem was ordered on Ada Baguley, and in her body (and later
also in that of Mrs Baguley) large quantities of morphia were
discovered. Sullivan and his mistress were jointly charged with
murder, but Sullivan was quickly found 'not guilty' and dis-
charged. The self-designated 'nurse' was executed, despite a
strangely soft-hearted jury's recommendation to mercy. One

account of this callous crime describes the accused's appearance in the dock as "forlorn and pathetic"—an appearance she was doubtless at pains to present. Dorothea Waddingham was, in fact, not only a murderess for financial gain, but a petty criminal with a record of thefts and frauds, one of them—stealing money from a servant she herself employed—of a particularly mean nature. In court the Baguleys' doctor requested that she should be referred to as 'Mrs Waddingham' (her real name Leech had disappeared beyond recovery) rather than 'Nurse'. "It is rather unfair to the nursing profession, and also misleading," he remarked reasonably. She continued to be known as 'Nurse', however, an added insult to the profession she disgraced.

On 2nd August 1951, 48-year-old Mrs Mabel Tattershaw, of Longmead Drive, Edwards Lane, Nottingham, went to the Roxy Cinema. A young man sat next to her and they began to talk. The next evening they went for a walk in Sherwood Vale. On 9th August, following a call to the crime reporter of the *News of the World*, the police contacted Herbert Leonard Mills, a 19-year-old clerk who lived in Mansfield Street, and were taken by him to the Orchard, an isolated wooded area off Sherwood Vale, where they found Mrs Tattershaw's body. Mills said he had stumbled over her but had no idea who she was. He added that he noticed a "sinister limping man" in the district. Mrs Tattershaw had been strangled, and there were indications that she had been beaten both before and after death.

During the next few days Mills had several meetings with Norman Rae, chief crime reporter on the *News of the World*, and described his discovery in an article that was published in the paper. Norman Rae, however, was strongly suspicious of the "cold, cocky, greedy" young man, and led him on to talk more and more unguardedly, until at last he wrote out a confession—on sheets of a hotel notepaper—which Rae forwarded to the police. Hairs and suit fibres found on the body were found to match his own. His trial opened on 11th November 1951, and he was executed in December. It was an attempt at the 'perfect crime', Mills claiming that if he had not reported finding the body he would never have been connected with the murder. "I am," he said, "quite proud of my achievement."

On 5th May 1760 Laurence Shirley, fourth Earl Ferrers, having been found guilty by his peers of the murder of his steward, dressed himself in a light-coloured suit embroidered with silver, drove in his own carriage from the Tower of London to Tyburn and, as a concession to his exalted rank, was accorded the privilege of being hanged with a silken rope. The scene of the crime was Staunton Hall, a mansion at Staunton Harold some 19 miles north-west of Leicester and three north of Ashby-de-la-Zouch (off the B587). Earl Ferrers was regarded as a man of violent temper. He had, for instance, beaten a footman on the head with a silver candlestick and stabbed him because a barrel of oysters sent from London was found to be uneatable. He had a habit of chasing his wife around the house with a loaded pistol, until, tired of dodging him round the furniture, she left and obtained an order for maintenance on the not unreasonable grounds of cruelty. The steward, John Johnson, who lived at a farm half a mile away called the Lount, was made Court Receiver, responsible for collecting the rents from which the income was to be paid to the Countess. Earl Ferrers had a say in the appointment and chose his steward, so it was suggested, because he thought he could turn such an arrangement to his own advantage. Johnson, however, proved to be a man of integrity, refusing to cook any books to please his master, and the latter conceived a violent hatred towards him. On 18th July 1759 he sent all the servants away ("except for three maids"), summoned Johnson and demanded that he sign a paper confessing to "numerous villainies". Indignantly, Johnson refused, whereupon Ferrers made him kneel down and shot him through the stomach. When a party of neighbours arrested him on his own bowling-green he was armed with a blunderbuss, two pistols and a dagger.

Staunton Hall was first built in Gothic style by Francis Shirley in 1566 and later rebuilt by Robert Shirley, first Earl of Ferrers, in the seventeenth century. During the Second World War it was occupied by the military and by Italian prisoners. Afterwards it remained empty, in poor condition, and there was a threat—fortunately unfulfilled—that opencast mining might be started in the grounds. In 1954 it was put up for sale, with every prospect of being demolished if no offer was received. Later, however, as a result of the courageous efforts of Group Captain Leonard Cheshire, it became famous as one of the Cheshire Homes for Incurables. At the time of writing it is still in full use, an inspiring development for the scene of one of the county's most notorious crimes.

Almost equally notorious, though in humbler surroundings, was the unsolved Green Bicycle case which occurred in the quiet country lanes and villages just east of Leicester in 1919. On the evening of 5th July Joseph Cowell, of Elms Farm, Little Stretton (called Stretton Parva in a contemporary police announcement) was driving his cattle along Gartree Road, also known by its Roman name of Via Devana. At the bottom of a small dip, close to the village, he saw the body of a young woman in the middle of the road, her bicycle lying beside her. She had been shot just below the left eye, and there was a bullet close by. She was identified as Bella Wright, a girl of 21 who lived at Stoughton and worked on a night shift in a Leicester factory. Earlier in the evening she had cycled over to see her uncle in Gaulby, a village reached by a turn-off from the road near Little Stretton. With her was a man whom she described as a stranger—but her uncle noticed that when she left the house the two of them rode off together. The man rode a green bicycle. This was the last seen of Bella Wright alive by anyone other than the man—and, perhaps, her murderer.

Little more developed for several months. Then, on 23rd February 1920 a canal boatman taking a load of coal to the factory where Bella had been employed saw his tow-rope dip beneath the water and tauten again bearing part of a bicycle—and it was green. It slipped back under the water, but the boatman knew all about the official interest in (and the reward offered for) green bicycles, and saw to it that it was recovered. Green bicycles were not uncommon in those days, but this one had certain peculiarities. It was traced to a man named Ronald Light, 34, who denied all knowledge of Bella and said that though he had once owned a green bicycle he had sold it long ago. At the time of the murder he had been living with his mother at 54 Highfield Road, Leicester, after being demobilized from the Honourable Artillery Company. Before the discovery of the bicycle he had obtained a post as a schoolmaster in Cheltenham. Despite these denials—and following the dredging up from the canal at a spot near where the bicycle was found, of a revolver holster containing live bullets—Light was charged and brought to trial. He was defended by Marshall Hall. Appearing as a junior counsel for the prosecution was Norman Birkett, in his first notable case.

When called to the witness-box Light sprang a carefully prepared surprise by admitting ownership of both bicycle and holster. The revolver belonging to the holster had been taken from him when he left the army after suffering shellshock. He also admitted meeting Bella Wright (for the first time) that evening. He had been to visit some family friends in West Drive, Leicester, he said, but found them away, and decided to go for a ride around the countryside. He took the main road out to Great Glen then turned off a side road to Little Stretton. From there he cycled towards Leicester, but having some time to spare turned

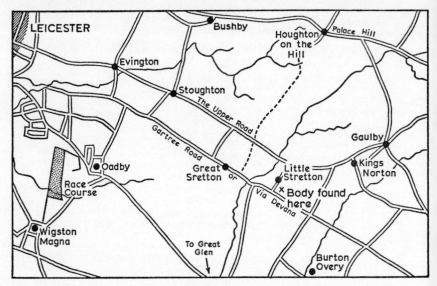

The Green Bicycle Case

off up a side lane on to the Upper Road. This was, in fact, a quicker route back to the city than the Via Devana, passing through the villages of Stoughton and Evington *en route*. With time still on his hands, however, he then turned away from Leicester towards Gaulby. A moment later he came across a girl (Bella Wright) who asked him for a spanner to adjust the freewheel of her bicycle. They chatted together and he cycled back with her to Gaulby. Having some trouble now with his own bicycle—a flat tyre—he repaired it while she visited her uncle and rejoined her when she came out. They started back along the Upper Road, but when they got to the fork that passed Little Stretton she surprised him by saying she was turning down it—and there they parted. He never saw her again.

Light made an excellent impression in the witness-box. He admitted frankly his foolishness in not going to the police when he knew they were looking for the man on the green bicycle— he admitted throwing both the bicycle and the holster away in panic—he admitted his lies and evasions when questioned. He made it apparent how anyone in his position might have been frightened into acting in the same way. Marshall Hall emphasized the complete lack of motive, and the fact that no-one had seen Light and Bella Wright actually on the Via Devana together that night. It is one of the minor mysteries of the case why Bella Wright, who lived at Stoughton on the Upper Road, should have chosen suddenly to take a roundabout way home: she was known to be a quiet, retiring girl of a type most unlikely to go in for secret assignations. Light was acquitted to popular acclaim and afterwards wrote a moving letter of thanks to his counsel.

One more character—suitably macabre in this oddly bizarre mystery—remains to be mentioned. Behind the hedge where Bella Wright's body lay there was found the corpse of a large black bird (probably a crow or a rook rather than the 'raven' suggested by a dramatically-minded constable), gorged with blood. From the girl's body to the dead bird ran a trail of twelve bloodstained claw marks.

Moving into Northamptonshire we are faced at once with (according to contemporary opinion) "one of the most appalling instances of human depravity". This was the murder in 1821 of John Clarke, a wealthy farmer who lived at Charwell House, Charwelton (about five miles south of Daventry on the B4036), by his wife and her lover, John Philip Haynes. The dastardly crime took place "after a long course of adultery". On 10th February Mr Clarke was busily cutting hay on one of his stacks as a good farmer should, when he was shot at from a barn only seven or eight feet away. His left arm was hit, and in spite of (or in those days perhaps because of) amputation of the injured limb, he died. During the two days before the fatal operation was performed Mr Clarke both made his will and expressed strong suspicions of Haynes, who had been employed by him and dismissed a short time previously. There were numerous points of evidence against the accused man, including the fact that he was seen hiding in the barn shortly after the murder, by a labourer in Mr Clarke's employment who lived at Hellidon close by. A striking feature of the case was a number of letters from Mrs Clarke found in the accused's possession, which left no doubt of her complicity—their constant theme being "do him in if you can". In one of them she asked Haynes to obtain some laudanum and send it to her. Allowing for the contrast between straightforward rural earthiness and sentimental suburban romanticizing in the respective correspondence, the similarity of this case to that of Thompson and Bywaters is noteworthy.

Towards the end of the last century Mr E. Macrae was a well-known Northampton provision merchant who used to label his sacks of goods for transit "E. MACRAE, NORTHAMPTON, L. & N.W.R.". One such label was to bring his brother Andrew to the gallows. Andrew, who worked in the family firm, had been living at 33 St John Street, Northampton, with a woman not his wife. They were known as Mr and Mrs Anderson. On 20th July 1892 Mrs Anderson was seen leaving a house to which she had moved in order to give birth to her child. Andrew was with her. On the 21st they were seen together again, with the baby, outside a warehouse in Dychurch Lane which was owned by E. Macrae and generally left in Andrew's charge. That was the last glimpse of either Mrs Anderson or the baby alive. Andrew took lodgings in Derby Street—alone.

On 6th August a man walking along a road in East Haddon, a village six miles north-west of Northampton (just off the A428) noticed a very unpleasant smell: after hunting around for the source he came across a bulky parcel wrapped in sacking. It consisted of a very decomposed torso, and on the sacking was Mr E. Macrae's label. The remains were identified by a Miss Lizzie Pritchard as those of her sister Annie. For two years the Pritchards and the Andrew Macraes had lived next door to one another in Highgate Road, Birmingham. Annie Pritchard had then become 'Mrs Anderson' and Andrew had deserted his wife. Further human remains were found in a copper in the Dychurch Street warehouse—Mr E. Macrae stated that it had been cleaned out several times and that many fires had been burnt in it since 21st July. To the last Andrew protested his innocence, but after debating the matter for 40 minutes the jury took the view that

this was one more instance of the callous disposal of an attachment that had become a burden, and Andrew was condemned.

A far more complicated burden, in fact a whole conglomera-
tion of burdens, led Alfred Arthur Rouse to attempt a far more
subtle means of disposal in the famous Blazing Car Murder of
1930. Rouse was a fine example of the music-hall (and largely
libellous) picture of the licentious commercial traveller, with a
girl—and possibly a child—in every town. The son of a hosier,
he was born in 1894 in Milkwood Road, Herne Hill, and before
the First World War worked in a London soft-furnishing firm.
He became a sacristan at St Saviour's Church, Stoke Newington,
and at the beginning of the war married Miss Lily Watkins at
St Saviour's Church, St Albans. On active service during the
war he suffered very severe head injuries and endured the subsequent hospital treatment with considerable courage. He was dis-
charged in 1916. The operation to the left side of his head was
subsequently put forward as the cause of the change in his character. He took up various jobs, eventually becoming a successful
commercial traveller. He was also an accomplished car driver
and mechanic—a skill that was to have some influence on his
fate. Around 1927 he moved with his wife to a small house in
Buxted Road, Finchley, where he was known as a keen gardener
and an entertaining companion—particularly popular at parties,
where his pleasant singing voice was much in demand for the
rendering of tender Victorian ballads.

He had, however, interests less innocuous than roses and
song. By 1930 he had, during his travels about the country,
bigamously married Helen Campbell (by whom he had first had
a child in 1921 when she was 15), was complying—very irregu-
larly—with maintenance orders in respect of children born to
him by Nellie Tucker, another lonely girl whom he had seduced,
and was trying to deal with the problem of Ivy Jenkins in distant
Gellygaer, Monmouthshire, who was looking forward to both a
child and a marriage certificate. These—among others. The
liaison with Ivy Jenkins was particularly risky for she was no
'lonely girl' but had a family (her father was a colliery proprietor)
that showed a close and inconvenient interest in their daughter's
welfare, believing that she was already married to Rouse who
was in the process of preparing a fine house for her in fashionable
Kingston-upon-Thames. In addition to all this his wife, long
suspicious of what was going on, was contemplating a separation.

It was, in fact, becoming an intolerable situation. Rouse decided to tolerate it no longer.

At about 2 a.m. on the morning of 6th November 1930 two young men, William Bailey and Alfred Brown, were walking home from Northampton after a Guy Fawkes' Night dance. They lived in the village of Hardingstone and their way lay along the main Northampton–Newport Pagnell road (A50). About three miles from Northampton they turned left into Hardingstone Lane, which during daylight hours was, despite its name, quite a busy thoroughfare. As they did so a car passed them on the main road and in its headlights they saw a man clambering out of a ditch. A few hundred yards down the lane, partly hidden by a bend, was a fiercely burning fire. Remarking in a rather breathless voice, "It looks as if someone has had a bonfire," the man went onto the main road where he paused uncertainly, looking back. Bailey and Brown found that the flames came from a blazing car in which lay—half in and half out of the seat —a charred body. The burning had rendered identification of the man impossible, but the car was traced to Rouse, and Rouse was the man in the ditch.

By a chance mistiming of a few seconds a whole elaborate plan had gone astray. In a 'confession' published the day after his execution and generally regarded as substantially true, he tells what he did—and what should have happened. The old Rouse must not only die, but must be seen to have died. Outside the Swan and Pyramids Hotel, 975 High Road, North Finchley, not far from Buxted Road, he met by chance a man who appeared to be completely alone, without friends, family or job. A few days later, on 5th November, he arranged to give the solitary stranger a lift to Leicester, picking him up at the same spot. On the way he turned off into Hardingstone Lane, drew up at the side of the road, strangled the man, whom he had previously made drunk on whisky, poured petrol over him, loosened the petrol joint in the car, removed the carburettor, then set fire to the car by a petrol trail from ten yards away. From that moment on, Rouse should have been presumed dead.

Once his plan was shattered by the inopportune meeting with the two young men his cunning seems to have deserted him. Instead of either summoning help or at least reporting to the police, he went home for a short while then travelled immediately by coach to Ivy Jenkins in Wales. Apparently he did not think the news of the burnt-out car would have spread so quickly, and was flabbergasted when Ivy's father showed him a picture in the newspaper and a description of the man seen by Bailey and Brown. He made a quick return to London, but the police had been forewarned by further developments, including a call from a Cardiff journalist, and he was arrested as he alighted at the Hammersmith terminus. He made a statement that he was stopped while in his car near St Albans by a man who wanted a lift. In Hardingstone Lane, when Rouse got out of the car to relieve himself, the man had accidently set fire to the petrol while emptying a can into the tank. Much of the trial was concerned with technical and scientific details in connection with the question as to whether the car was ignited by accident or on purpose. Rouse's behaviour in the witness-box, callous and boastful, did not help him. He was found guilty and sentenced to death.

In the opinion of Edgar Wallace, Rouse died for two reasons: (1) he told lies, (2) he ran away from the fire. The identity of the lonely victim was never discovered.

The circumstances surrounding the murder of Arthur Johnson, 53-year-old unmarried farmer, are commonplace enough, but the setting—a lonely stone cottage called Crow Tree Farm deep in the water-logged, dyke-checkered fen country—has all the properties of a mystery-thriller: and the clue that betrayed the killer has a bizarrerie that matches the rest. It was the smell of dry rot. Crow Tree Farm, a square, hard-faced building, can still be seen on the lane about $2\frac{1}{2}$ miles from the village of Farcet and seven from the City of Peterborough. From this isolated dwelling place Arthur Johnson, on the night of 15th October 1957, disappeared. He had last been seen at about 10 p.m. driving his van towards home. A reserved, taciturn man, he was reputed to have a considerable amount of money hidden about the house. The police, however, found only a number of separate small amounts. What they did notice, in the little used parlour, was a strong smell of dry rot. A 27-year-old lorry-driver, Morris Arthur Clarke, was questioned as a matter of routine. He had once stayed on the farm and his wife had worked for Johnson. Afterwards he had started up his own business, but this had failed and he was known to be in debt and short of funds. On 16th October he paid £200 in notes into the bank to meet a cheque that a creditor had already presented once, only to have it returned. Other notes, amounting to about £10, were found in his possession, and he had no alibi for the night of the 15th. Later he did produce one, but it was proved to be false and belonged to another evening. More significant than this was the condition of the notes—they smelt strongly of dry rot.

Johnson's body was discovered in a canal or dyke not far from his home. Though they still had very little to go on the police again visited Clarke, this time with a search warrant. In the loft was a tin containing over £641—and a strong smell of dry rot. Faced with this discovery Clarke confessed. He said he suspected an affair between the farmer and his wife and went to challenge him. A quarrel arose during which Johnson attacked him. Clarke then hit him with a piece of wood, killing him. He opened the safe with a key found in the dead man's clothing, and hid the body in the dyke. He was sentenced to death, but later reprieved. The Fens Murder must be a very rare instance in which a sense of smell (other than those which led to the finding of a decomposing corpse) was primarily responsible for the discovery of a killer. In his book *Occupied with Crime* Sir Richard Jackson mentions how Superintendent Wilfred Daws carefully wrapped up the cake tin in which the money was found, to ensure that the smell would still be present at the trial.

In 1827 occurred what might be called the Case of the Miserly Clergyman. The Reverend J. Waterhouse was rector of Coton and Little Stukeley (on the A14), and lived in the large Rectory which stood alone in a farm in the centre of Little Stukeley, about fifty yards from the road. He was famed for his meanness. He used the best rooms in the house to store grain from his farm, lived in the kitchen and cooked for himself and those who worked for him, and bricked up all but 2 of his 40 windows to avoid the tax. Every Saturday he drove his pigs to Huntingdon, about four miles away, bringing home his tea and other provisions for the week in a basket. He was reputed (once again the fatal rumour, which should be a warning to misers) to keep large sums of money in the house.

At 11 a.m. on 3rd July his body was discovered by two farm boys lying in a mash tub. He had been stabbed. A man named Joshua Slade, of no known occupation, who had been seen hovering around, was apprehended and questioned, and later charged.

It was proved that he had stolen a sword from the Horse and Jockey Inn at Huntingdon shortly before the murder. After conviction he confessed his guilt, telling a tale with an undeniable touch of black comedy. On the morning in question, he said, he climbed the Rectory wall with the sword thrust down inside his trousers—a noteworthy, not to say dangerous, feat—entered the house and hid himself in a room he called the wool chamber, intending to rob the Rector that night. Worn out with his exertions, however, he fell asleep, and snored. The Reverend Waterhouse investigated the noise, whereupon Slade leapt up and drew his sword. The Rector, somewhat optimistically, then expressed a desire to be allowed to go and get his blunderbuss. Slade, not unnaturally, refused permission. He said instead, "Mr Waterhouse, if you will forgive me, I will forgive you" The Rector, understandably surprised as he was not aware of having done anything to be forgiven about, said nothing. Impasse. After a frozen moment, the Reverend Waterhouse told Slade he wouldn't forgive him, and began to run away. Slade knocked him backwards into the mash tub. The Rector tried to scramble out, there was a struggle, and Slade stabbed him in the throat. The unfortunate Rector exclaimed, with no more than the truth, "I'm done", and fell back into the tub.

Slade met his richly deserved fate at Huntingdon on 1st September. It is reported that while awaiting execution he "applied himself zealously to the performance of his religious exercises". The Rector might have appreciated a somewhat earlier application.

Seventy years later, in another village close to Huntingdon, a farmer named Walter Horsford murdered his mistress. He lived at Spaldwick, about five miles west of the town (on the A604), and had been married only a few months. For some years previously he had been intimate with a widowed cousin, Mrs Annie Holmes. At the end of 1897 she asked him for an abortive drug as she was expecting another child to add to the three she already had. One of these could claim Horsford as father. On 5th January 1899 he went to see her. After he left she went to bed early with a glass of water, and during the night she died in agony—from strychnine poisoning. On the following day packets of strychnine were found beside her, together with a note saying, "Take a little in water. It is quite harmless." Horsford was proved to have purchased arsenic, prussic acid, carbolic acid and strychnine "to kill rats". There can seldom have been a murder so clumsily contrived.

An unsolved mystery still remembered in Cambridge was the death of 50-year-old Miss Lawn in her small shop (converted from a private house) in King Street on 27th July 1921. The house was separated from The Champion of the Thames pub by a small plot known as Christ's Piece—a sort of recreation ground used chiefly on market days. At 11 a.m. she was seen at her door; at 11.10 a customer found the shop closed; at 11.30 a woman heard a faint noise inside; at 3 p.m. a little girl saw the side door open and, knowing Miss Lawn to be particular about this, went and informed her brother. Miss Lawn was found at the foot of the staircase bound and gagged. She had been beaten on the head with a chopper. There was a bowl of bloodstained water and a towel in the sink. Money had been stolen from the till, but a large packet of notes hidden in a bedroom was untouched. Suspicion fell on a young labourer named Thomas Clanwaring, recently released from Bedford prison and known to have been near the shop selling postcards. He had also been seen at the Rose and Crown, a pub some distance away, and much depended on whether he could have travelled between the two spots within a certain time limit. The evidence against him was shaky: though the jury took 90 minutes to decide, their verdict was Not Guilty, and Clanwaring was released.

The notorious Sarah Dazeley, whose declared ambition was to achieve seven husbands in ten years, lived at the village of Wrestlingworth, about three miles from Potton (on the A603) where she was born. She married husband number one, Simeon Mead, in 1839 and in February 1840 they had a baby boy. By the end of the year both had died from some mysterious internal complaint. Number two, 23-year-old William Dazeley, was married in February 1841 and died in October 1842. So far so good— Sarah was well on schedule, and in January 1843 she was preparing number three, named Waldock. Nasty rumours, however, were beginning to make themselves heard, and Waldock wisely retired from the running. Enquiries were started, Sarah fled, was apprehended in London and brought back. The bodies of Mead, the baby and Dazeley were exhumed. Arsenic was found in the last two, the first being too far advanced in decomposition. She was convicted, and executed in Bedford gaol, aged 24. Sarah Dazeley seems to have been a sluttish wench and her success, such as it was, suggests a serious shortage of available brides in the district. In his book, *Murderess*,* an interesting detailed study of the women executed for murder since 1843, Patrick Wilson singles out Sarah Dazeley as the only case of a multiple murderess whose motives were predominantly sexual— she achieved no material advantages from the deaths she caused. She also, fortunately, fell far short of her statistical ambitions.

Mary Ann Crouch, 19, died on 26th September 1841 at Ridgmont House, Ridgmont, just under four miles from Ampthill (on the A418), after eating a cake. She was the daughter of William Crouch of Chalfont and was staying with her uncle, a wealthy farmer. A relative of Ann's wanted yeast for some cakes she was making, and when she could not find any she asked the cook, Ann Lee, for soda instead. This was found to contain arsenic, which had also got into the pepper. The whole family were taken ill—though only Mary Ann died—and suspicion fell on both Ann Lee and a worker named George Peppott, a recent purchaser of arsenic ("for rats"—needless to say). No real motive emerged, however, and the case remains unsolved. One might, perhaps, be permitted to wonder about the reason for Ann Lee's dismissal, and about any possible relation between her and Peppott the arsenic man.

The killer of the woman whose completely naked body was found on 19th November 1943 by the River Lea on the outskirts of Luton, Bedfordshire, had taken such pains to destroy identification that her own 17-year-old daughter failed to recognize photographs of her mother's partially restored face which were shown on cinema screens and elsewhere. It was not until after three months, and after the tracing of over 400 missing women, that the body was proved to be that of Mrs Rene Manton, of Regent Street, Luton. Horace William Manton, a lorry-driver in the Fire Service, had told everyone his wife had left him, and had even been writing letters, supposed to come from her, to her mother. As with Louis Voisin, the Charlotte Street butcher,† his spelling gave him away. The letters referred to Hampstead (where Rene Manton was supposed to be living, and where Manton had been on frequent trips to post them), as "Hamstead". Asked by the police to spell out the name, he again made the same error.

* Published by Michael Joseph, 1971.
† See *Murderers' London*.

Manton confessed to killing his wife in the course of a quarrel, wrapping her body in sacking and hiding it before the children came home from school, and later wheeling it on a bicycle to the river. He was sentenced to death, but reprieved and imprisoned at Parkhouse, Isle of Wight, where he died a few years later.

The murder of Michael Gregston and the brutal assault on Miss Valerie Storey on 22nd/23rd August 1961 (the 'A6 Murder') took place in a layby at a spot, unmarked on most maps, known as Deadman's Hill, near Silsoe. The gunman had surprised the couple sitting in Gregston's car in a deserted cornfield at Dorney Reach, by the river Thames near Slough. He forced them to drive to the A4, then turned towards Slough and London Airport. After stopping for petrol, the man keeping Gregston covered throughout, they went through Hayes onto the A4010, eventually reaching Western Avenue at Greenford. Changing the original plan, which was for Northolt, the man directed them towards Harrow and Stanmore. They passed through Radlett, on the A5 to St Albans and eventually to the A6—Gregston trying all the time to attract the attention of passing motorists as he drove. On the A6 they went through Luton, Barton-in-the-Clay and Silsoe, finally stopping at the Deadman's Hill layby after turning the car back to the direction of Luton. There the man shot Gregston dead, raped Valerie Storey in the back of the car, dragged her out, and shot her also. Leaving her for dead by the roadside he then drove off in the car. Valerie Storey recovered, but is doomed to spend the rest of her life in a wheelchair. The attention of the police was drawn to a man named Peter Louis Alphon, but he was later cleared by them and James Hanratty, self-confessed burglar, thief and car-stealer, was arrested. After his first alibi (that he was with three men in Liverpool at the time) had collapsed, he put forward another one—that he was in Rhyl. After a trial of unprecedented length he was found guilty, and executed on 4th April 1962.

Hanratty had been engaged in crime at least from the age of 18: he was proud of his proficiency, and declared his complete lack of remorse for the worry and often very real suffering he caused to the people into whose homes he broke in order to deprive them of their possessions. He lied frequently and fluently. Ever since his trial a vast amount has been both written and spoken for and against his innocence of the A6 crime—presenting a complicated story in far fuller detail than we have room for here. In 1963 the House of Commons debated a demand for a public enquiry. It was rejected and the motion defeated. In 1966 Roy Jenkins, Home Secretary, set up a special enquiry to investigate the Rhyl evidence: in 1967 it was announced that there were no grounds for further action. During this time Peter Louis Alphon confessed more than once to the murder, then retracted. In 1971 a public enquiry was called for in a book by Paul Foot (*Who Killed Hanratty?*) that strongly defends Hanratty's innocence: in a long review of the book in the *Sunday Times* Dick Taverne, Q.C., who was Parliamentary Under-Secretary, Home Office, at the time of the 1967 report, just as strongly defends the verdict. In 1972 the B.B.C. devoted a whole programme of over two hours to an account and discussion of the case under the chairmanship of Edgar Lustgarten. The pros and cons were about equally divided. It may well be that the A6 murder will become as lasting a battleground for criminologists and amateur detectives as that of Julia Wallace or the Bordens. When all the noise of argument and debate dies down, two facts remain: the grief of Hanratty's family and their natural desire—whatever else he may have done—to clear his name of murder; and Valerie Storey, crippled for life after seeing her lover shot before her eyes, who said, "I should know whether Hanratty was guilty—I was there".*

* *Who Killed Hanratty?* is published by Jonathan Cape. See also: *The A6 Murder*, Louis Blom-Cooper (Penguin Special, 1963); *Deadman's Hill—Was Hanratty Guilty?*, Lord Russell of Liverpool (Secker & Warburg, 1965); *Famous Criminal Cases 7*, Rupert Furneaux (Odhams, 1962); *The Meaning of Murder*, John Brophy (Corgi, 1967).

5

ON THE BEACH
Eastern England: Lincolnshire, Norfolk, Suffolk, Essex

On 19th December 1934 Ethel Lillie Major was executed at Hull for killing her husband in the most agonizing manner, by poisoning him with strychnine. It is difficult to understand why the case of this nasty little beady-eyed woman—whose combination of spite with silliness seems to add an extra horror to malice aforethought—should have aroused such interest, unless as an admonitory example of just how sinister female viciousness can be. At the time the Majors were living, with their son of 14, at 2 Council Houses, Kirkby-on-Bain, which is on a small road running parallel to the A153 between Coningsby and Horncastle. At first, despite her bad temper and tedious boasting, their married life seems to have been reasonably calm. Later, however, the revelation of a gross piece of deception on her part cast a gargantuan spanner into the matrimonial works. In 1914 or 1915, when she was about 24, Ethel Brown, as she was then, had an illegitimate daughter who had been brought up by her family as one of their own. She had already known Arthur Major when they were children together in Tumby, but he had since gone away. When they met again and he proposed marriage Ethel hid the fact that her presumed sister was in fact her child. He only became aware of the truth years later, when someone in Kirkby-on-Bain had the pleasure of informing him. Mrs Major, it appears, was extremely unpopular among her neighbours, who were doubtless not too unhappy at the thought that such a revelation might well cause her some dismay. Arthur was understandably indignant at her dishonesty and further angered when she refused to tell him the name of the father. Their relationship rapidly deteriorated. She was later to accuse him of being a bully-ing drunkard, and there seems to have been some truth in this assertion. She not infrequently took her son and slept elsewhere than at home. Neither Arthur's boss, however, nor the Rector (he was a parochial councillor) noticed any signs of undue drink-ing. Ethel also professed to have found two mildly worded 'love letters' in his pockets (there is considerable doubt as to their authenticity and it was thought she might very well have writ-ten them herself), and fuel was thrown on the fire of her resent-ment by an anonymous note warning her that her husband had got himself "a nice bit of fluff". The author of this was never discovered either, but considering the universal dislike of Mrs Major it may well have come from a genuine mischief-maker. She accused a next-door neighbour, Mrs Ruth Kettleborough, of carrying on with Arthur—an accusation Mrs Kettleborough was to deny indignantly in the witness-box. The infuriated woman then embarked on a sort of publicity campaign that combined malice and absurdity in almost equal proportions. She attempted to harass and embarrass the unfortunate Arthur in every possible way, writing or talking against him to the police, the solicitor, the doctor, even the sanitary inspector. She climaxed her campaign by trying to get him dismissed from his job as a lorry-driver. His employer snubbed her by informing her that he was a very good worker, which doubtless made her angrier still. Eventually she poisoned him with strychnine, to which it was later proved she had access. Just before the funeral proces-sion started out (with Ethel in a frantic hurry to get things over) a second anonymous letter arrived—this time for the police. It referred to the death of a neighbour's dog which had eaten something Mrs Major scraped from a plate after Arthur was taken ill. Mrs Major watched it enjoying the scraps, laughed, and went back to her house: the dog died in agony. The cere-mony was halted, and Mrs Major arrested. The defence alleged that she had been driven to a state of hysteria by the letters and her husband's general behaviour. However, she elected not to go into the witness-box to substantiate this—and face cross-examination. The jury recommended this strikingly merciless woman to mercy, without stating the reason.

At the village of Stickney, about seven miles east of Kirkby-on-Bain (on the A16 north from Boston), Priscilla Biggadike poisoned her husband on the 30th September 1868 by putting arsenic in his tea. She said at first that he had left a note (which she had burnt) expressing his intention of killing himself because of his debts, then later tried to put the blame on Thomas Proctor, one of two lodgers in their cottage, who worked as a ratcatcher. He was arrested, but was not sent for trial and later appeared for the prosecution. Neighbours told of constant feuding and of Priscilla's expressed desire to see her husband dead. It was proved that she possessed arsenic and had offered some to a neighbour "to kill mice". Priscilla Biggadike, aged 29, was executed at Lincoln at the end of December. Patrick Wilson names her in his book *Murderess* as the first woman to be hanged inside a prison after the cessation of public executions.

Finally in Lincolnshire, to Boston workhouse, where in 1844 Eliza Joyce, 31, admitted to killing three young children, a son and daughter of her husband by his first marriage, and her own daughter aged only three weeks. She had already been charged in 1843 with the murder of the boy, 15-year-old William Joyce, by giving him arsenic, but the name was incorrectly entered in the indictment. She reappeared in the dock a month or two later, with the charge reduced to attempted murder—William's death having occurred over two months after the alleged administration of the poison. She was acquitted, but her husband left her and she was taken to the workhouse. The two little girls had died before the trials (in October 1841 and January 1842) and it was no longer possible, when she confessed in 1844, to confirm her statement that she had given them laudanum. It was on this confession alone that she was found guilty of murder and executed at Lincoln in August 1844. She said she had killed the children rather than let them continue "in this troublesome world", and the deeds were now a burden on her conscience.

Lorenzo Beha was a German-Jewish watchmaker who lived at St Stephen's, Norwich. In November 1853 people on their way to market noticed trails of blood on the lane between the hamlets of Wellingham and Tittleshall (a mile or so east of the A1065 from Fakenham). The trail led to Mr Beha's body lying on the edge of the common; his head had been almost severed by a hatchet. Mr Beha was known to be in the habit of carrying a box of gold and silver jewellery and watches in a bag suspended from a stick across his shoulder, in addition to a large sum of money in his pockets. All had gone. A butcher named Webster said he had seen a man bending over the ditch by the side of the lane, but for some reason it was only much later that he added the essential information that he knew who it was—a labourer named William Thompson who lived in Tittleshall. Thompson's cottage was searched, with startling results. The place was crammed, almost festooned, with jewellery. Watches and trinkets and coins cascaded out of every nook and cranny, including the chimney, the oven and the privy. Gamely he declared he saw a stranger commit the crime, and was threatened with instant death unless he agreed to decorate his house with the proceeds and keep his mouth shut. This valiant effort, unhappily, availed him nothing. He was tried, found guilty: he confessed, and paid the penalty.

On 21st March 1929, the day before he was to be ejected for non-payment of mortgage interest on his small farm at Tilney St Lawrence (off the A47 between Wisbech and King's Lynn), Wallace Benton came across Thomas Williamson, the man who was to have the reversion of tenancy, near the small row of stables by the house, and shot him dead. Williamson had, in fact, already started working the farm and was about his lawful occasions when he was killed. It was the violent climax to a sort of campaign of non-violent resistance Benton had put up against his removal. Over 70 years of age, he was stubborn, argumentative, partially blind and almost totally deaf. The combination of his failing faculties and his aggressive garrulity caused chaos at his trial. Ignoring everything that was said to him, the old man insisted on re-enacting the circumstances of the case, using the Clerk of Assize as his dummy victim, and waving the muzzle of his gun about within a few inches of the unfortunate official's head. The death sentence had to be bellowed at him phrase by phrase through an ear-trumpet. To the solemn concluding words, "May the Lord have mercy on your soul", he doughtily replied, "I'm not at all sure of that. I don't see why he should." Benton's appeal was dismissed, but he was swiftly reprieved. "I was not sorry," comments Sir Travers Humphreys who presided at his trial, "to see the last of him."

Rival claims for Norfolk's best-known murder case are probably fairly evenly divided between the Great Yarmouth Mystery of 1900 and the Stanfield Hall Horror of 1848.

Stanfield Hall, which still stands today not very greatly altered, is to be found some three miles east of Wymondham (off the A11). Charles Dickens, who visited it shortly after the fatal night, described it in a letter to John Forster as having "a murderous look that seemed to invite such a crime", but this description may have been coloured by romantic hindsight. The following is a necessarily simplified outline of the very complicated events that led up to the murder. A full account may be found in the *Notable British Trials* volume on the case, or in a well-illustrated article in the *Norfolk Fair* magazine of July 1971. James Blondfield Rush was an illegitimate child who early on in life had started to indulge in various forms of criminal activity, including arson. In 1824, when he was about 23 years of age, he became tenant of a farm in Aylsham, about 14 miles north of Norwich. He married in 1828, and 8 years later became tenant of Stanfield Hall Farm, his landlord being the Reverend George Preston. In 1837 Preston died, and his eldest son took on the name of Jermy "to regularize ownership of the estate", there being disputed claims to the properties. In 1842 or 1843 Rush's wife died, leaving him with nine children. He went to London, advertised for a governess and brought a Miss Emily Sandford back to the farm, where he seduced her under promise of marriage. Later he took lodgings for her at 2 Mylne Street, Pentonville, London. In 1848—not surprisingly—he was badly in arrears with his rent. He was evicted, and went to live at Potash Farm about a mile from the Hall, bringing Emily back from London to live with him. This building also still exists, though a good deal altered. He was now bankrupt, and seething with rage against Jermy, who was still demanding mortgage arrears. There followed some extremely complicated financial juggling in the course of which Rush forged various agreements, plunging ever further into a morass of debt and deception. Things reached their tragic climax on 28th November 1848.

Jermy, his son, and the latter's wife, were in Stanford Hall, together with several servants. Jermy was alone in the dining-room, his son and daughter-in-law playing piquet in the drawing-room. Rush arrived at the house heavily disguised behind a bush of false hair. At 8.30 Jermy senior left the dining-room and walked through the hall to the front of the building. Rush, who was lurking in the porch, shot him dead. He then threatened the butler, who came running out on hearing the noise, and rushed through the hall towards a passage in the rear of the house. When young Jermy came from the drawing-room in alarm

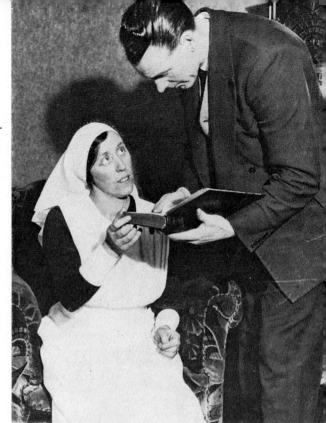

(*right*) 'Nurse' Dorothea Waddingham and R. J. Sullivan. (*below*) The Waddingham case: exhumation of the body of Louisa Baguley.

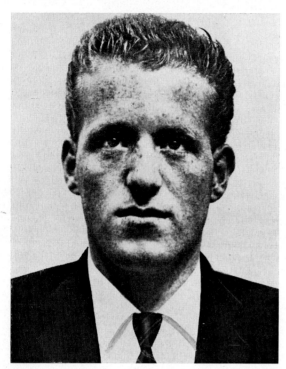

The A6 murder: (*left*) James Hanratty and (*below*) the scene of the crime.

Rush shot him also, killing him instantly, and seriously wounding his wife in the breast when she ran to the body. Meantime a servant plunged into the moat and swam across to summon help. Before it arrived Rush had caused another casualty—a maid named Eliza Chastney who bravely ran to aid her mistress. She was wounded in the thigh. Despite his cumbrous disguise and the confusion in which he made his escape, Rush had been clearly recognized and there was never any doubt as to his guilt and clear intention to slaughter the entire hated family. He was hanged in Norwich on 21st April 1849.

On 1st January 1869, his memories and conscience both perhaps strengthened by alcoholic New Year celebrations, William Sheward walked into Walworth Police Station, London, and confessed to having killed his first wife Martha by stabbing her with a pair of tailoring shears in Norwich 18 years previously. During that time he was eking out a precarious existence as a tailor, first in Ber Street, Norwich, then in White Lion Street, St Giles Street, and finally Tabernacle Street. The latter no longer exists, but ran then a little way to the east of St Martin's-at-Palace Church. Sheward was a shiftless, harddrinking man and his wife, a good deal older than her husband, was a querulous, nagging woman. Their quarrels were so familiar to the neighbours that when he announced she had up and left him nobody was particularly surprised. The truth was, however, that she had been distributed piecemeal around the district. A few fragments did in fact come to light. A hand was found in a road leading to Lakenham, a foot about 300 yards away, portions of flesh and bone in the outlying district of Hellesdon, in Martineau's Lane and in Hangman's Lane—later Heigham Road. These grim and unusual findings, though, were taken to be remains of a young girl, and no suspicion was attached to the tailor. His wife's long hair, he stated in his eventual confession, he "cut into small pieces, and they blew away as he walked along". In 1862 he married again, worked for a while as a pawnbroker in King Street, failed in that as he had in the tailoring business, but eventually did better as landlord of the modest Key and Castle Inn, St Martin's-at-Oak. It was while spending a few days with his sister in Walworth that remorse most unexpectedly overcame him. He informed the police that parts of the body were still preserved in spirits of wine at the Norwich Guildhall, and these were found, helping to confirm his grisly recital.

G

Later the voice of conscience weakened and he attempted to re-
tract but—as in other cases—he had gone too far to turn back,
and was convicted, sentenced to death, and executed on 20th
April 1869, having made a second full confession of his wickedness.

One day in the year 1898 a boy of 15, John Edward Casey,
who lived with his family at Stokesby (just north of the A47
between Acle and Great Yarmouth), stole some women's underclothing, dressed himself up in it, killed and dismembered a pig,
distributed some of the pieces around the house, then wrapped
the torso in the stolen garments and hung it up in the parlour.
It is not the sort of thing one likes to be reminded of, and when,
two years later, some friends chaffed him about the incident in
a neighbouring pub, the result was a tragedy. It happened that,
though he had never even spoken to her, Casey had become
enamoured from afar of a Mrs Thirza Kelly, a widow with a
young baby who had recently arrived at the village. That same
evening, 23rd December 1900, after bursting into tears over the
teasing he had received, he went to Mrs Kelly's cottage a couple
of miles away and broke in. She was in bed asleep when he disturbed her and, thinking he was about to harm the child, she
screamed and caught hold of him. There was a struggle, in the
course of which he stabbed at her savagely with a knife, and fled.
She was found lying on the floor by her mother who called the
following morning, and lived just long enough to tell what had
happened. Surprisingly, Casey was not considered to be insane,
but the death sentence was commuted to penal servitude for life
on account of his youth.

The case known as the Great Yarmouth murder, referred to
earlier, was closed on 21st March 1901, by the execution of
John Herbert Bennett, 22 but looking a good deal older, for the
murder of his wife Mary Jane on 22nd September of the previous
year. Her body was found by a boy of 14, John Norton, on
South Beach, then a lonely and scrubby area of grass and sand-
pits above the high-water mark. She was lying on her back, her
skirt above her knees, and had been strangled with a bootlace.
The young couple (she was about two years older than Bennett)
had first met when he went to take violin lessons from her, and
they were married in 1897. For a while they lived a somewhat
chequered life together and carried on a number of dubious joint
activities, including running a grocery business which was in-

sured and conveniently caught fire when losing money; selling fake 'old violins' from door to door to the accompaniment of hard-luck stories; and, on Bennett's part, an odd, never-explained trip to South Africa which led to suspicions that he had worked as a spy for the Boers. As time went by, however, they began to drift apart. Bennett had even found himself another girl, Alice Meadows, to whom he gave an engagement ring.

In the summer of 1900 he suggested that Mary Jane should take a holiday at Great Yarmouth (where he had already stayed, in the Crown and Anchor Hotel, with his new girl) and gave her the address of a Mrs Rudrum, 3, Row 104, South Quay—a lodging recommended by the obliging Alice. On 15th September Mary Jane arrived at Mrs Rudrum's—calling herself Mrs Hood and providing herself with a totally fictitious history according to which she was a widow with a brother-in-law who was infatuated with her. At 9 p.m. on 22nd September Mrs Rudrum noticed her standing outside the Town Hall. The next report was of her dead body on South Beach.

As soon as her true identity was established Bennett became, as a matter of course, the first suspect, but it was not until 6th November that he was arrested in Woolwich. The most damning clue against him was a gold chain found in his possession, which Mrs Rudrum stated emphatically she had seen Mary Jane wearing that evening. By chance a similar chain featured in a photograph taken of her by a beach photographer, and much discussion ensued at the trial as to whether the two were identical. Marshall Hall, who defended Bennett, strongly contended that the chain in the photograph had a different kind of link from that found in Bennett's lodgings. Unfortunately the print is so indistinct that no firm conclusion has ever been possible on the point. At a late stage in the judicial proceedings a Mr Sholto Douglas came forward to say that he had met a man named Bennett in Eltham at a time that would have made it impossible for him to have committed the crime in Great Yarmouth. Mr Douglas, a complete stranger to the accused, was firm in his assertion. To have made this alibi really convincing, however, it was necessary that Bennett should have been called to the witness-box—and thus faced with the ordeal of a relentless cross-examination. In view of Bennett's general character and of the lies he seemed unable to help telling, his defence counsel dared not take such a risk, with the result that the alibi lost any strength it might otherwise have had. Marshall Hall never ceased to believe in his client's innocence. The story of Bennett's movements on the days immediately preceding and following the crime was extremely complicated, and never really made clear. There was even a possibility, for instance, that he had been with his wife some of the time, wearing a wig and false moustache, both of which were found among his belongings. No less mysterious were the reasons for Mary Jane's apparently pointless pretence to Mrs Rudrum. It could be that she and her husband, despite the break-up of their life together, had been planning some new and dubious method of making money— perhaps involving blackmail—which was foiled by a murder of which he was completely innocent.*

Nearly twelve years later, on Monday 15th July 1912, an unsolved murder came to light on almost exactly the same spot, though a complete absence of any disturbance of the sand (in contrast to the Bennett case) seemed to suggest that the crime was committed elsewhere and the body brought to the beach later. The victim was 18-year-old Dora Grey, who lived with two ladies, Mrs Brooks and Miss Eastick, in a house near the cattle-market. She was an illegitimate child, born in Norwich, and originally taken under the care of Mrs Eastick, mother of the woman she now knew as her 'aunt'. During the day she worked in a boarding-house in Manby Road. On the Sunday before the crime she told a friend she had been to Lowestoft with "a gentleman" and was going to meet him again that evening. She was last seen by a girl-friend, Emily Blythe, walking towards South Beach wearing a big straw hat newly trimmed with roses. Dora Grey was found strangled with a bootlace (as Mary Jane Bennett had been), taken from one of her own shoes. Both shoes and stockings had been removed. Shortly after the murder a large stone was found lying on the spot. On it was written in pencil, "In memory of DORTHY [sic] MAUD GREY. May she be revenged. July 15th".

Just within the Suffolk border with Norfolk is Beccles, on the A146. In 1944 Arthur Heys, a Leading Aircraftsman at the aerodrome nearby, signed his own death warrant in an 'anonymous'

---

* For an excellent account of this involved story see Paul Capon's *The Great Yarmouth Mystery* (Harrap, 1965).

letter purporting to come from the killer of W.A.A.F. Winifred
Evans, 27, a murder with which he himself stood charged. On
8th November Miss Evans and her friend Corporal Margaret
Johns returned from a dance at an American base, reaching
their own station at about midnight. She left Margaret Johns
at the W.A.A.F. quarters and started to walk to the aerodrome,
where she was on duty. Margaret Johns entered an ablution hut,
and found a man in uniform standing in a corner. He said he
had lost his way back to the aerodrome. She warned him to
get off quick or he might find himself in trouble, and he went
away in the same direction as Miss Evans. The airman, a stranger
to her, was Arthur Heys. The following morning the body of
Winifred Evans was found by a policeman, lying in a ditch
by the roadside. She had been raped and then asphyxiated. Heys
was picked out by Margaret Johns at a pay parade and, when
further evidence mounted up against him, was charged with
murder and held at Norwich. The day before he was committed
for trial his commanding officer received an anonymous letter
in blue pencil. It contained a statement that the writer was responsible for the death of Winifred Evans, whom he had
arranged to meet in the lane. Before he arrived, an airman passed
him. Later "Winnie" came along and said that the airman was
drunk and had lost his way, and that a W.A.A.F. friend had
offered to go along with her. The letter then continued with
details of the girl's death which only the murderer could have
known. But the fatal slip was in the earlier part. Winifred Evans
had left Margaret Johns before Johns found Heys in the hut.
Winifred could therefore have known nothing about the meeting or that Heys was drunk and lost his way. Only Margaret
Johns—and the murderer—had such knowledge.

Heys went to very great trouble, smuggling the letter out
of prison, to set this final seal on his own condemnation. His
motive in visiting the W.A.A.F. quarters may be surmised but
his attack on Winifred Evans after being shown on his way
by her friend is—in view of the certainty of eventual discovery
—incomprehensible in its recklessness. Heys, a married man
with a family, was found guilty after the jury had been out just
under three-quarters of an hour.

Among murders committed by children, that which took
place in the Poorhouse at Eye, Suffolk, on the morning of 13th
May 1748 must rank high in horror. A boy of 10 had a quarrel

with a little girl five years younger than himself named Susan Mahew. He hit her and made her cry. She ran out of the building and hid in a dunghill opposite the door. Determined to kill her, the boy followed her with an iron hook, but dropped this on the way and grabbed a knife from a table. He cut her left wrist "all round it to the bone", slashed her arm above the elbow, then knocked her down, put his foot on her stomach, and cut her right arm in the same way. He then grabbed the hook and gashed her left thigh to the bone, after which he buried her in the dunghill and went in to breakfast, pleasant, cheerful and unconcerned. When questioned, all he would say in explanation was that she fouled the bed they shared and that he did not care for her sulkiness. He was sentenced to death, reprieved, and eventually pardoned on account of his "tender years".

The Rectory of Bacton (on the B1113 north of Stowmarket) was in 1853 a primitive establishment—a solitary, moated building on the edge of the village well over a mile from the church. The rector, the Reverend Mr Barker, and his housekeeper, Maria Steggles, were both in their eighties, and had as servants one young girl and an outdoor labourer. On Sunday 8th May of that year Mr Barker and the girl went off to church, leaving Mrs Steggles to carry on with cooking the midday meal, which they always ate together in the kitchen. On their return they found the old housekeeper lying on the floor covered in blood from blows on the head and with a gash across her throat. Blood was also spattered over her open prayer-book and her spectacles (which were broken) on the table. Suspicion fell on 18-year-old William Flack, recently dismissed from service at the Rectory on account of unsatisfactory behaviour. He lived near the church, was known to be short of money, and had been heard to say that one day he would "steal some of the old parson's mouldy sovereigns". A few days before the murder he had been caught gathering eggs from the Rectory henhouse. When arrested Flack tried hard to implicate another man, who was fortunately able to provide a complete alibi. Apart from the obvious motive of theft, he was known to harbour a personal grudge against Mrs Steggles, possibly in connection with his dismissal: after the murder, but before his arrest, he said that he had meant to kill her but "she's dead now, so that's all right". When convicted, Flack confessed. He said that he always lent a hand with the bellringing on Sundays before service: on this

particular day, after "chiming" parson and congregation safely
into church, he ran straight to the Rectory to commit
murder.

Peasenhall, a quiet, one-street village (on the A1120 a few
miles north of Saxmundham) has been linked for 70 years with
the name of Gardiner, and is likely to be remembered for some
time yet as the scene of the crime for which he was tried twice
before juries who could not agree. On 11th May 1901 William
Gardiner, carpenter, married man with several children, Primitive Methodist Elder, choirmaster, Sunday School superintendent,
ardent chapelgoer, who lived in a double-fronted cottage in the
main street, was summoned to a meeting at the chapel in Sibton,
a hamlet adjoining Peasenhall. He was to answer—and, it was
hoped, refute—rumours that he had been somewhat less than
discreet in his relationship with Miss Rose Harsent, 23, a member of his choir who worked as maid at Providence House, the
'big house' of Peasenhall wherein resided Deacon Crisp, a Baptist
Elder, and his wife. Sounds and remarks not strictly relevant
to its purpose had, it was alleged, been heard proceeding from
the Doctor's Chapel (as it was called), at an hour when it was
thought to be closed. Rose Harsent was reported to have referred
to the Bible in connection with "what we are doing tonight".
She then quoted Genesis 38—the reprehensible story of Onan
and Tamar. Though the young men who brought the charge
could not see what was going on inside the building, Rose's
mention of this particular Bible tale, together with certain rust-
ling noises, led them to draw their own conclusions. Gardiner
was, however, found pure in the sight of the congregation, but
warned to be more careful in future.

On Sunday 1st June 1902 Rose Harsent was discovered dead
at the bottom of a back stairway leading to the kitchen in
Providence House. Her throat had been cut and there were signs
that an attempt might have been made to burn the body, though
it was possible that the charring of her arms and legs might have
been caused by the accidental breaking of an oil lamp. A good
deal of evidence seemed to point towards Gardiner, particularly
when Rose Harsent was found to have been pregnant. The
scandal of a year previously was remembered. He was charged,
and put on trial at Ipswich in November. The jury failed to
agree—eleven being for conviction, one for acquittal. He was
tried again the following January. The jury failed to agree—

eleven being for acquittal, one (immovably) for conviction. The law gave up. A *nolle prosequi* was entered and Gardiner was released. Understandably, he wished to shake off the dust of Peasenhall. Shaving an impressive beard and whiskers, he took his family to London. Some years later, according to information given to John Rowland,* a man from Peasenhall was astonished to see him serving in a suburban grocer's shop. The mystery of Rose Harsent's death has never been solved. We may perhaps reach a tentative conclusion that William Gardiner, though he suffered greatly by enduring the ordeal of two trials, was—on the whole—fortunate.

So many melodramas, ballads and olden-time stories have been based (if that is not too precise a word) on our next crime over the years since its commission, that there are those who believe the characters concerned never existed outside the realms of lurid fiction. A visit to the lovely and tranquil little village of Polstead, however, will soon convince the doubter of the truth of the sad story of William Corder, Maria Marten and the Red Barn—even though the Barn itself is no longer to be seen. Maria, born in 1801, was the eldest daughter of a mole-catcher (an important and respected occupation in those days) who lived in a handsome cottage on the fringe of the village—the lane has been called Marten's Lane ever since her death made her name familiar to the wider world. Far from being the demure young maiden of melodrama, she had already had more than one lover and at least one child before she met Corder, and was, in addition, two years older than the man who was to hang for her murder. William Corder was a tenant farmer. His father had prospered, and the farmhouse—in the centre of the village—was (and is) a handsome building. Again contrary to theatrical tradition he was no hulking villain, but a very slightly built young man, no more than 5 feet 4 inches in height.

When he was 16 he formed a relationship with a girl named —gloriously, but surely by concoction—Hannah Fandango. He went with her to London. She was the daughter of a merchant vessel captain and a Creole woman, and almost certainly by the time they met had turned to prostitution. While in London she introduced him to the famous forger-poisoner Thomas Griffiths Wainewright, who was living next to her in Great Marlborough

* *The Peasenhall Mystery*, John Rowland (John Long, 1962).

Street.* After this jaunt Corder returned—penniless—to Polstead. It was some time around 1826 that he began his ill-fated
liaison with Maria. In March 1827 he took rooms for her with
a Mrs Goodwin in Plough Lane, Sudbury, and there she gave
birth to a boy. Soon after return to Polstead the baby died,
apparently from natural causes, but, with the connivance of
Mrs Marten, Maria's stepmother, it was buried secretly—no-one
has yet discovered where. On 18th May 1827 William told Maria
to make discreet preparations to travel with him to Ipswich,
where they would be quietly married. There was a perfectly
valid and unsensational reason for this secrecy that does not
appear in many dramatized versions, but that totally negates the
usually accepted story that William had worked out a cunning
plot to get rid of her. It is true that he had shown a good deal
of reluctance to tie himself for life to Maria, but the reason for
the hurry and concealment was that he had been informed that
a warrant was out for Maria in connection with her bastard
children. To aid her disguise he persuaded her to put on mascu-
line dress. Off her own bat—though apparently with no objec-
tion from William—she added to her male clothing two
ornamental combs, earrings and a large green umbrella—somewhat spoiling the total effect. The pair set out separately, having
arranged to meet at the Red Barn—and that was the last seen of
Maria, alive.

A short while afterwards Corder reappeared in Polstead, presumably from Ipswich, saying he had left Maria there. He then
departed for London, put up at the Bull Inn, Leadenhall Street
—and advertised for a wife. From over 50 replies he selected a
Miss Mary Moore, who ran a school in Gray's Inn Terrace.
There is some mystery shrouding this whole proceeding, as he had
already met, and apparently immediately fallen in love with,
Mary Moore: yet, after seeing her only a week or so previously,
he advertised for a wife—and she was among those who
answered. However it came about, he could not have made a
better choice, as she stood by him with the utmost loyalty until
the end. The marriage was a happy one, and the couple opened
a joint school called Grove House, Ealing Lane, Brentford, on
the east side of what is today called Ealing Road, a little north

* For a full and fascinating account of Corder's relations with Wainewright see Donald McCormick's *The Red Barn Mystery* (John Long 1967),
required reading for anyone interested in the history of Maria Marten.

of the M4 motorway. In Polstead, however, suspicions began to rear ugly heads. What had happened to Maria the mole-catcher's daughter? Where was William Corder? The famous dream of Mrs Marten—dramatic green-lit climax of many a stage version —is today treated with considerable reserve. It has been suggested, with certain evidence to back the theory, that she not only knew of Maria's death but may even have been in some way implicated. At all events, matters were taken in hand, a search was made in and around the Red Barn, Maria's body came to light. She had been shot, stabbed and possibly strangled. A warrant was issued for Corder's arrest, and in due course he was traced to Ealing, and brought to trial at Bury St Edmund's. After conviction he confessed to the shooting but denied emphatically and to the end of his life that he had stabbed Maria. He was publicly hanged at Bury St Edmunds on 11th August 1828.

Polstead, some ten miles east of Sudbury (between the A1071 and the B1068) is still remarkably unspoilt, a quiet little village by the river Box. Though the Red Barn (so-called because of its red roof which used to glow in a sinister manner under certain lights) is gone, its approximate site is known. Both Corder's house and Maria's cottage, lovingly preserved, still stand. Maria is buried in the quiet and lovely parish churchyard. Her gravestone was long ago chipped out of existence by souvenir-hunters, but a wooden plaque marks the approximate spot. In the circumstances of her death, as Donald McCormick cogently argues, is far more mystery than the audience of a Victorian melodrama might suspect.

Only a mile or two from the Red Barn, on 20th January 1961, the body of 12-year-old Linda Smith was found by a hawthorn hedge in a field adjoining Stackwood Road, The Heath, Polstead. She had been strangled, but except for one shoe that was missing her clothing was intact. Linda Smith left her grandmother's house in Earl's Colne, a village over the Essex border some 18 miles away from the spot where she was found, in order to buy a newspaper at the local shop, but she did not buy one, and did not return home. A woman stated that she saw a little girl resembling Linda sitting in a parked black van in the village about the time she disappeared, and the night before the body was discovered a black car was seen reversing down the road. A transport café owner at Great Leighs, some miles from Earl's Colne in the opposite direction from Polstead, came forward to say he saw a man with a small girl at about 5.30 that evening, and five miles from the same village some boys noticed a man trying to entice children into his car. A certain amount of evidence appeared to point to a man who worked near the place where Linda was last definitely identified, but it was not very strong, and he denied ever having known her. The murder was never solved.

The chief mystery about the Moat Farm murder of 1899 was how Miss Camille Holland, a delicate, devout, once-pretty-now-fading Victorian spinster of 56 living in a genteel boarding house (37 Elgin Crescent, London W11), could ever have allowed herself to become so infatuated with the man who was to kill her. Perhaps a pathetic hint lies in the fact that, in addition to ladylike accomplishments such as painting watercolours, composing little songs and playing them on the piano, she spent a good deal of time attempting—by such artificial means as were then available—to arrest at least the outward signs of time's relentless progress. Samuel Herbert Dougal, who swept her off her feet when they first met (as far as can be ascertained) at the Earls Court Exhibition, was a bluff, bearded, virile, soldierly figure who had spent a number of years in the army—and an equal number getting in and out of various scrapes. The set-up was, in fact, an ideal one for murder—just as Moat Farm was an ideal setting. The fated encounter occurred towards the end of 1898, and very soon afterwards Miss Holland, letting it be supposed among her somewhat sceptical fellow-boarders that she was married, went off with Dougal to stay at a house known as Parkmore, in Hassocks, Sussex. He then purchased Coldham's Farm, near Quendon, Essex, in his own name—but Camille, devoted 'wife' though she may have been, knew who held the purse-strings, and had the deeds changed to her own name, thus ensuring her death in due course. While the place was being put in order they stayed at 4 Market Row, Saffron Walden and then, on 27th April 1899, drove through Newport, turned along a couple of narrow lanes, and arrived at the solitary house surrounded by dark fir trees and its own moat. Dougal the romantic naturally renamed it Moat Farm—and very shortly indeed after arrival was up to his romantic tricks with one of the servant girls. Camille caught him at it, thereby hastening her demise. After only three weeks' joint residence Camille and Herbert went out in the pony-trap to do some shopping—Camille in a dark dress and a white sailor hat. That evening Dougal returned alone, informing the anxious servant girl that her mistress was paying a brief visit to London.

There now began an incredible period of almost four years during which Dougal, by a most skilful series of forgeries backed up with ingenious lies, took over all Camille Holland's possessions, including Moat Farm. The few enquirers at that exceedingly remote spot were told that she was still in London. Dougal began living it up as a sort of combination of traditional Turkish Sultan and English Squire—surrounding himself with a succession of attractive country servant girls (at least one of whom he enjoyed teaching to ride a bicycle naked), begetting progeny, driving the first motor-car in the district. He was a fine shot, popular among the neighbouring gentry, generous in his subscriptions to such worthy causes as the provision of a church clock to commemorate the coronation of King Edward VII. All good things, however, must come to an end. By March 1903, despite the general bonhomie, so much scandal, so many rumours, so many unanswered questions had arisen that Dougal was arrested. On 27th April, after a prolonged search, the decomposed body of poor little Camille was dug up from the farmyard grounds—four years to the day since her arrival there. Dougal was convicted of murder following his trial at the Old Bailey, and hanged at Chelmsford on 8th July 1903—having enjoyed a fairly good run for his (or rather Miss Holland's) money.

Moat Farm, now also referred to as Coldham's, is some 5 miles from Audley End Station and 6½ from Saffron Walden, between the A11 and the B1038 from Newport. There has been no major redevelopment in the area, which remains much as it was when Dougal, and what remained of Camille, left it for the last time. The two bay windows that adorned the front of the house then have gone, and there is a new bridge over the moat that still surrounds it. Though solitary still, it is today a pleasant, well-tended and comfortable house—a haven of quiet in a noisy world. And there are, as the charming lady who has lived there with her family for the past 14 years assured me, "no ghosts".

A mile or so from the Moat Farm is the village of Clavering
—home in the 1840s of Sarah Chesham, who was either the
luckiest (for a time) or the most persecuted of women. She lived
with her farm labourer husband and several children in conditions of wretched poverty. In the course of a few months around
1847 she was arrested for, charged with, and acquitted of no
fewer than three murders or attempts at murder—two of her
own sons and one of a neighbour's baby. It was discoveries in
connection with the last death that resulted in the bodies of the
two boys (who had died in 1845) being exhumed. Arsenic was
found in the organs—and in January of that same year Sarah
had sent out a neighbour to buy arsenic, to "kill rats", as usual.
Lack of motive was influential in bringing in a verdict of acquittal in the first two cases: in the third, that of the baby, the
evidence for the prosecution was so weak that the trial was
stopped. For all that, Sarah was known in the village by this
time as a "professional poisoner", so that when, in 1850, her
husband also died and a small amount of arsenic was found
inside him, she was arrested once more. A bag of rice in her
cottage was found to contain the poison, and this time Sarah was
condemned—for attempted murder. She was hanged at Chelmsford in March 1851. After her death her body was taken by
friends, for some reason unstated, to Wix, a village about 50
miles east of Clavering. (Oddly enough, Wix was the scene of
another arsenic poisoning in 1848 by a woman named Mary
May, who poisoned her half-brother seemingly to obtain "burial
money". An unconfirmed report alleged that she had been influenced by Sarah.) Before the interment of Sarah Chesham could
be completed, her body disappeared from its coffin. An interesting possibility suggested by Patrick Wilson to account for all
these strange events—and for the remarkable number of poison-
ings by women near Boston in Lincolnshire and Ipswich in
Suffolk—is that they may have had some connection with witchcraft and similar practices believed to be prevalent in these districts.

A tragic case with echoes of the murder of Vera Page in
Kensington in 1931* came to light with the discovery of the
body of 9-year-old Pamela Coventry in a ditch near Hornchurch,
Essex. She had been sexually assaulted and strangled after a des-

* See *Murderers' London*.

perate struggle. Her body, naked except for her dress which was tied loosely round her neck, was bound with insulated wire and tarred string. Pamela Coventry left her home in South Romford after lunch on 18th January 1939 to go back to her school in Benhurst Avenue. Her stepmother watched her along South End Road towards Coronation Drive and Elm Park Station. Two of her friends were waiting for her at the corner of Benhurst Avenue, but she never arrived. Somewhere in that short distance she had been enticed or forced away.

As in the case of Vera Page, the post-mortem examination was made by Sir Bernard Spilsbury. When Vera Page's body was moved a fingerstall was found in the crook of her elbow: caught up in Pamela Coventry's body was part of a home-made cigarette. Later her wellington boots were discovered in South End Road, and two buttons and her school badge near Elm Park Station. The buttons were wrapped in a copy of the *News Chronicle* for 11th January, together with a piece of insulated wire similar to that on the body. A man living in Coronation Drive was arrested. There were several coincidences in connection with the newspaper, the tarred string and the insulated wire that appeared at first sight to link him with the crime. He rolled his own cigarettes, using the same brand of paper and tobacco. All these items, however, were in common use and, though he was charged with murder, they were deemed insufficient, unsupported by further evidence, to warrant a conviction. In fact, the jury stopped the trial and the man, after being congratulated by the foreman, was released.

While serving in the army in 1943 Eric Brown, 19, attended lectures on the Hawkins 75 Grenade Mine, which was used against enemy tanks. While on leave in July of that year he put his knowledge to a more personal use. Brown lived with his father, mother and younger brother at a house in London Road, Rayleigh, Essex. Mr Brown was an invalid, paralysed from the waist down, and Nurse Mitchell, resident help with the family, used to take him out for a daily outing in a wheelchair. Despite his disability, or perhaps because of it, he seems to have been a stern, even a tyrannical parent, particularly towards Eric. On the afternoon of 3rd July, just after Nurse Mitchell had set off with him, there was a terrific explosion. The wheelchair disintegrated and Mr Brown was blown to pieces. Nurse Mitchell was lucky enough to survive, and told the police that Eric had

been very busy that morning doing something in the air-raid
shelter, where the chair was kept when not in use. On being
questioned, the young man confessed to having contrived to set
a grenade in the chair, saying that his father was now out of
his suffering. While in custody awaiting trial he tried to kill
himself. At Essex Assizes in November 1944 Eric Brown was
found guilty but insane.

Prittlewell, now merging into Southend-on-Sea, was in 1894 a
quiet little village to the landward of the resort. On Monday 25th
June of that year the body of Miss Florence Dennis, 23, whose
sister Mrs Ayriss ran a lodging-house in Southend, was discovered lying in a ditch by a path through some fields. She had
been shot. Police enquiries resulted in a search for John Canham
Read, a middle-aged clerk at the Royal Albert Docks, Woolwich,
who had left his wife and eight children and disappeared. He was
run to earth a fortnight later at Rose Cottage, Mitcham, living
as Edgar Benson, with a Mrs Benson and a baby. It transpired
that he had met 'Mrs Benson'—in reality a Miss Kempson—by
chance at Gloucester Road Station, where "they spoke". Miss
Kempson, a highly respectable but not over-wise young woman,
had allowed herself to be seduced by Read under promise of
matrimony, had introduced him to her parents as her affianced,
and had left her job in a confectioner's shop in London to go
and set up house with him in Mitcham. It was established that
Read had also had relations with Mrs Ayriss (Florence Dennis's
sister) when she was living with her husband at Maysoule Road
and St John's Hill, Wandsworth. He had in fact had a child
by her. One day on Clapham Common he encountered Florence,
and straightaway started to lay siege to her.

The police theory was that by June 1894 Read had tired of
Florence too and had found himself yet another girl friend.
Florence then wrote to him saying that a baby was on the way
and what did he propose to do about it? What he proposed
to do about it was as cruel as it was unoriginal. He arranged
to meet her, took her for a walk, shot her, and threw her body in
a ditch. There was much evidence against him. Various people
claimed to have seen him in the district at the critical time. He
was proved to have owned a gun, and could not now account
for its disappearance. Nor could be provide an alibi. On the
contrary, 'Mrs Benson' said that he spent only Saturdays and

Sundays with her, accounting for his absence during the week by saying he was a traveller: in the whole course of his association with her, she stated, he had missed only three week-ends. The fatal Sunday was one of them. Read, the insatiable clerk of Woolwich, was convicted of murder, and hanged.

(*above left*) A recent photograph of Mary Blandy's home at Henley-on-Thames. (*right*) Moat Farm (Coldham's Farm) where Camille Holland went to live with her murderer, Samuel Herbert Dougal, as it appears today.

(*below*) A contemporary picture of Marshall's cottage, Denham, with interested onlookers. From an old postcard.

The murder of Thomas Arden, Mayor of Faversham, by Black Will and Shagbag in 1550—a print of 1663.

Rooks Farm, Stocking Pelham—police searching for the body of Mrs Muriel Mackay.

The Luard murder mystery, 1908—a thoughtful constable paces by the gate close to the summerhouse.

6

"GENTLEMEN, DO NOT HANG ME HIGH"

The South and West Midlands: Warwickshire, Worcestershire, Herefordshire, Gloucestershire Oxfordshire, Buckinghamshire

On 26th May 1817 Mary Ashford, aged 20, left her uncle's house at Langley Green, a mile or so from Walmley, just north-east of Birmingham, where she worked as housekeeper, to go to a dance arranged by a local Friendly Society. The dance was held at the Three Tuns, Tyburn (generally known as Tyburn House), a large inn that adjoined the bridge carrying the Chester Road over the Birmingham and Fazeley Canal. Mary, whose father worked as a gardener in Erdington, was described as "sweet and amiable, mild, unassuming, strictly virtuous, lively, with a human form moulded into the finest symmetry". This charming female paragon left the dance at about 3 a.m. with a young man named Abraham Thornton, a far from worthy counterpart for such a girl, being squat, grossly fat, low-browed, with "a swollen shining face" and a distinctly dubious reputation. At 4 a.m. Mary looked in, alone, at the home of a girl friend in Erdington (to be welcomed at such an hour surely indicates that the above description was no exaggeration), and left half-an-hour later to walk back to Langley Green across the fields. She was last seen, alive and well, in Bell Lane. An hour or two later her body was found in a pit in a field off Penn's Mill Lane, into which Bell Lane turned. She had been sexually assaulted and then, apparently, flung into the pit to drown.

H

Abraham Thornton was tried for her murder. Despite his un-prepossessing appearance he was well known as the local Don Juan. He had been heard to remark that he had already been intimate with Mary's sister and "would have her too, or die in the attempt". His defence was an alibi: he had waited for her outside her friend's house in Erdington, and when she did not reappear had gone off towards his own home. This, surprisingly, was confirmed by several (admittedly somewhat vague and equivocal) witnesses. Abraham was acquitted, but so great was the feeling that he had escaped justice that an ancient law known as an Appeal of Murder was successfully invoked by Mary's brother, William Ashford. Thornton was arrested a second time. He himself now invoked the right, consequent on an Appeal of Murder, of Trial by Battle—by which the appellant and the accused literally fought it out until nightfall. William Ashford being a puny man, and Abraham Thornton a stocky and stalwart gymnast, the former put prudence before valiance, and dropped the charge. Abraham went free. A theory was put forward that no intended murder had been committed at all—that poor Mary, brutally raped, had gone to the pit to wash her-self, had fallen into the water, and drowned. Such an argument would, of course, have made little difference to the fate of her assailant, had he been found.

Despite the great changes in the district, the geography of this famous old crime can be followed very closely if the plan drawn in 1819 is compared with a modern map. There are the Tyburn bridge and crossroads, and the London and Chester Road now known as the Chester Road. Bell Lane is today called Orphanage Road. Penn's Mill Lane, turning off to the Lichfield and Birm-ingham Road, is Penn's Lane, and leads to Walmley and what was Langley Green beyond. A house known as Langley Hall, and a farm, Langley Heath Farm, still exist to the north-east of Walmley village. The footpath which Abraham said he took after leaving Mary and returning to his own home was a little south of Holly Lane, probably near Mason Road. The "Fatal Field", as it was christened, adjoined the south side of Penn's (Mill) Lane about one thousand yards from the junction with the Birmingham Road. There, close to the roadside, was the pit where pretty, virtuous, amiable, symmetrically moulded Mary Ashford, a century and a half ago, was cruelly drowned.

Moving further to the centre of Birmnigham, and much further forward in time, we come to Willows Crescent, Cannon Hill, the scene of a strange, still unexplained mystery on 24th October 1932. Marjorie Yellow, 19, already both married and separated, was living at number 63 with a man named Herbert Gwinnell. Her sister, Emily Thay, was spending the week-end with her. At a little after 7.30 p.m. Emily rushed into the street screaming, "Murder!" Marjorie Yellow followed asking for help to put a man out of the house. As passers-by ran up, a young man came out of the house and was just able to gasp out, "I have done nothing", before he collapsed in the porch-way, and died. He had been stabbed in the chest. The two sisters were charged with murder but the evidence was extraordinarily confused and conflicting. The deceased, identified as Sidney Marston, 21, a grocer's assistant, was a well-built and powerful man, hardly the type to succumb to an attack without putting up a struggle—of which there were no signs. In his pocket was the blade of a knife, the handle lay on the ground near by. Marjorie Yellow said that he had stabbed himself, and she took the handle from him. There was talk about a missing ten-shilling note, which was found in his pocket. Some witnesses said that Marjorie denied knowing Marston, others that she admitted having met him at a dance. Another remark she was supposed to have made was, "He's only shamming. He's done that before" —yet another, "They don't hang women, do they?" It was one of those Janus cases where everything—even the evidence of the expert, Sir Bernard Spilsbury—seems to face both ways. In the event the judge, Sir Travers Humphreys, decided there was insufficient evidence against Marjorie Yellow and none at all against Emily Thay, and by his direction a formal verdict of Not Guilty was returned. The whole story remains clouded in doubt, for it seems certain that the wound could not have been self-inflicted.

Among the most horrible of all crimes in the district was the murder and mutilation by Patrick Byrne of Stephanie Baird at the Y.W.C.A. hostel in Wheeley's Road, Edgbaston, on 23rd December 1959. The discovery of her body led to one of the most intensive police hunts ever organized. Forces not only throughout Britain but also on the Continent co-operated, but the only clue the killer had left was a scribbled note: "This was the thing I thought would never happen." Byrne was found on 7th February staying with his mother in Birchall Road, Warrington. He was a 28-year-old labourer who had been working in Hagley Road, close to Wheeley's Road, at the time of the murder. On 24th December he had left his lodgings to spend Christmas in his home—in fact, he had at first intended to go there after finishing work on the 23rd and had already written to his mother telling her to expect him. The police, when they arrived to question him, had no particular reason to suspect him. His landlady had given them the Warrington address, and the visit was merely part of the vast enquiry embracing everyone known to have been in the vicinity of the hostel. Almost at once, however, Byrne made a full confession.

After finishing work on the 23rd, he said, he had a drink at the Ivy Bush in Hagley Road, returned to the site for an hour or two, then left to go to his lodgings. Noticing a light in one of the hostel windows as he passed by, he went and peered in. He had done this on several occasions previously, and once had actually entered the hostel and gone into a room where a girl was in bed. For some reason, perhaps owing to the calm presence of mind she showed, he walked out again without touching her, merely saying that he was looking for someone else. On the night of 23rd December he saw Stephanie Baird, 29-year-old office worker, in a red pullover and underskirt, packing a suitcase. He made his way into the corridor and stood on a chair to look through the fanlight. When she heard him she opened the door to find out what was going on. He tried to kiss her, and when she resisted he pushed her into the room, strangled her, raped her while she was unconscious—or possibly after her death—then performed the most ghastly mutilations on her body, using a tableknife he found in a drawer. Finally he cut off her head and held it up by the hair, watching himself in the mirror. He wrote the note referred to and then, hearing a noise in the corridor, ran outside. In the yard he picked up a heavy stone, wrapped it in a brassiere he found hanging on a clothes-line, and crept back to another part of the building where he saw a girl in the hostel ironing room. He pushed open the door and switched off the light. When she came up to see what was happening he hit out at her with the stone. It slipped in his hand and he missed her. She screamed, and he ran off to his lodgings. Several people were in the house when he arrived, but no-one noticed anything unusual in his manner. In his confes-

sion Byrne stated that he had indulged in sadistic fantasies since
he was 17—on the night of 23rd December a chance combination of circumstances drove him to turn them into dreadful
reality. He stated that he felt a compulsion to terrify women
"to get my own back on them for causing my nervous tension
through sex". Byrne was found to be sexually abnormal, but
sane. He appealed against his conviction for murder and the
term was changed to that of manslaughter—but the sentence,
imprisonment for life, remained the same.

During their investigations in the case the police heard of a
man who got on a number eight bus in Birmingham covered in
—in fact dripping with—blood. They were never able to estab-
lish his identity. Such was the stoicism—or self-absorption—of
his fellow-travellers that no-one appears to have taken the
slightest notice of his appearance, except to avoid the place he
sat in.

Lower Quinton lies about a mile to the east of the A46 from
Stratford-on-Avon to Cheltenham and about eight miles south
of the former town. It is in the heart of the famous Warwick-
shire witch country, where even today their legend, if not their
influence, lives on. Little Compton, Long Marston, Compton
Wynyates, the Rollrights, Meon Hill—the names themselves
can still conjure up the dark secrets of the coven. Consequently
when, on St Valentine's Day 1945, the body of a 74-year-old
hedge-cutter, Charles Walton, was found under an oak tree near
Lower Quinton, skewered to the ground with his own hayfork,
it was inevitable that the case should become known as the
Witchcraft Murder. In addition his slashing-hook was stuck
deep in his body and a rough sign of the Cross had been
cut across his throat. The spot was at the foot of Meon Hill
itself.

Though Walton seems to have been regarded as a somewhat
morose and unsociable man, there appeared to be no real motive
for his murder except one that reached back to the dark ages
of ancient ritual. In 1875 at Long Compton a half-witted youth
named Thomas Haywood was tried for murder of Ann
Turner, aged 80, said to have bewitched him. He, too, used a
bill-hook and cut her throat in the shape of a cross. Walton's
killer remains unknown.

On 27th May 1827 Abraham Pratt was walking along the edge of Harbury Pond by the village of Bishop's Itchington (on the B4451 from Southam), when he noticed an umbrella sticking out of the water. He investigated further and found the body of Mary Ann Lane—well known in the district as a wet-nurse. Before long suspicion centred on a 28-year-old labourer, William Miller. On being apprehended he confessed to the killing, pleading that he had been drunk at the time. He said that when he "attempted some familiarities" Mary Ann began to make noises of protest, so he put his hand on her neck "to prevent her hootin". She fainted, and he threw her into the pond. When she revived and tried to scramble out he pushed her back and held her down. For this futile and callous crime, drunk or not, Miller was despatched.

On midsummer's day 1806 two people heard a shot and a cry of "Murder!" from the garden of the Reverend Mr Parker, rector of Oddingley, a village about four miles south of Droitwich. They rushed to the spot and found him dead, his clothes alight from gun wadding. One of them pursued the murderer, who turned to threaten him then threw a gun into the hedge and made off. He had, however, been recognized as Richard Heming (or Hemming), a carpenter and wheelwright who lived in Droitwich. Fifty guineas were offered for his capture, but he disappeared and was never seen again.

The rector had been an unpopular man among his flock of farmers, largely on account of his aggressiveness in the matter of tithes. There seemed little motive, however, for Heming, a comparative stranger, to kill him.

Twenty-four years passed during which the village—relieved of the burden of the Reverend Parker, seems to have flourished. One man, however, Thomas Clewes, had not done so well. He had become a confirmed drunkard, and was no longer capable of keeping his farm going. Netherwood Farm, as it was called, was therefore sold. One day the new owner was making alterations to a barn on the grounds when he came across a skeleton under the floor. Mrs Heming identified it by the teeth as that of her husband. Clewes was arrested and charged with murder. Under questioning he poured out the whole strange story. Together with five other farmers he had hired Heming to kill the hated clergyman and afterwards, either as a safety measure or as a result of blackmail, the group had murdered the murderer. Since then all save Clewes had prospered. Three were now dead. The other two, now highly respected village worthies, were charged with being accessories after the fact. In the end the jury decided that Clewes was no more and no less responsible than the rest, and no further action was taken against any of them.

Our two Herefordshire cases are both concerned with servants and mistresses, and both occurred in country houses within three years of each other. The first, in 1929, was at Burghill Court, about three miles north-west of Hereford, the home of the two Misses Woodhouse—Elinor Drinkwater and Martha Gordon. For over twenty years Charles Houghton had been their butler and for most of that long period had—it may be presumed—given them satisfaction. Of late, however, he had taken to giving himself satisfaction—out of a bottle. After much heart-searching the ladies decided that steps must be taken, and on 6th September Houghton received his notice—only 24 hours, but accompanied by a golden handshake in the form of two months' wages. He seemed to be accepting his dismissal with equanimity until the following morning, when he walked into the kitchen where Miss Elinor was giving the cook instructions for the day's meals and shot her dead. He then went and shot Miss Martha, ran to his own room and tried, ineffectually, to cut his throat. On being arrested he said that the whole thing was a bad job—which it undeniably was—then added, rather mysteriously, "It is passion". He pleaded a tendency to epileptic fits, but was found gulity and sentenced to death.

In the second case the position was reversed—mistress killing man. Mrs Edith Dampier lived at Hunter's Hall, Lea, a village at the junction of several roads (the main one being the A40) to the east of Ross-on-Wye. On a night in January 1932 the police were sumoned to deal with the body of Benjamin Parry, 31, a servant in the house who, according to Mrs Dampier, had committed suicide. He was sitting in an armchair with a gun between his knees and a wound in his neck. Sir Bernard Spilsbury, however, gave the lie to the suicide theory, giving it as his opinion that the wound could not have been self-inflicted. Robert Churchill, the ballistics expert who accompanied him on so many cases, agreed. There were rumours around that Mrs Dampier's relations with her manservant went deeper than appeared on the domestic surface. She was charged with murder but—unlike the butler Houghton—was found unfit to plead.

In Gloucestershire, overlooking the Severn some ten miles north of the Bridge, is Berkeley Castle, where King Edward II was horribly and bestially (but from all accounts not inappositely) done to death, a sordid end to a treacherous reign. The room where the murder took place can still be seen, looking much as it did when the deed was perpetrated.

Of less national import, but far more interesting as a mystery, are the events that occurred in 1660 around the still enchanting little town of Chipping Campden. Already in those days it had lost some of its earlier importance as a centre for the wool trade, but it was still an active and flourishing place. In one of its houses—unidentifiable today—lived 70-year-old William Harrison, steward to Viscountess Campden and responsible for collecting the rent of her tenants. On 16th August 1660 he did not return from his journey around the adjoining villages, and Mrs Harrison sent her manservant, John Perry, to search for him. He too failed to return. The following morning Edward Harrison, William's son, set out to find the missing men, and met John Perry apparently returning to the house. He said he had been able to discover no sign of his master. By this time, however, the old man's hat and comb had been found on the roadside, and Perry was arrested on suspicion of robbery and murder. Under restraint—and no doubt persuasion—he soon began to talk. He said he was convinced that his master had been murdered by someone (other than himself, of course) and the body hidden in a certain bean rick. There was, however, no body in the bean rick. He then changed his story and said that his mother, Joan, and his brother, Richard, had persuaded him to report William's movements so that they could ambush and rob him at a time when it was known he would be carrying a large sum of money. It was, said John, Richard who had killed him, by strangulation, and then thrown his body into a millpond. It was dragged, but there was no body in the millpond either. Nevertheless, Joan and Richard now joined John in confinement. John later declared that they tried—perhaps understandably—to poison him while awaiting trial.

They were all three charged with murder and robbery, but with no corpse to be seen, the judge ordered the murder charge to be dropped. The idea continued to grow that they knew more about William's death than they had admitted, and they were brought to trial a second time before another judge, who was not in the least worried about whether there was a corpse to be seen or not. John then belatedly declared that he had been mad and had not known what he was saying, but this retraction came too late to save him. The three Perrys were hanged together on Broadway Hill, a little way outside the town, near the spot where the Fish Inn stands today.

This might seem to be the end of the story. Far from it. Two years later William Harrison turned up—with a fantastic tale to tell. He said that he had been kidnapped, carried to Deal, taken aboard a ship to Turkey and sold to a Turkish doctor in Smyrna as a slave, the price paid being in the region of £7. After his purchaser's death the redoubtable old man managed to escape and make his way back to England. It seems a story that calls for a prodigious suspension of disbelief, but it is all that has ever come to light. Ingenious theories have been, and will doubtless continue to be put forward to account for both John Perry's behaviour and William Harrison's yarn—each as inexplicable as the other—but the mystery will probably continue for ever to be known as the Campden Wonder.

Readers of newspapers in the generally drab post-war year of 1947 will probably not need much reminding of the 'Mad Parson', who escaped from Broadmoor wearing a clerical collar which he had used as a prop in a concert party run by the inmates and called the Broadhumoorists. He remained at liberty for nearly two years, his presence being reported from almost every county in the kingdom. The undoubted ingenuity and comedy of his successful venture (he described the escape operation as "incredibly simple", and took a job while free) tended to obscure the tragic events that preceded it. On 19th June 1937 the body of 17-month-old Kathleen Woodward was found lying by the side of a road at Fulbrook, Oxfordshire, a small village about a mile from Burford (on the A361). The child had been strangled with a piece of clothes-line, and was clutching two pennies in her hand. Her parents worked at the Lamb Hotel, Burford, and for some months had been friendly with John Edward Allen, 25, employed as assistant chef in the same building. The young man had often played with Kathleen and seemed very fond of her. On the day of her death he gave the baby two pennies, and told Mrs Woodward that her husband had asked him to take the child out for an airing. Mrs Woodward asked him to take good care of her, and let her go. She said later that Allen was jealous because she had been given the responsibility of preparing cakes for a banquet. During the trial it was revealed that Allen had previously been in a mental hospital, and at its conclusion he was committed to Broadmoor. For the appalling consequences of a similarly easy escape from the same institution, see the case of J. J. Straffen on page 175.

Just outside Burford on 19th December 1931 Mrs Mabel Matthews was found dying on the side of the road by two cyclists. A cousin of Sir Alfred Matthews, she lived at Windrush Mill, and was known to have gone shopping that day in the village only a short distance away. Beside her lay her damaged bicycle, its acetylene lamp missing. According to Sir Bernard Spilsbury's findings she had been savagely kicked about the face and neck as well as being partially strangled, and she died before reaching hospital. Close at hand was a man's bloodstained macintosh and a packet of sandwiches containing sausage-meat. A mile and a half further along the road lay a shopping-basket belonging to Mrs Matthews, and an electric bicycle lamp.

A radio appeal was broadcast for information from anyone who might have seen her, and from anyone who might have supplied a man with sausage-meat sandwiches. In due course a report was received from a sailor in Northolt that a soldier, Private G. T. Pople, who had been staying in the same house, had gone away with just such a packet of sandwiches, riding a bicycle with an electric lamp. Gradually and persistently this man's movements were traced. Near Oxford he had met another cyclist, telling him that his lamp battery had run down and he had no money to replace it. In Oxford itself he had asked a policeman how far it was to Gloucester. On the night of the 19th he had paid 4s. 6d. for a lodging—at that time he had an acetylene lamp on the bicycle. Despite these pointers Pople had reached Abergavenny in Wales before he was tracked down and arrested. His story at the trial was that he had made up his mind to get hold of a lamp from someone, and when a woman cyclist passed him he made a grab for the one on her bicycle. As he did so, his trousers caught in a pedal and he fell onto the other cyclist, tumbled off his own machine and rolled down into a dip. When he got up he found the woman lying unconscious and, in a panic, grabbed her lamp, together with some articles that had spilled from her basket, and quickly rode away. For all his ingenious tale, it took the jury only 40 minutes to find him guilty, and he was hanged at Oxford on 10th March 1932.

In 1931 Mrs Annie Louisa Kempson, 58, widow of a local tradesman, was living in a small semi-detached house called The Boundary in St Clement's Street, off the High Street and Iffley Road on the outskirts of Oxford. During the August Bank Holiday, her lodger, Miss Williams, being away for a few days, she had made arrangements to visit a friend in London. She did not turn up, and on the holiday Monday her brother, who worked at Jesus College, found her lying dead on the dining-room floor, with head wounds that suggested she had been attacked with a hammer. The house had been ransacked, but Mrs Kempson was very poorly off and there was little of value to be had, and probably only two or three pounds in cash. Information was received from a Mrs Andrews, of Headington Hill, concerning a vacuum-cleaner salesman named Seymour of whom she had been a customer. He had borrowed money from her the previous Friday, saying his wallet had been stolen, and later had further imposed on her kindness to borrow a bed for the night in the house where she and her husband lived. She noticed the next morning that he had purchased a hammer and chisel with the money he had borrowed—the wrapped, open-ended parcel was on her hall table. He left about 9.45 a.m. on the Saturday and was next noticed at a bus station in Headington at a little after 11. Mrs Kempson had also been a customer of Seymour's, and it would have been possible for him between these times to have called at her house, made some excuse to get himself admitted, killed her and gone on to the bus station. Seymour's movements were traced to the Greyhound Hotel at Aylesbury. He had already left there, but because he had been unable to pay his bill the manager had retained his suitcase. In it were found a hammer and chisel, newly washed. The police knew now whom they were after. Seymour, the son of a doctor, was a man of about 50, with a record for housebreaking and robbery. He was eventually traced to a house in Brighton owned by a widow. In his bedroom floor he had bored two holes, with a new chisel, in the hope of being able to discover where she kept her money. He put up a poor performance in the witness-box, and the verdict of Guilty caused little surprise. He was executed at Oxford prison.

The ominously-named Gallows Tree Common is almost equidistant from Henley-on-Thames and Pangbourne (close alongside the B479). In 1922 the licensee of the Crown and Anchor Inn on the Common was a 55-year-old widow named Mrs Sarah Ann Blake. On the morning of 4th March she was discovered dead in her kitchen with her skull fractured in four places, her neck gashed and more than sixty wounds on her face, hands and arms, caused by a heavy iron bar and a knife. She had last been seen alive at about 6.30 the previous evening. Among those who approached the police with offers of help was 15-year-old Jack Hewett, who had been sent to fetch some beer from the Inn the night before. He said he had been unable to get in and the place was in darkness, so he got his beer from another pub. After a 'confession' from a man named Robert Shepperd had been proved false, suspicion became directed to Hewett himself. On being arrested he admitted the crime, saying he didn't know what made him do it, and blaming "the pictures". Later he withdrew this statement, saying he was unaware of what he was signing, but the jury preferred to believe it, and found him guilty of murder. He was sentenced, for this brutal and vicious assault, to be detained during His Majesty's pleasure, being too young to suffer the full penalty of the law.

After more than 200 years Oxfordshire's most famous crime is still probably that of Miss Mary Blandy, executed in 1752 for the murder of her father. A villainess of the first order she most certainly was, but after so long a mellowing passage of time it is difficult not to feel for her something akin to pity—if only for the pathetic clumsiness with which she set about her wicked work. Mr Blandy was a prosperous attorney-at-law who lived in a handsome house close to the river at Henley-on-Thames—St Mary's Church standing between. His daughter, born in 1720, seems to have been an attractive girl—marks of smallpox on her face were her chief disfigurement, and in those days this was a minor blemish. Mr Blandy was determined to do his very best for his daughter: ironically, it was this very solicitude that led to his undoing. Nobody—but nobody—satisfied him as a possible suitor for his daughter and her £10,000 fortune, and at the age of 26 she was still unattached. In 1746, of course, Henley was far less accessible than today, with correspondingly less opportunity for social life. In that year, however, Mary found someone on her own account—someone, unfortunately, altogether unworthy of her. The Hon. William Cranstoun, fifth son of a Scots peer, was puny, ungainly, freckled and of a sandy hue. He was also penniless and of a weak character. But Mary loved him, and Mr Blandy at first was flattered at the thought of connections with an Hon. For six months Cranstoun was a guest in the Blandy home. There was, however, another drawback to the Hon. W. apart from his depressing physical and personal attributes. He was married. His wife was a fervent supporter of the Jacobite cause and consequently, in 1746 of all years, distinctly out of favour—so much so that her husband kept very quiet about her, and had even tried—unsuccessfully—to pass her off as a mere mistress.

The news burst on Mr Blandy like a thunderclap, and the Hon. W. was no longer welcome in his house. Mary, however, remained infatuated, and strangely enough she had her mother strongly on her side. When Mrs Blandy died, quite shortly after this shattering news (and from natural causes), the lovers lost their chief support. Cranstoun then began making odd suggestion to Mary about a "magic potion" which, introduced into Mr Blandy's digestive system, would change him from a malevolent despot into a benevolent ally. Even foolish Mary seems to have been sceptical at first, but at last consented to lace the old man's tea with the mixture. Astonishingly, it appeared to work. For a brief while (the true reasons remain unknown) Mr Blandy became affable and amenable. Mary was delighted, and even the discovery of a couple of letters in her lover's pockets revealing that he was running a mistress in London did not seriously upset her remarkably placid and generous nature.

The Hon. W., however, was growing impatient, and sent Mary doses of "magic potion", this time labelled "Powder to clean Scotch pebbles". This was probably done with an eye to his future safety should anything go wrong, Scotch pebbles being a popular form of ornament at the time. It was from this moment, June 1751, that the real mischief began. Mary, however, showed herself singularly unskilled as a villainess. Mr Blandy became increasingly unwell, but so did everybody else, for owing to Mary's culpable carelessness most of the household were finishing off his left-overs and suffering in consequence. This was a complication she should surely have taken pains to prevent. First a servant and a charwoman who shared the remains of his special "tea dish" were violently sick, then a housemaid helped herself to his gruel and was taken ill also. The latter, indeed, became suspicious of what was going on, and warned first the cook and then the master himself. Hoping to stop any further damage, both Blandy and his doctor made Mary aware of their concern, but at this she lost completely what little head she had left, and began frantically throwing bundles of letters and packets of powder into the kitchen fire—from which they were promptly rescued by the cook. She then wrote a thoroughly compromising letter to Cranstoun (who had prudently if unchivalrously kept well away during all this) and gave it to—of all people—Mr Blandy's clerk to post. He of course opened and read it, and even more fat was in the fire. Mr Blandy, now *in extremis*, behaved with the greatest kindliness, dignity and generosity towards his erring daughter. "I forgive thee, dear," he said movingly, "and I hope God will forgive thee: but thou shouldst have considered better than to have attempted anything against thy father." Weeping, Mary admitted she had put the powder into his gruel, but said "it was given me with another intent".

Mr Blandy died on 14th August 1751, and Mary continued to behave with reckless stupidity. On the very day of her father's death she tried to bribe one of the servants to help her to run away. Inevitably, she was charged with murder by the administration of arsenic, and the jury at her trial took only five minutes to reach their verdict. As she mounted the scaffold she made her celebrated remark, "Gentlemen, do not hang me high, for the sake of decency".

The Hon. W. escaped from the country, and died from an unspecified but apparently agonizing illness in 1752, only a few months after Mary was executed. The handsome Blandy house still stands in Hart Street, Henley-on-Thames, and is still known by that name. It is now inhabited by a firm of dentists. Some parts have of course been rebuilt, but others—the cellars, for instance—are almost unchanged.

In Windsor Road, one of the main thoroughfares of Slough, Buckinghamshire, a Mr Hezekiah Reville, 40, owned a butcher's shop which he ran with his wife and two assistants, Alfred

Payne, 16, and Philip Glass, 15. Official closing time was 8 p.m., but as was sometimes the practice in those more accommodating days (the year is 1881), it was his habit to leave the door on the latch for a while in case of tardy customers. He himself would go off to what was then the village inn, the White Hart, while Payne and Glass (a pleasing combination of surnames) put the shop to rights and Mrs Reville entered up the books. On Monday 11th April Glass left the shop at 8.25, and Payne a few minutes later. Both men were seen leaving by passers-by. Payne went to the Royal Oak Tavern, which was run by his father. A few minutes after they had gone Mrs Reville's small daughter came downstairs for a drink of water. She saw her mother lying across the desk with blood coming from her head, and ran back to her bed in terror. A few moments later a neighbour looked through the window and saw the same horrible sight. Mrs Reville had been beaten to death with a heavy chopper. Money was scattered around, and lying on the desk was a scribbled note purporting to come from a Mr Collins and threatening dire consequences to Mrs Reville for having sold him bad meat. This was an obvious blind, and Payne, as the last person known to have seen her alive, was arrested. The case was not at all a clear one, however, and Reville himself was regarded with some suspicion. He had been much later than usual arriving at the White Hart, and explained this by saying he waited outside a tobacconist's for a friend who took a long time making his purchase. The money could have been scattered around as a blind, and an accusation of dishonesty that Reville had made publicly against Payne the previous day could have had the same underlying purpose. No bloodstains were found on the clothing of either suspect. Payne's remarkable coolness of manner at his trial could have indicated either callousness or the calm of innocence. It is one of those tantalizing cases with an equal balance of evidence, together with the possibility of an unknown factor that never came to light. Payne was acquitted after half-an-hour's deliberation by the jury, and the question remains unanswered.

Salt Hill, long since swallowed up by the maw of Slough, was described one hundred years ago as a pleasant, quiet and genteel hamlet a little west of the town. It was the *mons* or mound of the Eton *montem*—a gala day involving a parade from the school to the spot and the levying or 'salting' of contributions on the spectators. A coloured ticket was given to each contributor so that a second demand should not be made, rather after the manner of a present-time flag day. After deduction of expenses the balance was presented to the Captain of the School. In 1844 this amounted to some £1,400, but this was not as generous as it sounds: when payment for various entertainments and remunerations had been made there was not much left. The ceremony, much spoiled when the advent of the railway brought in 'undesirable visitors', was abolished in 1847, two years after the murder of Sarah Hadler, with whom we are now concerned.

At the time the best hotel in the district was the Windmill, or Botham's Inn, and the young woman dwelt in a cottage close beside it. She was the mistress of John Tawell, a wealthy tradesman who, after being transported to Sydney for forgery, had returned to build up a successful business as a chemist, as well as interesting himself in a number of other concerns. He was, or outwardly appeared to be, a Quaker, and always dressed as such. He first met Sarah when she was a servant girl and their relationship, during which she bore him two children, outlasted his first marriage, which was ended by the death of his wife. By September 1843 he had remarried and was living in Paddington, London. During that month Sarah was suddenly taken ill after drinking a glass of stout given to her by Tawell. She recovered, and on 1st January, fifteen months later, he was again in Salt Hill and again plying her with stout. This 'long time between drinks' might have been a cautionary measure taken by Tawell or might simply have been due to lack of opportunity. Whatever the reason for the interval, this latter occasion was poor Sarah's last glass. In the evening a neighbour heard muffled screams and a moment later Tawell (whom she recognized by his Quaker garb) hurried from the cottage. Sarah was found lying in agony on the floor and died almost immediately, poisoned by prussic acid. A telegram had already been sent to the authorities in Paddington (the first use of such a means in the apprehension of a murderer), and Tawell was arrested the next morning. He was identified as having bought prussic acid from a shop in Bishopsgate. His story was that Sarah had died from the cyanide contained in apple pips and that she had committed suicide in front of him by this method. This somewhat improbable story was totally rejected and Tawell was condemned to death. He afterwards confessed to the murder, giving as his reason fears that his wife might come to learn of his mistress. It seems more likely that the motive was a financial one, since Sarah's death would have relieved him of having to continue paying her an allowance of £1 per week. Tawell was hanged at Aylesbury at the end of March 1845, still wearing the clothing of a Quaker. It would have been interesting to know his thoughts as he donned for the last time the dress of the faith he had so signally betrayed—and whether it struck him that it was this very dress that had to a large extent, because it was so easily recognized, brought him to justice.

The pleasant little village of Denham has been the incongruous setting for a particularly brutal murder. This was the killing, in 1870, of the village blacksmith, Emmanuel Marshall, and his entire family, comprising his wife, mother, sister, and three children. Two other children were fortunately away at the time. The killer was a middle-aged tramp or travelling blacksmith named Owen, who came from Wolverhampton. In March of that year he had done a certain amount of casual labour for Marshall but considered his wages inadequate. He decided on a fearful, indeed an insane, revenge. Breaking into the blacksmith's cottage at night, he armed himself with his erstwhile employer's axe and systematically beat out the brains of everyone in the place as they came downstairs in turn to see what was happening. He then dressed himself in Marshall's suit and boots, smashed his portrait, and left the house, explaining to one old lady who saw him in the lane that he was a member of the family—his victim's brother, in fact. The following day a little girl knocked on the door of the cottage, got no reply, peered through the window and saw a child's body lying in the ashes of the fireplace. The old lady was able to give a fair description of the man she had seen, and after a notable piece of detective work by Superintendent Dunham, Owen was discovered at the Oxford Arms, Silver Street, Reading. As he was arrested he attempted to shoot the Superintendent with a gun stolen from Marshall's house, but was overpowered. He must have carried out his frightful slaughter with considerable cunning and precision as there were no signs of a struggle by any of the victims, and apparently no outcry.

Marshall's cottage and adjoining smithy existed up until the the early 1960s in Cheapside Lane, opposite the village Junior

I

School. The blacksmith and his family lie buried in the church-yard, and particulars of their cruel death may still be read on the stone that covers them.*

* The weapon used by Owen has almost always been referred to as a sledgehammer. I am indebted to Mr Geoffrey F. Hadrill, who lives in Denham close to the site of the cottage, for the information that it was, in fact, an axe. Mr Hadrill not only has a letter from relatives of the Superintendent of Police in charge of the case guaranteeing that an axe was used, but was actually able to purchase it, and now has it in his possession.

7

DEEP-FROZEN OR SMOKED
The South East: (1)
Hertfordshire, Middlesex, Kent

The small hamlet of Tring, Hertfordshire (we are speaking of the year 1751) shared fully in the universal dread of witch-power. On 18th April a gang attacked an elderly couple, Ruth and John Osborne, suspected of casting the evil eye on the local crops and livestock. The two were stripped and bound, and finally flung into Marlston Mere, a pond just outside the village. The old woman died as a result, choked with water and mud: the fact that she drowned was accepted as proof that she was innocent. Had she survived, and thereby shown herself guilty, she would have been thrown into the pond again, and so on until death mercifully intervened. Thomas Colley, ringleader of the gang, was hanged and his body exhibited in chains at a nearby spot known by the oddly sinister name of Gubblecut.

A novel and bizarre way of concealing the body of a victim is thought to have been introduced into the murder of 17-year-old Anne Noblett, who was found in dense undergrowth between Kimpton and Whitwell (on the B651 south of Hitchin) on 31st January 1958. Five weeks previously, on 20th December 1957, she left a dancing class at Harpenden and caught the 5.50 p.m. bus to her home in Marshall's Heath, Wheathampstead, but never arrived. She had been sexually assaulted before dying of strangulation, and her body, when found, was frozen solid—far colder than the surrounding temperatures. The spot where she was discovered had already been thoroughly searched during earlier investigations and it was considered unlikely that her body could have been missed. The supposition is that during those five weeks it had been kept in a deep-freeze unit, and dumped in the undergrowth only shortly before it was found. A man who had been living in Southend and whose company dealt in deep freeze equipment underwent a lengthy questioning when traced to Bruges, but he put up an unassailable alibi for the period in question and the murder joined those as yet unsolved.

Stocking Pelham lies on the borders of Hertfordshire and Essex, almost half-way between the A10 and A11, and just south of the B1038. In the early months of 1970 this small village (its odd name probably deriving from 'Peotla's log-built homestead') was brought into a glare of publicity by what has been referred to as the country's first case of kidnapping. On 29th December 1969 Mr Alick McKay returned to his home, St Mary House, Arthur Road, Wimbledon, to find his wife missing and signs that she had been forcibly abducted. At 1.15 a.m. a telephone call was made from a kiosk at Bell Common, Epping, from a man announcing himself as a member of Mafia Group 3 and demanding a ransom of one million pounds for the return of Mrs McKay. During the next weeks over a dozen calls were received from 'M3' (among a mass of malicious and cruel hoaxes) and several letters were received written by Mrs McKay—though the dating of some of these was certainly faked. After two abortive rendezvous at which it was hoped to trap the kidnappers (the first at the junction of the A10 and the road to Dane End; the second at Gates' Used Car Salesrooms, Bishop's Stortford, on the A11) the police, through noting the registration number of a Volvo car, were led to Rooks Farm, standing isolated even from the lonely village of Stocking Pelham itself. The farm was inhabited by an immigrant tailor from Trinidad, Arthur Hosein, 34, his wife, two children and teen-age sister. In the middle of December Mrs Hosein, who was of German extraction, had left with the family to visit her parents on the Continent, where they were to stay until 3rd January. With Arthur at Rooks Farm, however, was his younger brother Nizamodeen, or Nizam, 22, who had arrived in England in May 1969 on a temporary visit that had been extended but was due to expire in January 1970. There was no sign of Mrs McKay—nor has there been any sign since—but a great deal of evidence appeared to link the Hosein brothers with her disappearance. On 6th October 1970 they were found guilty on several charges relating to the kidnapping and murder, and sentenced to long terms of imprisonment.

The grim irony of the McKay case is that her murderers abducted the wrong woman. In October 1969 Rupert Murdoch, proprietor of the *News of the World*, appeared on a television programme in which references were made both to his wealth and to his wife, Anna. It has since been presumed that the Hoseins watched this programme and thought they saw a way to acquire both money and a standing in a district into which they fitted somewhat incongruously. They worked out an ingenious plan to trace Mr Murdoch's home address through follow his blue Rolls Royce car from the office to his house. What they did not realize was that on 19th December the Murdochs had left for a holiday in Australia. Use of the car was offered to his colleague—Alick McKay.

In 1955 a Pole named Onufrejczyk was convicted of the murder of Stanislaw Sykut on an isolated farm in South Wales. The body was never found, and rumours arose that the killer had fed it to the pigs on his farm. The same hideous possibility—though there has never been the smallest proof to substantiate it—could not fail to increase the horror felt over the case of Muriel McKay. Whatever her fate, the judge, Justice Sebag Shaw, was, if anything, moderate in his description of her abduction and murder as "a cold-blooded and abominable crime".*

In the autumn of 1972 Rooks Farm was once again in the news, when the owner, Anthony Lewis Wyatt, licensee of the Black Boy public house in Stepney, East London, was charged with the murder of John Scott, 26, a tailor's cutter whose body was found stabbed and dumped in a van at Leytonstone. He was last seen alive at the farm.†

Just north of the village of Markyate (on the A5) is Markyate Cell, built in its present form about 150 years ago, and incorporating part of a Tudor manor house on the site of an ancient nunnery. Here in 1660, in the gardens close by one of the windows, was discovered the body of Katherine Ferrers, Lady Katherine Fanshawe, better known to posterity (and filmgoers) as The Wicked Lady. She had apparently died from loss of blood

---

* In the autumn of 1972 it was announced that Arthur Hosein had been given permission to have enquiries re-opened into the case of Mrs McKay.
† Wyatt was found guilty of manslaughter and jailed for three years. Rooks Farm was reported to have been sold in June 1973 for £46,500 to an undisclosed buyer.

caused by a gunshot wound—and she was in male attire. The actual cause of her death was never solved, but legend quickly filled the gaps left by unrevealed truth. At the age of 12 Lady Ferrers, heiress to the fortune of the Markyate branch of her famous family, was married off to 16-year-old Thomas Fanshawe, whose relatives rapidly acquired most of her property. By the age of 18 she was living alone, except for a small retinue of servants, in the old house. According to the story, she became involved in highway robbery with a farmer named Ralph Chaplin. After his execution (on Finchley Common) she dressed as a man and was responsible for a reign of terror in the neighbourhood—harmless people were killed or injured, though apparently little or no attempt at actual robbery was made. A possible explanation of her death was that she was shot while attacking a wagon crossing Normansland Common, near Wheathampstead. The story goes that a rider suddenly appeared, killed the wagoner, was fired on in turn by a man lying in the cart, and galloped away as if hit. The mysterious rider may have been none other than the Wicked Lady.*

Shortly before three o'clock on the afternoon of 7th September 1956 two 14-year-old boys noticed a car parked near Leverstock Green, Hemel Hempstead: in the back seat a man was bending over a woman. At 5 minutes past 3, in Green Lane about a mile away, three more boys watched a man (described as wearing horn-rimmed glasses, a blue pin-striped suit and kid gloves) take a body from a car and drop it into some bushes. Going closer, they saw a shoeless foot under a macintosh, then hurried to the police. The body was identified as that of Winifred Suttey, a 36-year-old nurse of Pinner Road, Harrow. She had been strangled with her own scarf, and there were teeth marks in her neck. Mrs Suttey had been seen leaving the Crow's Nest Café, Markyate, earlier that afternoon, and had accepted a lift from a man driving a Rover car. It was thought likely that she had an appointment with someone else and had been dropped by the driver of the Rover near the prearranged spot. There she was picked up in the smaller car that was seen by the boys. The police had plaster casts made of the teeth marks on the victim's

---

* An interesting account of the exploits of Katherine Ferrers, written and illustrated by V. W. Lea, may be found in the *Hertfordshire Countryside* magazine, December 1967 issue.

body and circulated them to numbers of dentists, but despite such steps as this, and the fact that the small car was noticed by several people in the neighbourhood, the murderer has never been traced.

Murder in order to pay a visit to the zoo was committed in the village of Redbourn (on the A5 about four miles north of St Albans) on 27th January 1921. Donald Litton, 13, had been promised the trip by a schoolmaster if he could provide 7 shillings to cover his expenses. He was given sixpence by his mother. To obtain the rest he picked up a hammer and broke into the cottage next door to his own. The occupant, 71-year-old Sara Seabrook, was having an afternoon nap on her bed. While searching for her money he made a disturbance and she suddenly appeared in the bedroom doorway. He hit her with the hammer and a frantic struggle took place, until eventually Mrs Seabrook collapsed on the floor. Litton went out, buried the hammer in a neighbouring garden, and returned to find the old lady still alive and stumbling downstairs. He picked up a poker and attacked her again. No fewer than 28 wounds were found on her head. He then tried to drown himself in a well, clambered out again, returned to his home, took off his clothes and put them in a bucket, then sat down before the fire. All this horrifying story he later told to the police. In his defence it was put forward that he attacked Mrs Seabrook first in fear and then in a frenzy, and that he was too young to have knowledge of guilt. The jury however found that he had committed murder, and he was ordered to be detained.

St Albans has a connection with the famous Red Max case, described in my book *Murderers' London*: his dead body was found on 24th January 1936 under a hedge in the then rural Cell Barnes Lane. It had been taken there in a car from the room in Little Newport Street, London WC2, where he had been killed—a journey of some 20 miles.

Finally in Hertfordshire we enter the grim precincts of Leavesden Mental Asylum as it was in the year 1899 during a serious outbreak of typhoid. One of the inmates of Ward 7 was Caroline Ansell, who had been there about 15 months. On 22nd February she received a parcel of tea and sugar, on 9th March a cake. The tea had been thrown away because of its bitter taste, but Caroline and several of her fellow patients shared the cake. All were taken slightly ill and Caroline, who presumably gave herself the largest slice, seriously so. With so much illness raging it was not until some days later that she was properly examined and taken to the infirmary. She died 12 hours later, blaming the cake. A post-mortem revealed the presence of phosphorus, and enquiries led to the arrest of her sister Mary Ann, 22, a maid-servant employed at a house in Great Coram Street (now demoted to Coram Street), London WC1. She was identified as the purchaser of phosphorus at a shop near by saying—with the usual lack of originality—that she needed it "to kill rats". This the lady of the house indignantly denied. It was discovered that Mary Ann had taken out an insurance on Caroline's life, stating that she was a servant working at the Asylum, instead of an inmate. By paying 3d. per week premium she could look forward, if Caroline died within a specified period, to the princely sum of £11 5s. She was engaged to be married, but the wedding had been postponed until more funds were available. Questions were asked about Mary Ann's mental condition (her deceased sister, after all, had been an inmate of an insane asylum), but these did not affect her fate. On 19th July 1899 Mary Ann paid the penalty of her contaminated confectionery at St Albans prison.

Lionel Rupert Nathan Watson was a bakelite-moulder. He was also a murderer. On 19th May 1941 he killed Phyllis Elizabeth Crocker, to whom he was bigamously 'married', and her daughter of 18 months, by poisoning them with prussic acid. A few days later he buried them in the garden of his house in Goring Way, Greenford, Middlesex. His digging operations had been noticed, however, and at the end of June the bodies were exhumed from two feet of earth beneath flagstones. He alleged that on arriving at the house that day he found both mother and child already dead, and buried them to avoid the irregular relationship being discovered. By now more than bigamy had been discovered, and Watson was hanged at Pentonville on 12th November 1941.

On an evening in October 1962 Carol Ann White, 16, went to a telephone kiosk in West Drayton to wait by arrangement for a call from her boy-friend, Peter Watson, who lived in Guildford and had arranged to ring the box at 9 p.m. He was unable to get into his own kiosk, which was occupied by a garrulous woman. Carol Ann White went to her home in East Road, West Drayton, for her purse, returned to the kiosk, and rang Peter Watson's neighbours. They told his father, who went along to fetch his son. He found that he had managed to get into his kiosk and dial, but was now, of course, getting the engaged signal from Carol White's kiosk, where she was holding the line to the neighbour's telephone. Peter Watson returned to the neighbour's house, and found to his surprise that Carol Ann had rung off. This unfortunate series of mistimings had tragic results. Carol Ann White did not return home and her father, becoming worried, went to look for her. All he found at the telephone kiosk were her purse and a pencil. Now thoroughly alarmed he contacted the police.

The following afternoon Edward Donald Garlick, a 25-year-old storeman of Princes Park Lane, Hayes, was out walking with his wife, two children and their dog. They were on their way to visit his mother. At the corner of Stockley Road and Cherry Lane, West Drayton, close to London Airport, the dog ran off into a field of artichokes. Garlick followed, as he said later, in order to put it on its lead. In doing so he stumbled over the body of a girl lying on her back. Her clothes were orderly but covered in blood. He at once raised the alarm. Examination showed that she had been fiercely stabbed several times in the back with a thin-bladed knife, and a gag had been pushed down her throat. She had been dead for about 18 hours. The body was identified as that of Carol Ann White. After the police arrived Garlick was permitted to leave, but later, in the normal course of enquiries, he and his wife were questioned. The police were not happy about some of his statements. He had been seen walking home between 9.45 and 10 o'clock the previous evening, and said he had been trying in several pubs to get aspirin for his wife; but two of those at which he said he had been unable to obtain any could, in fact, have supplied him. It seemed to the detectives odd, too, that he should choose that particular moment of the walk (two miles from the start) to run after the dog in order to secure it on the lead. The real reason might have been that he wanted to explain any blood found on his shoes or clothing, by pretending to trip over the body. In addition, he was known to be in the habit of carrying a knife about with him, and was unable to explain satisfactorily the fact that it had disappeared.

It was remembered that some time ago he had, according to his own story, entered into a suicide pact with his first wife:

she had died from gas poisoning, and he had been charged with murder but acquitted. Eventually Garlick made a confession (which he later retracted), and showed the police where he had buried his knife by thrusting it deep into the ground. He said he had known Carol Ann for some months. On the evening of the murder he had seen her standing by the kiosk and suggested a walk, during which he took her into the field. He killed her, he said, because she mocked him about his "lack of experience". It was considered probable, however, bearing in mind the type of wounds inflicted, that he had threatened her with the knife and then stabbed her in a sadistic fury: she had been sexually assaulted. At the beginning of February 1963 Garlick was sentenced to life imprisonment.

We move now to Kent, and the Dickens country surrounding Rochester—firstly to a tragedy of which he may well have known. On 29th August 1843 the body of a middle-aged man was found in Cobham Park, on the margin of a deep depression known as Paddock's Hole. There were signs that he had put up a desperate struggle for his life. He was quickly identified as Robert Dadd, a well-known chemist of Chatham. At about six o'clock the previous evening he and his son Richard had arrived at the Ship Inn, Cobham, travelling by chaise. After eating supper they had gone out for a walk—from which neither returned. Richard Dadd, rapidly making his way as an artist, had for a long time been known as mentally unstable, and it quickly became only too clear that he had killed his father. He was traced to France. There, while travelling in a *diligence*, he tried to cut the throat of a fellow passenger, and this led to his being recognized. After detention for some months in a French asylum he was brought back to England. By now his insanity was so obvious that he was never actually brought to trial but, after a formal commitment, was placed in Bethlehem Hospital, which was then in Southwark. In 1864 he was transferred to the new Broadmoor Institution. Throughout his long confinement he continued to paint—not only canvases but murals, stage designs and pictures and patterns on glass. His work, alongside but apart from the PreRaphaelites, is remarkable for its microscopic detail and its strangely 'innocent' imagination. In his book on *Victorian Painters*,* Graham Reynolds comments, "In his childlike vision Dadd looks forward to Beatrix Potter—in his overall con-

* Studio Vista, 1966.

struction and assemblage of discordant facts, to the Surrealists".
Dadd died in 1886, at the age of 68.

Murder of a 13-year-old boy by a 14-year-old came to light
with the discovery on 11th May 1831 of the body of Richard
Taylor on the edge of a wood called Bridgewood, about three
miles from Stroud (now spelt Strood), near Rochester. There
was a huge gash in his throat and his body was badly decomposed, but his father recognized it by "a bunch of currants"
with which he had been born on his chest. On 4th March
Richard had been sent into Aylesford, near Maidstone, to collect
his father's allowance money, but never returned. The murder
was traced to his friend, John Bird Bell. On being charged, he
confessed, saying he did it to obtain the cash. Richard, he said,
fell on his knees, offering him the money, his cap, his knife,
anything he wanted, if he would only let him go. Bird, however,
refused, and killed him. He was hanged at Maidstone. According to a contemporary report, as he mounted the scaffold the
14-year-old boy cried out, "All people before me take warning
by me : Lord have mercy on my poor soul."

At about 9.30 p.m. on 9th October 1942 Mrs Ellen Symes left
her parents' home in Dickens Terrace, Frindsbury Road, Strood,
to walk some 20 minutes through the black-out to her home,
Thames Mount, Brompton Farm Road, wheeling her 4-year-old
son in his pushcart. Quite close to Thames Mount was a house
with the resounding name of Valhalla. Its owner heard screams,
and found Mrs Symes collapsed in the road outside. She had
been stabbed in the neck, and died almost at once. Though the
pushcart was overturned the little boy was unharmed, and was
able to say that his mother had been attacked by a soldier. A
trail of blood led along the road to a hedge some yards away.

On the following morning a policeman questioned a soldier
in the Gravesend Road who, he considered, was acting strangely.
The man admitted he was an absentee and was taken to Rochester police station. His name was Reginald Sidney Buckfield, a
married man with three children. After working before the war
as a labourer, he served first in Africa, then as a gunner in an
anti-aircraft unit at Tollgate, Gravesend. While absent without
leave he had been doing odd jobs on various farms including,
just before the murder, Beluncle Farm, Hoo, some three miles
from Strood. On account of his perpetual grin and general air

of bonhomie he was nicknamed "Smiler". He spent the time of his detention at Rochester furiously scribbling on sheets of paper, eventually handing the whole pile to a detective telling him he should read them "very very carefully as they were very interesting". This was no less than the truth. Certain suspicions had already arisen concerning Buckfield's possible connection with the death of Mrs Symes: the papers, consisting of chapters from a thriller with a leading character (presented in highly flattering terms) named "Smiler", showed knowledge of the details of the murder of which only the killer himself could be aware. The real give-away, however, was in the title—*The Mystery of the Brompton Road Murders*, by "Gunner Buckfield". Further evidence came to hand, including the discovery of a table-knife (identified as Buckfield's) in a garden near the murder spot. On 9th November he was charged. An alibi put forward by the defence collapsed under scrutiny, and the accused's plea that the Brompton Road in his story was the one in Knightsbridge, London, was held to be singularly unconvincing. Buckfield was found guilty, despite lack of apparent motive, but reprieved and sent to Broadmoor—smiling to the last, and possibly the only murderer who ever, to all intents and purposes, convicted himself by writing up his crime in the form of a mystery story.

Turning back over four hundred years, we next visit Faversham in 1550, year of the murder of the Mayor of the town, Thomas Arden—a crime commemorated in the anonymous (perhaps partly Shakespearean) tragedy *Arden of Faversham*. In early days Faversham was a place of considerable importance, referred to in 812 as "The King's little town of Faversham". Later, King Stephen and Queen Matilda founded a Cluniac Abbey and both were buried in it. Later still "Queen Elizabeth Slept Here"—for two nights in 1573. Consequently its Mayor was a gentleman of some substance: and Thomas Arden, it appears, was extremely fond of substance. He married Alice North for money rather than love. Her father was Sir Richard North, and her brother Thomas the famous translator of Plutarch. Her lover (taken, it appears, very shortly after her marriage) represented a downward slide in the social scale, being a mere tailor, by name Thomas Mosbie (or Mosby, or Morsby—they didn't worry much in those days), who worked for her father. In an early example of Design for Living, Arden invited the tailor to share his house as well as his wife while he occupied himself with making more money—a sixteenth-century *mari complaisant*. Even this accommodating attitude, however, did not prevent Alice and her Thomas from wishing him out of the way. After various fiendishly complicated attempts to poison him, they engaged two villains with the unsurpassable names of Black Will and Shakebag (or, better still, Shagbag), to help in their nasty work. Together with Morsby, Black Will and Shagbag battered the unfortunate Mayor to death at his own dining-table and then dumped his body in a field. They were a stupid group, however, and left all manner of incriminating clues behind them, and in a very short while the dead man was very thoroughly avenged. Alice was burnt alive at Canterbury, and everyone who could be even remotely connected with the crime was disposed of by a variety of efficiently deterrent means. Though inevitably much changed, Arden's House still stands at the Abbey Gate, a private residence now, and preserved by the Historic Buildings Council.

In 1946 a 47-year-old spinster with the formidable name of Dagmar Petrzywalski (known to her neighbours as Peters), lived alone in a hut on the Hever Estate near Kingsdown (on the A20 between Maidstone and London). She was generally regarded as an eccentric, and was also something of a recluse. She had, however, a mother of 80 who lived near by, and every week she would visit her brother in London, hitch-hiking on lorries. Towards the end of October 1946 she set off as usual, carrying a small case with sandwiches and a rather distinctive yellow-string bag crocheted for her by her sister-in-law. Round her neck she wore a man's woollen vest to keep warm, for she started her journey at the appalling hour of 5 a.m. She did not, on this occasion, complete it. On 31st October her body was found in some bushes on the edge of the A20 near Wrotham, at a place known as Labour-in-Vain Hill. She had been strangled with the vest, but there was no sign of a struggle. This seemed to indicate that the crime had been committed elsewhere and the body brought to the spot, particularly as Wrotham is in the wrong direction for a trip to London. Both case and string-bag were missing. Chief Inspector Robert Fabian, as he then was, ingeniously had an exact copy of the string-bag made and publicized it in the press. As a result the original was traced—it had been found floating in Clare Park Lake, some way off the A20 between Maidstone and Wrotham. Still more ingeniously he discovered, helped by the experience of some girl guides, that if articles were thrown into an old millstream at East Malling they were carried by underground currents to the Lake, arriving there two or three hours later. This turned attention to the mill, which had recently been converted to a cider works. On the day the body was discovered a load of bricks had been delivered on a lorry driven by a man known to his firm as Sinclair. Questioned, he admitted he was really Harold Hagger, a man with a long police record, including a charge of assault on a woman. He further admitted giving Miss Peters a lift, saying that a struggle occurred when she tried to steal his wallet, and in the course of it he accidentally killed her. His story broke down under examination and he was hanged at Wandsworth on 18th March 1947—one more example of a murder committed with seemingly incomprehensible lack of motive.

One of the cruellest crimes of the county of Kent, in which the cruelty was no means confined to the unknown killer, occurred in 1908 in the countryside near Sevenoaks. Between the villages of Seal and Ightham (on the A25) Major-General Luard and his wife lived in a house called Ightham Knoll. Their neighbour, Horace Wilkinson, had fairly extensive grounds surrounding his home, Frankfield, and in between the two houses, at a spot known as Fish Pond Woods, was a large summerhouse with a verandah and several rooms, known as Casa Ponza. Luard, 69, was still a very active man, and for 14 years after his retirement from the Army had been County Councillor for the district of Kent. He had been married to his wife, Mary Caroline, 58, for 33 years and they were known as a devoted and very popular couple. At 2.30 p.m. on 24th August they left Ightham Knoll together with their small dog and walked towards Godden Green golf links, about 3 miles distant, where the General wanted to pick up some clubs. They parted near a wicket gate leading through thick undergrowth to the Casa, arranging to meet back at the Knoll for a tea engagement with a Mrs Stewart at 4.30. This was another way home for Mrs Luard, who often liked to spend a few minutes looking at the view from the summerhouse. The General went on to Godden Green with his dog, picked up the clubs and returned home by the main road, arriving about 4.30. When his wife did not appear he became anxious and, with his guest, went to look for her, taking a route to the summerhouse that avoided the main road.

Near the Casa Ponza they parted, his guest having another appointment, and Luard went on alone. He found his wife lying dead on the verandah steps, shot twice through the head. Her rings had been wrenched from her fingers and a pocket of her dress containing a purse had been actually cut away. The moment of the shooting was fixed at 3.15 by a gardener who heard the sound. A coachman's wife also heard shots. The timing provided a perfect alibi, as Luard could not possibly have had time to shoot his wife and be at the club when he arrived there.

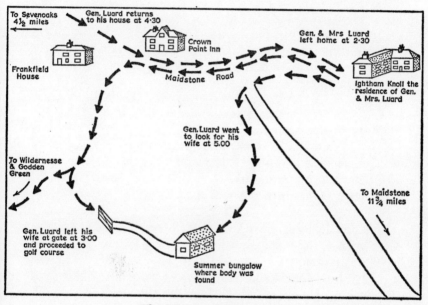

The Murder of Mrs Luard

In addition, there seemed absolutely no motive for him to have done so. Superintendent Percy Savage, who was in charge of the case, wrote of his complete conviction that Luard was innocent. Yet, as time passed and enquiries led nowhere, the elderly man became the victim of an obscene stream of abusive letters and anonymous accusations. These so preyed on his mind that a month later, when Ightham Knoll had been put up for sale and he was staying with his friend Colonel C. E. Warde, Chief Constable of Kent, he went out early one morning and threw himself on the railway line in the path of an approaching train, leaving behind a pathetic note to say he could not stand the strain of the vicious attacks any longer: ". . . somehow in the last day or two something seems to have snapped. The strength has left me and I care for nothing except to join her again. So good-bye, my dear friends, to both of us."

The murderer of Mrs Luard has never been discovered, though various theories have been put forward. The idea of a casual encounter with a tramp bent on robbery is one, but against this is the impossibility of such a person knowing anyone would be at the Casa and the unlikelihood of meeting anyone at all in so lonely and overgrown a spot. There is undoubtedly some mystery about Mrs Luard's last visit to the summerhouse, and of her remaining so long when she had an engagement and was supposed to be hurrying home. It is possible she had arranged to meet someone, known to either her husband or anyone else. In this connection Colin Wilson has a most interesting note in the appendix to his book *An Encyclopedia of Murder*, linking the case with J. A. Dickman, who was executed in 1910 for the "railway murder" of John Nisbet (see page 15).

Ightham Knoll still stands and the grounds are still thickly wooded. The Casa Ponza was accidentally burnt down in 1920. The Crown Point Inn, which the Luards passed on their last walk together, has been renamed the "Sir Jeffrey Amherst".

A white hogskin glove dropped at the scene betrayed the identity of a triple murderess in the village of Matfield, some eight miles from Tunbridge Wells (on the B2160). Before the Second World War Walter Fisher and his wife were living with their two daughters in Twickenham, but the family was breaking up, and each party had a lover. Mr Fisher's was a widow who had been christened Florence Iris Ouida Ransom and was generally known as Julia. He took a cottage in Matfield called Crittenden where he spent his week-ends—his weekdays being passed, presumably on reasonably friendly terms, with Mrs Fisher at home. In due course the elder daughter got married and with the coming of the war the household finally dispersed. Fisher went to live with Mrs Ransom at a farm she had at Piddington, near Bicester, called Carramore, while Mrs Fisher and the younger daughter took over the Matfield Cottage where they lived with Miss Saunders, 50, who acted as housekeeper. On 9th July 1940 Mrs Ransom put on a pair of white hogskin gloves, borrowed a

gun from a man named Fred Guilford, went to Matfield, and shot
Mrs Fisher and her daughter in the cottage, then traced Miss
Saunders to a wood near by and shot her also. She then returned
to Bicester, but obliged the police by dropping her glove. She
was arrested on 13th July and eventually convicted. Later she
was found to be mentally unbalanced, and committed to Broadmoor. It is probable that she had become morbidly jealous of
the Matfield cottage household, to which Fisher paid several
visits. She had certainly prepared the crime with some care.
There were even indications that she had procured herself an
invitation to pay a visit to the cottage and have tea—odd though
this may seem even in the generally odd circumstances of the
family set-up. It was, indeed, an odder set-up than had already
appeared. The Fred Guilford who provided the gun turned out to
be Mrs Ransom's brother. Together with her mother, Mrs Guilford, he had been brought in to help on the Bicester farm, Mr
Fisher remaining blissfully unaware of the relationship.

Moving on to the Kent sea-coast we pause first at Whitstable
for a tragic case famous in the 1920s as the Stella Maris trial.
Stella Maris was the name of a small villa inhabited in 1926 by
Alfonso Francis Austin Smith and his wife Kathleen. Smith, son
of a Canadian millionaire, educated at Eton and Cambridge, had
been an officer in the Dragoon Guards, with a notable record for
courage during the 1914–18 war. Early that year he became
friendly with John Derham, a fellow Etonian. Unfortunately
Derham fell head over heels in love with Mrs Smith, and Smith
saw their marriage heading for disaster. On 12th August he
sent Derham a telegram, in his wife's name, asking him to Stella
Maris to try to sort things out. At 11 p.m. Mrs Smith's younger
sister, who was staying in the house, heard a shot. She ran
downstairs and saw Derham holding Smith down on the floor
and hitting him with a revolver, while Kathleen Smith tried
frantically to stop him. After a moment Derham staggered
away, badly wounded, and collapsed out in the street. He died
from a gunshot wound in his left side. Smith's defence was that
the revolver went off in a struggle. It all happened in a moment,
as Derham and Kathleen were about to start a game of cards. It
seems an unlikely occupation in the circumstances, but playing
cards were certainly found scattered about the room. Smith then
pulled out the gun and said he was going to commit suicide.

K

Derham jumped at him to prevent it, and the weapon went off. Considerable sympathy was felt for the accused man, which was perhaps why Mr Justice Avory in his summing-up referred to "what is erroneously called the Unwritten Law. That is merely a name for no law at all." The jury found Smith not guilty of either murder or manslaughter. The judge, however, had the last word. "Stay," he said coldly as Smith was about to leave the dock. "There is another charge against the prisoner." Smith pleaded guilty to possessing arms and ammunition with intent to endanger life, and was sentenced to twelve months' imprisonment with hard labour.

Herne Bay, about 5 miles east of Whitstable, was the scene of the first (known) murder by Brides-in-the-Bath Smith. It was to number 80 High Street that he brought Beatrice Constance Annie Mundy in 1912, and there, on Sunday morning 13th July, she was found dead in the bedroom, drowned in a zinc bath which he had purchased a couple of days previously for £1 17s. 6d., having knocked the price down from £2. He originally met Miss Mundy in Clifton in 1910, bigamously married her in the name of Williams, found her capital securely inaccessible, and deserted her, leaving a disgustingly callous note accusing her of giving him a "disease". In March 1912, by an astonishing and tragic coincidence, they met by chance on the sea-front at Weston-super-Mare and Beatrice, determined to seal her own fate properly this time, agreed to return to him. He leased the house in Herne Bay, setting up as an art dealer and advertising apartments to let. He induced Bessie to sign a will in his favour (as he himself did, with nothing to leave, in hers), and prepared the way for her death by taking her to a local doctor and saying she had had a fit. The docile Bessie appeared totally unconscious of the fit, but admitted to a headache. After drowning her, and obtaining the coroner's verdict through his jury that death was due to 'misadventure', he had her buried as quickly as possible, sold up the house and furniture, and left Herne Bay to proceed on his eventful career elsewhere. Bessie's family had their strong suspicions of Mr Williams, but were powerless to prevent him obtaining her property. The bath was returned to the dealer two days after the tragedy—no money having changed hands, as Smith had wanted to try it out before deciding on a purchase.

It was in room 66 of the Hotel Metropole, Margate, that the

strange career of 31-year-old Sidney Fox and his mother came
to an abrupt end on 23rd October 1929, the night he murdered
her. For several years they had been living a nomadic existence
travelling from one luxury hotel to another leaving a trail of un-
paid bills—or bills paid by worthless cheques—behind them. Sidney's mother, who was 63 when she died, came from Great Frans-
ham in Norfolk, and was married to, and separated from, a railway signalman. She seems to have given her son a reasonably
efficient education in petty crime, and he had by this time a
record of thieving and swindling behind him. Between them they
had an income of 18 shillings a week—10 shillings from the
death of an elder son on active service, 8 shillings received by
Sidney for a war-wound of somewhat doubtful authenticity.
They seem to have managed their hotel odyssey with considerable ingenuity, patronizing among others the Grand, Dover, the
Royal Pavilion, Folkestone, and the County, Canterbury. Hotel
bilking, however, is not a pensionable career, and mother was
getting on in years, so on 21st April 1929 Sidney persuaded her
to make a will in his favour, and on 1st May he insured her
life by a policy due to expire at midnight on 23rd October.
Twenty minutes before the hour of expiry struck, Sidney rushed
into the hotel lobby screaming that there was a fire "in my
mummy's room"—which adjoined his own. She was found lying
across her bed, dead from suffocation and shock, enveloped in
black smoke.

The insurance company was not surprisingly suspicious of a
decease so conveniently timed: there were also many unusual
features about the fire, such as an unburnt piece of carpet between a blazing armchair and the gas-fire which was supposed
to have started it burning. Mrs Fox's body was exhumed from
its grave in Great Fansham, and Sir Bernard Spilsbury found that
the true cause of death was strangulation. Fox was anything but
helpful to himself in the witness-box. For instance, on being
asked why he had closed the door on his mother in the smoke-
filled room instead of giving her all the air he could, he made
the classic reply, "So that the smoke should not spread into the
hotel". So great an anxiety to avoid polluting the lounge at such
a moment appeared—to put it mildly—unnatural, and undoubtedly weighed on the side of the verdict of Guilty which
was eventually returned. Fox, a self-proclaimed homosexual
(though not above making love to a woman if he could thereby

get his hands on her jewellery) was hanged at Maidstone in April 1930.

On 10th August 1865 Stephen Forwood called at the Camden Arms, Ramsgate, to ask for the whereabouts of his wife and two children, whom he had left some time ago to go and live in London under the name of Ernest Southey. He was given an address, and the following day called on the house of William Ellis, dyer, in King Street. He was wearing a false beard, false moustaches and green spectacles. His wife, doubtless startled by his changed appearance, asked why he had deserted her—she would have perished but for the kindness of her friends. Forwood shouted wildly that he had saved up £1,172 and been done out of the whole amount, and instantly shot both his wife and daughter with a gun of which five chambers had been loaded with ball. He then, for some reason, removed his disguise before starting to recharge the gun. By this time people who had heard the shots from the street ran into the house, secured the demented man and led him away. As he passed his child's dead body he laid his hand on her hair and burst into tears. He showed no interest or emotion at the trial, and a plea of insanity was put forward. This, however, was dismissed and Stephen Forwood was executed at Maidstone—adding one more puzzle to the mysteries of human motivation.

Finally, a tragedy of 1856 on the beach between Folkestone and Dover. On 2nd August the bodies of two young women—sisters named Caroline and Maria Back—were found lying within 15 yards of each other by a spot known as Steddy Hole. This is immediately south-east of Warren Halt Station, about two miles along the coast east from Folkestone, where a zigzag pathway (cut, it is pleasant to record, through the generosity of Mr William Morris of Abbott's Cliff) ran from the cliff head to the beach below. Both girls had been shot in the chest. Caroline's fingers were cut, and Maria's clothing was torn. The murder was very soon traced to one Dedea Redanies, a Serb who was a private in the British Swiss Legion, part of the Foreign Legion that had been training at Shorncliffe. He had become acquainted with Caroline and Maria and their family several months previously.

After a speedy conviction, he wrote a long letter of confession to "Dearest Mother Back". The cause, he said, was his jealousy of the elder sister, Caroline, who wanted to break off a relationship that had grown up between them in order to go away to Woolwich. Maria he was forced to kill because she had been a witness to Caroline's death. "On the first lines," his letter begins, "I pray to forgive me the awful accident to the unlucky Dedea Redanies which I committed upon my very dear Caroline and Maria Back yesterday morning at five o'clock". (One may perhaps wonder what they were all doing on the beach at such an hour.) The letter concludes, "Scarcely am I able to write by heartbreak for my ever memorable Caroline and Mary Ann".

Despite these touching expressions of remorse, the unlucky Redanies was executed at Maidstone gaol.

8

WATCH YOUR STEP
The South-East: (2)
Surrey, Sussex

The Blue Anchor, Byfleet, Surrey, a large, solidly imposing pub in the centre of the town, was the scene of a notorious poisoning case in 1924. The licensee at that time was a Mr Alfred Poynter Jones, aged 37. On 23rd November 1924 he sent his wife Mabel off to the Hotel Victoria, Biarritz, for a holiday following certain financial worries she had encountered. There she had the extreme misfortune to meet Monsieur Jean-Pierre Vaquier (or Vacquier), a voluble, excitable gentleman employed by the hotel to give concerts with a new-fangled wireless set of his own invention. A passionate love affair developed between them—so passionate that it practically transcended the need for conversation, which was carried on ingeniously if haltingly by means of a two-way dictionary. When, in the following February, Mabel Jones returned to the Blue Anchor, Vaquier took up quarters in London the very next day. The reason he gave for his journey was his anxiety to secure the patent rights for his great invention, a new type of sausage-mincer. The trimmings of this fervid romance—dictionaries, sausage-machines—have an incongruously un-romantic air. After spending a night with Mabs (as he called her) at the Hotel Russell, Russell Square, WC1, the ardent Frenchman turned up at the Blue Anchor and settled in for a considerable time. At length, however, Mrs Jones began to tire of Vaquier, his arrogance, his excitability, his boasting, his in-creasingly insistent pleas that she should run away with him to a lifetime of semi-unintelligible conversation, mincing machines and penury. She refused to leave her husband. Vaquier decided to take steps to make it easier for her. He went up to London and visited a chemist's shop at 134 Southampton Row, close to the

Hotel Russell, which was run by a man of the same name as his prospective victim, Jones. There he purchased a large quantity of strychnine, saying he wanted it, among other chemicals, for his experimental work with "the wireless". The strangely unsuspecting manager handed over enough poison to kill several people, and Vaquier signed the poison book as "J. Wanker". On 29th March Alfred Jones took a sizeable dose of salts to offset the results of a heavily alcoholic party the previous night, and a little later—calmly watched by Vaquier—died in agonizing convulsions. Surprisingly it was not until 19th April, following a communication from the chemist, who had recognized a photograph of Mr Wanker, that the police arrested Vaquier, who was then at the Railway Hotel, Woking. Throughout his trial, for which he had to be provided with an interpreter, he preened, postured and argued. He was supremely confident of acquittal, and when—as all but he expected—the verdict of Guilty was returned, he yelled abuse at the cold and implacable Mr Justice Avory, then struggled all the way from the dock. Cruel, conceited, stupid and mean, Vaquier was hanged at Wandsworth prison on 12th August 1924. The Blue Anchor, still very much in use, stands on the site of a much older building, still known by that name back in 1839, but previously as Hollydays. Mr Leonard Stevens, in an account published in the *Woking Review* 1953, suggests that the name really refers to an 'anker', an old measure of wine and spirits, as there is no particular link between Byfleet and the sea.

In 1904 Kingswood Rectory was referred to as a large, old-fashioned red-brick building four miles from Reigate, sheltered from other houses in the village (on the A217) by shrubs and trees. In the summer of 1861, while the rector and his wife were away on holiday, the house was left in the care of a 55-year-old housekeeper, Mrs Halliday. On the morning of 12th June her body was discovered lying on the floor of her bedroom, clothed only in her nightdress. A piece of rag had been thrust down her throat and her hands and feet were tightly tied with string. Beside the body was a heavy branch recently broken from a tree, and under the bed a packet of six papers evidently dropped by the intruder. It seemed fairly clear that here was a case of housebreakers disturbed on the job. Three of the papers were found to concern a German named Carl Franz of Saxony and one of these, a form of identity certificate, contained a detailed description of his appearance. The other three papers were a list of names and addresses, an unposted begging letter signed Adolphe Krohn, and an answer to another begging letter, from a well-known singer of the day named Madame Titiens. German tramps were known to have been in the neighbourhood, and in fact two had put up at an Inn in Reigate called the Cricketers' Arms. One of the two men matched the description on the certificate, and the hunt was up. After several weeks a German arrested in London on some minor charge, who gave his name as Salzmann, was seen to resemble the official description of Franz. On being confronted by a detective brought over from Saxony he confessed to being the wanted man but denied all knowledge of the crime. He had changed his name, he said, because he knew a Carl Franz was being sought, and he was frightened. He thereupon told the following story.

A few months previously he had landed in Hull from Germany on his way to America to seek for work in the golden land. When he reached Liverpool he could not obtain a passage so he started to make his way to London on foot. As he trudged along the road he fell in with two men, also German, one called Adolphe Krohn. The name of the other he never discovered. This latter was very similar in build and appearance to himself. On the way they decided to spend the night on some straw in a Northamptonshire field, and settled down to sleep. The following morning Franz found not only his companions gone, but also his bundle of clothing (including a suit) and his precious papers. The two men, he declared, must have gone on to Kingswood Rectory (the unknown one wearing Carl's suit) and there committed the crime, dropping the papers in their haste. As might be expected, no-one believed so tall a story—which was a pity, for it happened to be perfectly true. This was proved by an astonishing chance.

While Franz was despondently awaiting trial some tramps went into a shed by a lane in Northamptonshire for a kip. Under the straw they found a little book filled with writing they could not understand, and passed it on to the police. Their honesty saved an innocent man's life. The book turned out to be a diary written in German—the diary that Franz kept with scrupulous regularity, and that his companions had thrown away as of no value. It was valuable indeed to the prisoner for it contained entries confirming every detail of his story, right up to the very moment when he turned over to sleep the night his belonging were stolen. Franz said later that as he was scribbling away Krohn had actually asked him what he was doing. What he was doing, though he did not realize it, was insuring his future. Further confirmation of the story now came from Madame Titiens, who knew both Krohn and his companion by sight and declared that, though remarkably similar in appearance, Franz was not the man. Franz was brought to trial as a matter of form, but speedily acquitted. The murderer was never found. Those often derided nightly scribblers of the day's events may take heart from the adventures of Carl Franz, and continue to put pen to little book—it might one day save their lives.

Though all accounts of the Kingswood murder that I have traced follow the original report in referring to the 'Rectory', it appears that this in fact is incorrect and that the building was in fact a vicarage. The Cricketers' Arms has proved extremely elusive. It was said to have stood opposite the police station of the time, which was in London Road. A directory of 1839 refers to a "Cricketers" run by John James Baker of London Lane, Reigate, but there is no reference to this in records of a few years earlier. In 1824 a public house called the Bat and Ball stood in London Road near the junction with the High Street: it may well be that these two inns were one and the same. Wherever the true site of the mysterious pub may have been, however, no trace of it remains today.

Early on the morning of Tuesday 11th November 1817 the inhabitants of the charming little town of Godalming were horrified to hear of the double murder of one of its most respected citizens and his housekeeper. George Chennell was a shoemaker and small farmer, owner of a modest amount of property. His home was in a small passage adjoining the Little George public house. There, on that Tuesday morning, a man called for some shoes he had ordered and on opening the door found the housekeeper, Mrs Wilson, lying on the floor with her throat cut. He summoned the neighbours, who went upstairs to the bedroom and discovered the body of Chennell, his head almost severed by a frightful gash. His son, George junior,

was quickly suspected, and on 12th August 1818 was brought
to trial at the Town Hall, Guildford, together with the dead
man's carter, J. Chalcraft. George was known as a drunkard
and wastrel, his father's sorrow, who had—as an old broadsheet
graphically puts it—"said many times to his sotty companions
that he wished his father dead and out of the way, he should
then have plenty to spend on beer and bacca". After the murder
two banknotes, one of them bloodstained, were found in his
lodgings. J. Chalcraft, his associate in the crime, was described
in one grandly sweeping phrase as a man of "universal bad
character". Evidence at the trial proved that on the night in
question George left the Richmond Arms where he had been
sitting drinking, shortly after nine, met Chalcraft by arrangement, entered his father's house, went upstairs and killed the
old man by smashing his head in with a shoemaker's hammer,
and then cut his throat. They then went down and killed Mrs Wilson as she was sitting by the fire mending her murderer's shirt.
After grabbing any valuables they could find, Chalcraft went
home and George returned to his drinking at the Richmond
Arms. The whole procedure had taken well under an hour. The
trial closed at 9.30 p.m. of the same day on which it opened—
the verdicts of guilty a foregone conclusion. Chennell and Chalcraft were hanged by Jack Ketch on a meadow just outside
the town in the presence of about 20,000 people, some of whom
climbed trees on Frith Hill and hung on the roofs of houses to
get a better view. It was the last public hanging in Godalming.
The accused reduced the two officiating clergymen to tears,
it is reported, by their refusal to confess, but they "communi-
cated with every appearance of reverence and awe". "Appearance" would seem to be the operative word: the crime was
despicable in conception and imbecilic in execution.

The Richmond Arms, where Chennell drank before and after
the murder, may still be visited on the corner of Holloway Hill.
The Little George in the High Street has gone and is now replaced by a branch of Timothy White's, but the doorway in
the narrow passage that ran by the house is still pointed out.

Another Godalming murder was that of a young woman
named Emily Joy, who was done to death on 7th January
1889 in a studio in Brighton Road. Her killer, E. B. Jenkins, was
hanged at Wandsworth the following March. Emily Joy was
buried at Farncombe, a little north of the town: though little

is known of the circumstances of the case it is agreeable to
record that an appropriate tombstone to the poor girl's memory
was erected by a Mr Patrick of Guildford—free of expense.

About six miles south-west of Godalming (off the A3), is the
village of Thursley, and a mile from the village is Hankley Common, once famed as a beauty spot and therefore as a matter of
course taken over as a training ground for the military. On 7th
October 1942 troops exercising over its devasted remains came
across the badly decomposed body of a girl lying in a shallow
grave. She had been murdered with barbarous brutality: stab
wounds were found on her skull and forearm (made with an unusual type of hook-bladed knife) and there was a single violent
blow on the back of her head, undoubtedly made by a thick
birch stake which was found near by with a number of fine hairs
still clinging to it. Personal belongings discovered later identified
her as Joan Wolfe, 19, a girl last seen alive over three weeks
previously. There was also a letter, written by her, saying that
she was pregnant and hoping that the man to whom it was
addressed would soon be able to keep his word to marry her.
For some time she had been carrying on an affair with a French-
Canadian of part Cree Indian ancestry named August Sangret
who was stationed at Witley camp about two miles away. She
had run away from home and throughout the spring and summer of 1942 was living near the camp in primitive shelters of
branches and clumps of heather which Sangret constructed for
her. These came to be known, in popular accounts of the case,
as "wigwams". For part of the time also she lived in a deserted
cricket pavilion near Thursley, the walls of which she covered
in drawings, sentimental poems, signatures and prayers—she
was a strict Roman Catholic. Though Sangret was supposed to
be trying to overcome various obstacles in the way of his marrying her, there is no doubt that in reality he was anxious to rid
himself of an increasingly irksome encumbrance. When questioned by the police he admitted the relationship (he could not
well do otherwise) but said he had last had an appointment with
her on 14th September, which she had failed to keep. He referred
to a knife of his that had been stolen (before any official information concerning the weapon was released), and later a knife with
a peculiarly hooked blade was found down a washhouse drain
and identified as his. It was then remembered that during an
early interview by the police he had requested permission to go

to the lavatory attached to this washhouse. The trial of August
Sangret opened towards the end of February 1943. It was suggested, from the evidence of the injuries, that he attacked Joan
Wolfe, and as she ran away she fell over an army trip wire.
He then killed her and—for some reason not explained—dragged
her body some 400 yards before burying it. It transpired that
Sangret already had a record in Canada of violence against
women. There was little difficulty in establishing his guilt and
he was executed on 2nd April 1943 in Wandsworth prison.

Uncertainty has often been expressed about the verdict in the
case of Norman Thorne, generally referred to as the Crowborough murderer. Sir Arthur Conan Doyle, who was living in
Crowborough during the last years of his life, was one who
shared such doubts, and Helena Normanton, who edited the trial
transcript for the *Notable British Trials* series, was another. An
account of the case by her actually appears in a series of "Great
Unsolved Mysteries".

On his demobilization after the First World War Norman
Thorne, 24 years old at the time of the murder, set up as a
chicken farmer in what was then a lonely spot outside the village of Crowborough called Blackness. He was the son of a respectable, conventionally suburban family, a one-time scoutmaster, regular chapelgoer and Sunday School teacher. He had
drifted into a relationship with a pale, bespectacled, characterless,
neurotic and irritatingly pathetic little 23-year-old typist from
Kensal Green called Elsie Cameron. By 1924 both marital and
material ventures were foundering and Thorne was beset by
difficulties. He had recently, to make things still more complicated, fallen in love with a local girl who was very opposite,
physically and mentally, of his ineffectual fiancée. To crown
everything, Elsie Cameron was now pleading pregnancy and
demanding marriage. On 5th December 1924 she arrived at the
chicken farm with a new jumper, a fresh hair-do, and a small
case carrying the sum of her possessions. She had come to stay—
though of how conclusive that stay was to be she had mercifully
no idea. It was an embarrassing situation for Thorne as he had
an appointment with his new love that same evening—a fact
that would not go down well with Elsie. However, according to
Thorne's own story later, they had a meal together in the squalid
hut that served him as home, and at a quarter to ten he told her
he had to meet someone at the station—a statement she accepted,

if without enthusiasm. On his return to the hut at 11.30 he found her hanging from a crossbeam, her feet just scraping the floor. Realizing she was dead, he stated, he panicked and, instead of fetching doctor, neighbours or police, stripped her, burnt her clothes, cut the body into several pieces and buried them around his small plot of land.

It was not long before the inevitable enquiries as to Elsie's whereabouts started, and they led straight to Thorne. Elsie had been seen near the farm, one witness actually watched her turn into Thorne's gate. A stringent search was made, Thorne at first appearing only too eager to help the police in their enquiries. He insisted, against all who said otherwise, that Elsie had been nowhere near the chicken farm that night. At last, however, the ghastly remains were brought to light, and Thorne recounted the story told above, sticking relentlessly throughout to the claim that she had committed suicide. Formidable evidence against this was given by Sir Bernard Spilsbury who said he had found eight bruises all inflicted before death, the inference being that Thorne had attacked her and then attempted to make her death resemble a self-inflicted hanging. Spilsbury's findings were strongly challenged by the defence, whose chief expert witness Dr Robert Brontë never afterwards altered his opinion that Thorne was innocent of murder. Elsie Cameron was said by her fellow-employees to have shown suicidal tendencies on several occasions —in her obsessed mentally unstable condition she might well have taken her own life. But Thorne was found guilty; his appeal, and an application for a review of the medical evidence both failed to save him from execution.

Thorne's dismembering of his fiancée's body was a horrible act and undoubtedly weighed heavily against him, but had he not stuck so obstinately to his defence of suicide he might have been convicted of manslaughter rather than of murder. Opinions on the case will always differ, but as Helena Normanton says in the closing words of her account of the case, ". . . in the long run one pities them both, caught in the grip of forces too strong for either of them".

The exact position of the tragic chicken farm is now uncertain, but it was apparently situated on what is now an overgrown site by the junction of Luxford Road and Luxford Lane. It is rumoured that Thorne's hut is still in use somewhere in the Crowborough area: one cannot help wondering whether the owner is ever conscious of a slight shiver when he opens the door after dark and sees the crossbeam gleaming in the shadowy moonlight.

On Saturday morning, 31st July 1948, Joan Mary Woodhouse, a 27-year-old librarian at the National Central Library, Bloomsbury, London WC, left her Y.W.C.A. hostel at Bennett Park, near Blackheath, after telling a friend she was going to spend the August Bank Holiday with her parents in Barnsley, Yorkshire. Ten days later her partially clothed body was found in Box Copse, a small dense wood of beech trees and box bushes in Arundel Park, Sussex. She had been raped and strangled. Her murderer, after the biggest search of the post-war years, was never discovered: nor was the reason for her sudden decision to travel south rather than north, though she knew the district well and was particularly fond of this particular spot. An attaché case containing some of her possessions was found deposited in the left-luggage office at Worthing Central Station. The fact that her outer clothing was folded into a neat pile by her side caused some puzzlement (she was a deeply religious girl of high moral principles, the last person likely to have been indulging in a secret love affair), until it was revealed that she was ardent sunbather and had probably chosen this secluded spot to bask in the summer afternoon.

In 1950, two years after a formal verdict had been returned, Joan Woodhouse's father was granted a private warrant (the first time such an application had been made in 85 years), as a result of which the man who originally reported finding her body faced a charge of murdering her. The evidence against him, however, was found insufficient to justify bringing him to trial.

In the early evening of 9th October 1912 a taxi-driver arrived at 6 Southcliffe Avenue, Eastbourne, to take the occupant, Countess Sztaray, to the Burlington Hotel. He told her he had noticed a man crouching on the portico above the front door, evidently waiting a chance to break in, and she telephoned the police. When Inspector Arthur Walls arrived and told him to come down, the man instantly shot him dead. The murderer was George Mackay, alias John Williams. He came of a good family and received an excellent education, but had afterwards settled for a life of petty crime. During the confusion that followed the killing he escaped to the beach where he had left a girl with whom he was living, named Florence Seymour. Together they buried the gun beneath the shingle. Mackay then wrote to his brother in London, explaining what had happened and asking for money. The latter showed this note to a man named Edgar Power, a friend of both the brothers. It happened, however, that Power was also in love with Florence Seymour, a girl of unusual beauty, despite the fact that she was expecting George Mackay's child. Power thereupon embarked on a cunning plan to get rid of his rival. He gave some cash to Mackay, who went off to London, then informed the police what had occurred. As Power was himself a known criminal the police knew they would need more than his uncorroborated word as evidence. A further plan—perfectly justifiable on their part but somewhat malodorous on his —was worked out between them. Posing as a loyal friend, Power persuaded Florence that the revolver must be moved as detectives would certainly find it very shortly. She agreed to go along with him to retrieve it, and when they arrived the police were waiting for them. Florence, terrified, confessed. Meantime Power went to London and, still in his pose as well-wisher, induced Mackay to come out of hiding and meet him—for some purpose unstated— at Moorgate Underground Station. The same betrayal procedure was followed, and Mackay was arrested and charged. Florence retracted her confession but it was too late, and Mackay was tried and convicted of murder.

The fact that for an unspecified reason the accused man was brought to and from court with a hood over his head inevitably resulted in the case becoming known as that of The Hooded Man. Florence's baby was born before its father was executed. In his account of the case Sir Patrick Hastings, who defended him, relates how the condemned man was allowed to see his child and placed a piece of prison bread in his hand murmuring, "Now no-one can say your father never gave you anything".* This genuinely touching little moment, and the fact that Power's motives for bringing the murderer to justice were less than disinterested, have to some extent obscured the cold truth that Mackay was just another callous and stupid criminal who killed a police officer to avoid arrest. If there is one person in the whole miserable affair deserving of sympathy it is the unhappy Florence Seymour.

* *Cases in Court* (Heinemann, 1949).

During the 1920s the Crumbles, a desolate and unbeautiful stretch of shingle between Eastbourne and Pevensey, acquired a sinister reputation on account of two notorious murders committed on its inhospitable beach. The first was that of 17-year-old Irene Munro on 19th August 1920. Miss Munro worked as a shorthand typist in London and arrived in Eastbourne on 16th August for her annual holiday, staying in a single room at 393 Seaside (30s. per week, bed and breakfast), a long, dull road leading from the town towards Pevensey. On the afternoon of the 19th she was seen by the Archery, a large public house about seventy yards from her lodgings, talking to two young men. The following day her body was discovered under some stones on the Crumbles. She had been beaten on the head with a heavy stone, and her handbag was missing, but there was no sign of sexual assault. Enquiries from several people who had seen the trio resulted in the arrest of William Gray, 29, and Jack Field, 19, two unemployed men who had been spending most of their time chasing girls or drinking at the Albemarle Hotel on the Parade. Gray, married to a girl who worked as a daily servant, was totally illiterate, unable to read or write. Field, a better educated man, lived with his family at 23 Susans Road, close to Gray's home in Longstone Road. His father was a head waiter in London and his mother let rooms during the summer season.

It was discovered that within an hour of Irene Munro's body being found, Field and Gray went to a recruiting office and tried to enlist immediately. A barmaid at the Albemarle said they had not returned to the place since the evening of the 19th, but on that occasion they had seemed to be unusually affluent, standing drinks all round and inviting her to the Hippodrome. Both men were found guilty, and by the time the appeal was heard each was violently accusing the other. They were executed at Wandsworth on 4th February 1921. Whether the reason for the crime was simple robbery or a sexual assault which Irene Munro resisted remains unknown. The verdict at the trial contained a recommendation to mercy on the strange ground that the murder was not premeditated.

The second Crumbles crime took place in 1924, when Patrick Herbert Mahon was charged with the murder of Emily Kaye in a bungalow on the same melancholy shore. Mahon, who lived with his wife and daughter at Richmond, had met Miss Kaye in the course of his business as a soda-fountain salesman and embarked on an affair with her. He was a handsome, well-mannered, cultured, lively man (and was well aware of it), four years younger than the 37-year-old typist who was swept metaphorically and literally off her feet. She did not know that behind the pleasant façade was a record of imprisonment for forgery, bank robbery and assault—nor that he already had another girl in the offing. By the spring of 1924 Miss Kaye had become a burden to him—a burden rendered no less heavy by the fact that she was expecting his child and demanding that he leave his wife and go away with her to South Africa. On 12th April he bought a chef's knife and saw from a kitchen utensils shop in Victoria Street, Westminster, and met Emily at Eastbourne. They went to the small bungalow he had taken at the Pevensey end of the Crumbles. It stood near the Wallsend Road and had once been part of the Langney Coastguard Station. A stone wall surrounded the place, which stood lonely and solitary right against the shingle, only a couple of hundred yards from the spot where Miss Munro's body had been discovered four years previously. A few days later, after a violent quarrel over his refusal to fall in with her plans, he killed her by a blow on the head. There followed a period of sheer ghastly nightmare, as he tried to dispose of the body. After cutting it up he boiled some parts and burnt others. He made up parcels of flesh to scatter about the countryside. Over the week-end he took a rest and invited his new girl to stay with him in the bungalow. She spent the time in blissful ignorance of the horrors hidden in a trunk and elsewhere all around her. "I wanted human companionship," he said later, and one may well believe him.

The crime came to light after his wife (long suspicious of his activities) found a Waterloo Station cloakroom ticket in his pocket and asked a friend to retrieve the bag left there. The friend, an ex-police officer, managed to force the bag open sufficiently to see what it contained—a blood-stained apron, a chef's knife, a tennis-racquet case and other articles spattered with blood. The bag was returned to the cloakroom, and when Mahon came to claim it the following day he was detained. By the beginning of May the dreadful contents of the bungalow were revealed: Bernard Spilsbury said afterwards they were the most gruesome human remains he had ever seen. Mahon alleged that Miss Kaye had run at him with a coal axe, he had defended himself, and she had fallen down, cracking her head against the

L

coalscuttle. The evidence was heavily against this, and the coal-scuttle was shown to be far too flimsy to have caused a fatal injury to anyone falling onto it. Mahon's famous description of how he burnt his mistress's head in the grate during a thunder-storm (another storm, by dramatic chance, was raging overhead as he spoke), and ran out of the house in terror as the eyes sprang open in the heat, formed a ghastly climax to a story as dreadful as any heard in a court of law until the playing of the tape in the trial of the Moor murderers.

On 27th February 1966 John Trevor Preston, 25, murdered his 78-year-old landlady, Miss Hilda Couchman, at her boarding-house in Channel View Road, Eastbourne. Her naked body was found lying on a bed in one of the rooms. He was sentenced to life imprisonment, but six years later, in 1972, was found hanged in his cell at Wakefield prison, Yorkshire.

The earliest of our Brighton-centred crimes occurred in 1831, when the streets were lit only by the occasional oil lamp, and the ornamental Royal Pavilion and grand houses of the Marine Parade hid a morass of squalid poverty. John William Holloway, born in 1806 and educated at two church schools in Alfriston, had by the age of 20 developed into an ill-featured but apparently successful Don Juan among the local girls. In 1826 he formed a relationship in Brighton with Celia Bashford, whom he had met on the racecourse. She herself was no beauty, barely four feet in height, with an overlarge head and a plain face, but when she became pregnant he married her (under duress), and eventu-ally she bore him two children. In 1830 he left her and went to work in the blockade service at Winchelsea, calling himself William Goldsmith. During a visit to Rye he fell in with a fine handsome girl named Ann Kennett, and bigamously 'married' her, settling at Pagham Harbour, near Bognor. In 1831, after moving around to various places and working at various jobs (including coiner and forger) 'Mr and Mrs Goldsmith' came to live in Brighton, lodging at 7 Margaret Street. There he found himself a job as painter on the Chain Pier. Here Celia, not for the first time, tracked him down and was able to force him by law to make her regular payments. Two shillings a week was con-sidered by the authorities to be sufficient to maintain herself and her two children. Holloway sent the money each week by—of all people—Ann Kennett, who seemed to be in physical terror of her 'husband'. This convenient go-between arrangement ended, as might have been expected, in a first-class row, Holloway joining in by visiting his wife and hurling threats and abuse at her. On 14th July, under pretence of being a reformed and remorseful character, he lured her into a hovel in an alley known as Donkey Row. There he killed her by some means not stated and, in the presence of Ann Kennett, cut up her body. Part of it he buried under the trees of an avenue in the village of Preston known as Lovers' Walk. The rest he threw into a cesspool close to the tenements where he and Ann were living. Both gruesome packages soon came to light and were identified. 'Mr and Mrs Goldsmith' were arrested and charged with murder. Ann, who appeared genuinely shattered by the turn of events, was acquitted. Holloway, doubtless realizing his case was hopeless, made no secret of his guilt, and had the grace to affirm his partner's innocence. He was hanged at Lewes on 16th December, spending the preceding night invoking the Deity with such vociferous fervour that he could be heard all over the prison yard and no-one could get a wink of sleep. On the scaffold he made the customary appeal to the crowd to take warning by his fate, which it is to be hoped they one and all did. A story is told that among the watchers was a countryman who suffered from a swelling on his forehead: with the permission of the executioner he untied the dead man's hand and rubbed it over the spot in the belief that the contact would cure him. It is not, unfortunately, recorded how successful this novel and somewhat grisly treatment for bumps proved to be.

On 13th April 1839 a Mrs Johnson was found dead in bed at 80 Nottingham Street, Brighton, "one of the most notorious parts of the town". Her throat had been cut. The Johnsons kept a lodging-house for tramps. For more than a week before her death Mrs Johnson had been almost constantly drunk, but this does not seem to have prevented her from rising betimes in the morning. They were, in fact, noted locally as a couple who could not wait to get out of bed in the morning. When the neighbours found the house door still locked around ten o'clock, therefore, they put a ladder against the window and looked in—to be met with the grim tableau described. Johnson was nowhere to be seen, but an old man said he had met him between 8 and 9 that morning, walking to Worthing with some clothes for his son. He was later run to earth in a beershop in that sedate resort, and told enquirers that he had left his wife in good health. When informed of the distinct change in her condition he remarked calmly that he was not in the least surprised—she had frequently tried to make off with herself. It appeared, however, that if Mr Johnson's suggestion was to be accepted, Mrs Johnson had not only cut her own throat, but had afterwards cleaned the razor as best she could, closed it up, and neatly hung a cloak over a shutter to conceal a number of bloodstains. Further bloodstains were also found on Johnson and he was in due course charged, tried, convicted and hanged.

An early case of murder of a senior police officer took place on 6th March 1844 when John Lawrence (described as a "reckless vagabond") was brought in to Brighton "Police Office" on a charge of stealing a carpet. While they were awaiting the arrival of a witness Chief Police Constable Solomon turned to speak to a man standing beside him. Instantly Lawrence (who had just asked, and been refused, permission to cut his own throat because life was a burden to him) seized the poker from the hearth and beat Solomon on the head. The unfortunate officer died the next morning: and the burden of life was lifted from Lawrence at Lewes Assizes.

One of the most famous Brighton crimes is that known as the Poisoned Chocolates Case of 1871. Christiana Edmunds, destined to die in Broadmoor, was born in 1828 in Margate, Kent. By 1870 she was the only surviving child of her family, living with her widowed mother in Gloucester Place, facing the new parish church of St Peter. One day while walking on the sea front she received a passing glance from a local physician, Dr Beard, and promptly fell violently in love with him—it was evidently a glance of devastating power. She wrote him long effusive letters with an Italian tinge, calling him Caro Mio, referring to Mrs Beard as La Sposa, and signing herself Dorothea. These grand operatic terms set the atmosphere for what was to follow. In March 1871 she visited Dr Beard's house and offered his wife a chocolate cream. Mrs Beard became violently ill and the doctor, suspicious and alarmed, forbade Miss Edmunds to have anything further to do with him or his family. He did not know his Dorothea. She threatened an action for slander (against the advice of her wiser mother) and when this brought no response embarked on a wild and terrible scheme to convince Dr Beard that, if there was a poisoner in Brighton, it was not his maligned and devoted female friend. She sent a child into a well-known sweet shop to buy some chocolate creams, injected them with arsenic or strychnine, and later despatched another child back to the shop to have them changed for another kind of confectionery. The shopkeeper obliged, and added the poisoned chocolates to his store. This procedure she repeated more than once, with inevitably tragic consequences. Sidney Albert Barker, a 4-year-old boy, died as a result of eating a chocolate from the shop in question, whereupon with sublime effrontery Christiana herself accused the shopkeeper of selling contaminated goods. Protesting that he had never before had such a complaint, the unfortunate man destroyed his entire stock. She also berated the police for not heeding warnings she had given them, and left the inquest on the child in a blaze of indignation and to ringing acclamations from the populace. For a while there was a lull, then people all over Brighton began to receive gifts of cakes, sweets and fruit, accompanied by letters written in a strange hand, but apparently by someone who knew each recipient. Some of the presents were posted in Brighton, others in London. Among those who received them was Christiana Edmunds herself. Many of the favoured ones who were rash enough to taste the contents became seriously ill, though Miss Edmunds, it seems, was happily spared. Eventually the Chief Constable—spurred on no doubt by Christiana's unrelenting attacks on his force ("idiots" was one of her milder terms)—offered a reward for information about the mysterious purveyor of poison. This chanced to be read by a chemist who had supplied Miss Edmunds with strychnine. Dr Beard also became interested. Handwritings were compared: letters she had used in order to obtain poison were found to be forgeries.

The final result was the appearance of Christiana in the dock, charged with murdering little Sidney Barker and attempting to murder Mrs Beard. She was found guilty and, after a plea of pregnancy proved false, was condemned to death. There was a long history of family insanity behind her, however, and she was committed for life to an asylum. She died in Broadmoor at the age of 78.

Two bodies found in trunks in the same town within a month may seem excessive, but in 1934 these grim discoveries were made at Brighton. On 17th June an unpleasant smell was noticed in the left-luggage office, and traced to a plywood trunk deposited there 11 days previously. When opened it was found to contain the torso of a woman wrapped in brown paper and tied with venetian blind cord. Head and limbs were missing, so also was the tray of the trunk. Notices were sent to other left-luggage offices, resulting in the finding of legs that fitted the Brighton torso, in a suitcase at King's Cross. These were wrapped in paper that had been soaked with olive oil. The remains were those of a pregnant girl in her twenties. There was no indication of the cause of death. Neither the identity of the girl nor any clue to her killer has ever been discovered.

The news of this trunk murder had a decisive effect on the behaviour of Tony Mancini, alias Jack Notyre, alias Hyman Gold, real name (probably) Cecil Lois England, aged 26. He was a petty crook who probably chose his best-known name from admiration of Chicago gangsterdom and had lived since 1933 with, and on, Violette Kaye (real name Violet Saunders), once a dancer, now a prostitute. They set up house together at 44 Park Crescent, Mancini working in a café near the front while Violette Kaye carried on her more lucrative profession in his absence—but with his knowledge. On 10th May the pair had a quarrel, and the next day Mancini announced that Miss Kaye had left for Paris. He then moved to 52 Kemp Street, taking with him a large, black second-hand trunk (price 7s. 6d.). For no less than two months he lived with this object in his room, despite an increasingly pungent smell that led one visitor to ask whether he was keeping rabbits.

Mancini was among the hundreds of people questioned in regard to the cloakroom trunk. The following day he fled. The police called again, following up some routine point, saw (and smelt) the trunk, opened it, and found Miss Kaye dead inside it, killed by severe wounds in the head. Two days later Mancini was arrested on the road from Maidstone to London. His story was that he returned from work to find Violette lying dead on the bed. Frightened of facing the police on account of his record, he panicked, hid the body in a cupboard, then took it in the trunk to Kemp Street, hoping for a chance, presumably, to dispose of it later. Mancini was brilliant defended by Norman Birkett. Suggestions were put forward that the woman could have fallen down the admittedly dangerous basement steps, injuring her head but able to stagger into her room: or, if it was murder, that any one of her many clients could have committed it. As Mancini said, he had nothing to gain from her death, and much to lose. "Strange as it is," he said, "I used to love her." Which may well have been true. He was acquitted, seeming as bemused as he must have been relieved, when he heard the verdict.

On 7th February 1954 Margaret Spevick, aged 9, whose home was at Embankment Gardens, Chelsea, was found raped and strangled on a divan in a one-room flat in Western Avenue, Hove. An unfinished portrait of her stood on an easel close by. A few days previously she had gone to stay with William Sanchez Hepper, 62, at one time on the staff of the B.B.C. as news typist and translator. Hepper's wife was friendly with Mrs Spevick, their two daughters had been to the same Chelsea school, and when Margaret broke her arm Hepper suggested it might do her good to stay a few days with him by the sea. He was living there apart from his family, but said a nurse who was resident in the flats would look after the little girl. On the 7th Mrs Spevick arrived at Brighton station to meet her daughter, but the girl did not arrive. Her mother, who had forgotten the Hove address, went back to London for it, and on her return found the girl dead, and Hepper gone. His portrait was broadcast on television, and he was eventually traced to Spain, where he had family connections. He was extradited to Britain and faced trial at Lewes in July. Seven doctors were called to reinforce a plea of insanity, and it was said that injuries in a car accident caused amnesia, and that when he attacked Margaret he was under the impression that she was his wife. Hepper however was convicted of murder, and hanged.

In the early 1930s Number 1 Clarence Street, Portslade, was an old junk shop owned by a man of 80 named Joseph Bedford, who described himself a trifle euphemistically as a leather merchant. Like many solitary livers, he had the reputation of a miser, though in fact he was liked in the district for his pleasant habit of handing small coins to the children. On a November night in 1933 the old man, feeble and hard of hearing, was violently set upon by two thugs, Frederick Parker, 21, and Albert Probert, 26. He died the next day from pressure of a blood clot on the brain. The motive was money—the haul was £6. Parker told the police the job was not worth doing for so small a return. As so often in these despicable crimes, each vicious party blamed the other. Both were found equally guilty, both were hanged. Among other points of evidence, the humble farthing (a coin he must often in his kindness have given to the children) played its part in bringing his killers to justice. Numbers of them were found scattered about on the shop floor—nearly thirty were found in the pocket of one of his murderers.

We close our south-eastern survey with a railway murder: that of Mr Frederick Isaac Gold, who was killed on the London Bridge to Brighton line on 27th June 1881 as the train passed through Merstham Tunnel, near Redhill in Surrey—scene of the death of Mary Sophia Money in 1905.* The case opened with the arrival of the train at Preston Park, Brighton, when a young man was discovered covered with blood, in a bloodstained compartment. He said he had been attacked and robbed—though it was noticeable that, despite his mauled appearance, he was able to move freely and apparently without pain. Surprise was caused also by the sight of a gold watch and chain sticking out from one of his shoes. He explained that he kept it there for safety. "What a peculiar place to put it," was the station inspector's mild comment. Incredible though it seems, the watch was then handed back to the young man, he was gently returned to the train by sympathetic officials and, with their best wishes, continued his dramatically broken journey. Further kindness was showered on him by the Brighton police, to whom he gave his name as Arthur Lefroy, actor and dramatist, *en route* to the Theatre Royal for an appointment with its well-known lessee, Mrs Nye Chart. No-one seems to have bothered to check his story, but he was advised to return to his home in Cathcart Road, Wallington, near Croydon, to rest and recover from his unpleasant ordeal. A plain-clothes officer was detailed to accompany him to see that he was provided with every care and comfort. The officer, after seeing his charge safely home, returned to East Croydon station to catch the next train back to Brighton. There, however, a telegram awaited him that completely changed the picture.

The body of a man who showed signs of putting up a desperate struggle before he was killed had been found on the railway line —Lefroy was to be brought back at once—the time for solicitude was over. The officer returned to Cathcart Road, but even then was loth to disturb the young actor-dramatist, who might be resting. Instead, he waited outside the house for a solid hour—

* See *Murderers' London*.

giving his late friend ample time to decamp, which in fact he had done the moment he found himself alone. The dead man was identified as the respectable, affluent and well-known Mr Gold, and the hunt was up. Lefroy was traced to Stepney and charged with murder. He admitted to no more than that his real name was Percy Mapleton, and added that he regretted running away. "It puts such a different complexion on the case." It did indeed. There was really no defence: the motive was obviously robbery, as Mapleton, like many another stage aspirant, was very short of money. Mrs Nye Chart, incidentally, had never heard of him. The story pieced together at the trial was that Lefroy boarded the train at East Croydon with a single ticket to Brighton, a knife and a revolver, bent on selecting someone to rob. The train was not due to stop again until Preston Park, which suited his purpose. He picked on Mr Gold, alone in a first-class carriage, and attacked him as the train entered Merstham Tunnel. Gold, though 64, was a powerful man and put up an unexpectedly fierce fight—which was actually heard in the next compartment and put down to fog signals. As the train passed Horley a woman in a cottage by the line saw two men "fighting or larking". In Balcombe Tunnel, south of Crawley, Lefroy, having robbed his victim, ejected the body onto the line.

Dreadful though the crime was, the trial was not without its lighter moments. The wretched watch-in-shoe business was brought up to plague the unfortunate station superintendent.

"And what was your notion of that?" asked the judge, referring to the incident.

"I thought the young man had attempted to commit suicide," replied the superinterdent.

"But why should he have his watch in his shoe?" the judge enquired, understandably puzzled.

"Well, my lord," was all the superintendent could say blankly, "the train was going off and I hadn't time to think about it."

The plain-clothes officer also had his moment. On the way back to Wallington, he said, he had asked the young man casually if he knew the number of the famous watch.

"Certainly—56312," was the immediate reply.

The officer looked inside. "But," he said heavily, "it is written here 16261."

"Oh, yes," said Mr Lefroy, unperturbed. "I'd forgotten."

And that was the end of the matter.

9

WATERBABIES
Southern England: Berkshire, Wiltshire, Hampshire, Dorset, Isle of Wight

Our first Berkshire case takes us back to the year 1560 and one of the most famous 'unsolved' crimes of history—the death of Amy Robsart at Cumnor Place, near Abingdon. Amy Robsart (she signed herself Amye, and her name has been variously spelt Robsert, Robesart, Robsarte, Robsesarte and Robertsett), was the daughter (and only legitimate child) of Sir John Robsart of Siderstern Manor, Norfolk. In 1550, at the age of 18, she was married to Lord Robert Dudley, who was only a few months older than his bride; and they spent their early years together in Norfolk. In 1560 she was staying in Cumnor Place, a house that belonged originally to the Abingdon monastery. It was given by Henry VIII to his physician, Dr Owen, who settled it on his son William. In 1560 it was leased to Anthony Forster, M.P. for Abingdon and agent for Robert Dudley. It was, one may note, on Dudley's directions that Amy went to stay there. What actually happened on the evening of 8th September is, of course, shrouded in mystery that now will never clear. Amy is said to have directed the whole household to visit Abingdon Fair. Three ladies staying in the place refused to go, but it seems that only one of them, Mrs Owen, wife of Mr Forster's landlord, dined with her hostess. When the servants returned from merrymaking they found their mistress lying dead at the foot of a circular stone staircase. The story put out was that she had been playing cards with the other ladies, had suddenly—for no given reason—risen and left the room, fallen downstairs and broken her neck. Dudley, soon to become Earl of Leicester, was with the Queen at

Windsor when the news was brought to him. As soon as she mounted the throne the Tudor Elizabeth had started lavishing favours on him. Her infatuation with this unscrupulous adventurer (described by the coolly appraising Spanish envoy Quadra as "heartless, spiritless, treacherous and violent") is as incomprehensible as it was discreditable, and may well have played its part in the fate of his unfortunate wife. Lord Cecil wrote a few years later that Dudley was "infamed by his wife's death". He certainly deserved to be. For some time before the event occurred he was talking of divorcing or poisoning her, so eager was he to get to his benefit-disposing Queen. There seems little doubt as to whether Amy Robsart fell or was pushed. Opinions differ concerning Elizabeth's participation in the loathsome plot. Ardent Tudorphiles shake their heads indignantly. Virginal infatuation, however, can be a strong emotive force, and Elizabeth's remark to another envoy, made a few days before the tragedy, that Amy was dying when in fact she was in perfectly good health, is, to put it mildly, oddly coincidental. The inquest, not surprisingly, was permitted to reveal little or nothing: there was talk that Dudley's brother-in-law covered up for him in some way and lived comfortably on the proceeds for the rest of his life.

Walter Scott softened and romanticized the story in *Kenilworth*, an account criticized by the historian Philip Sidney, whose excellent booklet *Who Killed Amy Robsart?** is a detailed 'for-and-against' examination. Cumnor Place was not nearly so large or lofty as Scott depicted. It has long since disappeared: in 1810 nearly the whole building, then a ruin, was demolished and the materials used for rebuilding Wytham Church, just north of Oxford. The East Window is supposed to be that of the room in which Amy Robsart slept just before she was done to death.

Moving forward from the murky deeds of the age of Merrie England, we reach 1948 in Maidenhead, where an old lady—her age given variously as 94 and 96—carried on a solitary and dwindling existence in a large, mouldering house in Ray Park Avenue, called Wynford. On 1st June the milkman, wondering why her bottles had not been taken in for two days, peered through the letterbox and saw a black trunk, a shoe and some keys on the hall floor. The police found that the old lady had

* Pub. Eliot Stock, 1901.

been knocked on the head, tied up and forced inside the trunk, where she had suffocated to death. Her name was Minnie Freeman Lee. Forty years previously she had come to the house as a wealthy woman, wife of a successful barrister. She became known for her hospitality and the 17-room house was filled with life and light. In the years that followed her family died and her friends departed, until she was left living completely alone on a small grant from a Benevolent Society. As so often in similar cases, there were rumours that she had great wealth hidden about the house, and the motive for her murder was clearly robbery. In fact, the place was crammed with rotting clothing, mouldering, old-fashioned furniture and cobwebbed junk. In this Miss Havisham-type dwelling a long, wearisome search revealed nothing in the way of clues, until Chief Superintendent Cherrill noticed a small cardboard box on the bed. On the floor underneath lay the lid, flattened by somebody's foot, and on its edge were two fingerprints—ill-defined and fragmentary, but enough to lead the police to George Russell, a man with a long record of theft and housebreaking, though not, hitherto, of violence. When arrested a few days later in St Albans Russell admitted going to see Mrs Lee about the possibility of doing some work in her overgrown garden, but he said he decided against this. Later, he stated, he was told by someone that she was very rich, but instead of going back to the house he went to Staines, sang hymns in the street, and went to Brighton on the proceeds. He gave himself away, however, by protesting indignantly that he would not dream of killing the "poor aged woman" for money she was reported to have, when in fact she had nothing at all but a load of old rubbish. Since, if innocent, he would not have known the details of Mrs Lee's poverty, this statement weighed heavily in favour of his guilt, and Russell was sentenced to death.

For a few moments in Reading gaol Oscar Wilde was moved to compassion for someone other than himself, and the result was the famous Ballad written in France after his release and dedicated to the memory of "C.T.W., sometime trooper of the Royal Horse Guards". C.T.W. was Charles Thomas Woolridge, 30, quartered with his regiment in Regent's Park, London. His wife Ellen, 23, lived with a companion named Alice Cox, who was her husband's niece, in a small house in Arthur Road, Windsor, which leads from near the railway station towards the village of Clewer. At first the couple seemed happy enough. Woolridge visited his wife whenever he could get leave, and she worked in a post office at Eton. Ellen (or Nellie as he called her) was apparently of a somewhat flighty disposition, however, and disquieting rumours reached her husband as to her deportment. He was not pleased, either, to discover that at work she used her maiden name of Glendell. Quarrels flared up, followed by remorse and repentance. Once he confessed to his niece that he had even knocked Nellie down, protesting how sorry he was afterwards and how bewildered he was becoming at the way she was "trying my temper". On Friday 27th March 1896 Nellie handed him a document to sign stating that he would not molest her again. The following Sunday, after she had failed to keep an appointment with him at the barracks, he went to Windsor, telling the sentry, "I must go—I am going to do some damage". On arrival at Arthur Road he asked Alice Cox to send his wife downstairs to him. A few moments later the girl heard a scream and the sound of someone running out of the house. She looked from the window and saw Nellie lying in the road and Woolridge bending over her. A crowd quickly gathered, among them a policeman to whom Woolridge said, "Take me! I have killed my wife". Ellen lay dead, her throat cut. A plea was put forward that the charge be reduced to manslaughter because of provocation through his wife's unfaithfulness, but the unhappy soldier was found guilty of murder and hanged in Reading on 7th July 1896. Along one side of Arthur Road still stands a row of small houses, in one of which very possibly lived flighty Ellen whose tragedy, and that of her tormented husband, was to be commemorated in so famous and moving a poem.

Saturday 22nd June 1929 was the date of the famous, still unsolved, Reading Shop Murder. Alfred Oliver, 60-year-old tobacconist, was left alone in his shop at 15 Cross Street while his wife took the dog for a run. The time was about six o'clock. Ten minutes or so later she returned to find him lying on the floor behind the counter with blood pouring from his head. Paper money had been grabbed from the open till, but the coins had been left. Oliver was unable to give any coherent account of what happened to him, and died 24 hours later. It was Ascot Week and the town was full of racing crowds, but no-one was seen to enter or leave the shop. Suspicion fell on an actor named

Philip Yale Drew, and it is with his name that the Reading shop murder has been unjustly linked ever since. Drew was a member of a touring company run by Frank and Marion Lindo, and was playing the lead that week at the Royal County Theatre in a play called *The Monster*. He was a man of unusual personality and striking appearance, and several people claimed to have seen him near the shop at about the time of the murder. One witness even said she had seen him standing on the doorstep wiping blood from his face. Drew's make-up for the play—a comedy-horror-thriller—was a heavy one, and much importance was attached to the question whether he could have gone from the Cross Street shop to the theatre in Friar Street and completed it between the time of the murder and his first entrance on the stage. He underwent a searing examination at the inquest from the coroner (who was a personal friend of the dead man), but much of the evidence against him was trivial and none of it in any way conclusive. Even so, he might have found himself in a highly dangerous situation had it not been for a last-minute witness, a butcher's assistant named Alfred John Wells who had seen a man resembling Drew in Cross Street a few minutes before six o'clock. After the return of a verdict of "Murder by person or persons unknown"—and indeed during the progress of the inquest—Reading was swept by a sort of pro-Drew hysteria, with yelling crowds surging through the streets and the actor appearing on a balcony to a cheerful throng like a leader celebrating the successful conclusion of some particularly unedifying war. It was an exhibition of mob fervour that appears bitterly ironical in view of Drew's subsequent life, a drab descent into anonymous destitution. The Royal County Theatre, unhappily, has been destroyed and its site given over to multiple stores.*

During the nineteenth century baby-farming was a profitable trade, and doubtless the cover for many more child murders than are ever likely to come to light. High in the list of its most infamous practitioners is the name of Amelia Elizabeth Dyer, hanged at Newgate on 10th June 1896. After activities in and around Bristol (where she was born and lived most of her life) she arrived in Caversham, now a residential district of Reading

---

* For a full account of Philip Yale Drew's life and the Reading murder see Richard Whittington-Egan's excellent and compassionate study *The Ordeal of Philip Yale Drew* (Harrap, 1972).

north of the Thames, during September 1895. With her came her daughter and son-in-law, Alfred Palmer, together with an old woman named Granny Smith whom she had met in a workhouse. Shortly afterwards the party moved to Piggotts Road near by, and from there she advertised in the local press offering board for babies. During the next few months about a dozen small children were delivered into her tender care. In January the young Palmers went to live in London, and later Mrs Dyer moved again, to Kensington Road, Caversham. Mr Dyer, of whom little is known, remained behind in Bristol, fortunately for himself, where he worked in a factory.

On 30th March 1896 the body of a baby girl, strangled with tape and parcelled up in brown paper, was found in the Thames. A label on the wrapping showed a Bristol Railway marking and an address to Mrs Thomas, Piggotts Road, Lower Caversham. By this time, of course, Mrs Dyer had moved to Kensington Road and the name Thomas was one of her many aliases. Thus it was not until 4th April that she was arrested, by which time two more babies had been found in the river, squeezed together into a carpet-bag. Her son-in-law was arrested with her as accessory after the fact in spite of Mrs Dyer's declaration that he had nothing to do with the death of the babies. With this declaration Mrs Dyer confessed her own guilt. By the end of April seven bodies had been recovered from the Thames: Mrs Dyer was put on trial for the murder of one, Doris Marmon. Palmer was acquitted in respect of complicity in the murders, but sent to prison for three months on a charge of abandoning a little girl, to which he pleaded guilty. A plea of insanity failed to save Mrs Dyer from execution. When asked after the trial how many babies she had flung into the Thames she replied non-committally that all hers could be recognized by the tape tied round their necks.

On the afternoon of 29th April 1952 J. T. Straffen, 22, escaped from Broadmoor Institution near Crowthorne, Berkshire. By about 5.30 he was at Farley Hill, a village some seven miles away and about four miles south of Reading. At just after 6.30 p.m. he was found and detained by Bramshill Hunt public house, a short distance from the village, having been free for a little over four hours. During that period he had approached 5-year-old Linda Bawyer, of Pillar Box Cottage, Farley Hill, when she was cycling in the road near the local school, persuaded her to go with him to a field between the High Street and Farley Hill House, and there strangled her.

Straffen had been committed to Broadmoor in 1951 following the murder of two little girls in Bath, Somerset, where he was living with his parents at Fountain Buildings after being released on licence from a hostel for mental defectives. The first child, Brenda Goddard, he saw picking flowers in a field behind Camden Crescent. He took her to a nearby copse, put his arms round her neck, strangled her and beat her head against a stone. Afterwards he went to the Beau Nash cinema. This was on 15th July. On 8th August he spoke to 9-year-old Cicely Batstone at the Forum Cinema, where they happened to be sitting next to each other watching a Tarzan film. He asked her if she would like to see some more pictures, and took her to the Scala. Afterwards they went to a meadow known as the Tumps, off Broomfield Road, where he strangled her. When arrested he made some confused statements, then confessed to the murder of Brenda Goddard but said he had left the other little girl asleep in the meadow.

Straffen was then arrested and charged with murder, but found unfit to plead. He escaped from Broadmoor when taking part in a regular chore of cleaning certain outbuildings. Going into a yard on the pretext of shaking out his duster, he waited until his companion had returned inside, then climbed onto the roof of a shed and over a 10-foot wall. He said later he had killed to annoy the police. Straffen was convicted of the murder of Linda Bowyer and sentenced to death, but later reprieved and committed to Wandsworth prison.

On 10th July 1951, only a few days before the murder of Brenda Goddard, the body of 7-year-old Christine Butcher, of Peascod Road, Windsor, had been found in Stevens Meadow, Windsor Park. She had been criminally assaulted and strangled with the belt of her raincoat. Beside her lay her black-faced plastic doll. Headlined news of the discovery was widely published in the press, and it is very possible that reading about the murder had influenced Straffen. The killer of Christine Butcher was never discovered.

The ease with which Straffen escaped from Broadmoor caused great public indignation and alarm, and resulted in the setting up of a committee to enquire into the security precautions of the institution.

The village of Rode (variously spelt through the ages Roade and Road, and signifying a clearing) is now in Somerset (on the A361 between Trowbridge and Frome), but at the time when Constance Kent first brought it an unenviable notoriety it was included in the neighbouring county of Wiltshire. In 1852 Mr Samuel Savile Kent, inspector of factories, lost his wife. He was left with two children, Constance aged 8, and William, 7. In 1853 he married their governess, Mary Pratt, and the following year went to live in Road-Hill House, contemporarily described as "a handsome, commodious, modern residence". By 1860 three more children had been added to the family. Kent seems to have been a hard-natured man, generally disliked in the neighbourhood, and his eldest daughter, Constance, was regarded as somewhat unstable and enigmatic. When she was 13 she had cut short her red hair, dressed herself as a boy and run away from home with her brother William, demonstrating by that short, sharp episode that whatever her feelings towards her father she was certainly not the sort to take kindly to an ex-governess stepmother as she grew older. Life in the large comfortable house seethed and simmered under its placid Victorian middle-class exterior. It boiled over in horrible fashion on the morning of 30th June 1860, when the pretty nursemaid, Elizabeth Gough, noticed that the 4-year-old boy Francis, eldest of the second instalment of children, who slept in the same room with her, was not in his cot. An hour later his body, wrapped in a bloodstained blanket, was found forced deep into a disused privy near a shrubbery in the grounds. His throat had been cut with such violence that the head was almost severed and there was a deep gash in the left side.

The protracted inquest revealed little, and resulted in a verdict of murder against some person or persons unknown. The unpopularity of Mr Kent directed local suspicion towards him as the killer of his own son. The police however arrested Elizabeth Gough, only to release her for lack of evidence. Constance's turn came next, largely owing to the zeal of Inspector Whicher, who had discovered that one of her nightdresses (presumably blood-stained) was unaccountably missing. She also was released, and Elizabeth arrested a second time. All charges eventually came to nothing, and the excitement died down. Mr Kent moved to Weston-super-Mare with his family, and thence to Wales. With his family, that is, except for Constance. She elected to

M

go to a convent at Dinan. Later, rather strangely, her father sent her to a fashionable French finishing school. In 1863 she returned to England and entered an Anglican Sisterhood, St Mary's Convent—or Hospital—in Queen's Square, Brighton, founded by a leading clergyman of the town, the Reverend A. D. Wagner. Then, in April 1865, five years after the murder and when the storm it created had long died down, came the thunderclap. Constance Kent, accompanied by the Reverend A. D. Wagner and a member of St Mary's called Miss (or Sister) Graeme, arrived at Bow Street police court and announced that she was the murderess and wished to give herself up. On her repeated assurance that no pressure had been put on her to confess she was brought to trial, found guilty, and sentenced to death. This was commuted to life imprisonment: she was released in 1885 at the age of 41 and spent the rest of her life in obscurity. Despite her confession, doubts about her guilt persist. In one of a number of full-length studies of the murder Yseult Bridges makes out a strong case for the guilt of Mr Kent with the connivance of Elizabeth Gough, with whom he was supposedly having an affair. In it she quotes a letter from Dickens to Wilkie Collins, written in October 1860, in which he says, "Mr Kent intriguing with the nursemaid, poor little child awakes in crib and sits up contemplating blissful proceedings, nursemaid strangles him then and there. Mr Kent gashes body to mystify discoverers and disposes of same."*

Road-Hill House, a beautiful example of period architecture still stands, known now as Langham House. There is a Rode Hill House today, but this was not the scene of the crime. The older part of the village, despite housing developments in the area, probably looks much as it did at the time of the death of little Francis Kent.

As a suspected murderess, the name of Constance Kent is preserved for posterity. As a mere victim, few will remember poor 77-year-old Joseph Grimes, found lying in his lonely cottage in a lonely lane in a lonely village, with his head cloven almost in twain by a billhook. The date was April 1874, the place was Purton (on the B4041 about five miles west of Swindon), which at that time could claim only a fraction of the present 3,000 inhabitants: its name signifies an enclosure of pear trees. A little girl discovered the dead old man. No valuables had been taken,

* *Saint—with Red Hands?* (Jarrolds, 1954; Arrow Books, 1958).

no furniture disturbed. His life's savings, amounting to the sum of £4, lay untouched. His murderer was never discovered. Of his long life, only death was deemed worthy of record.

On 24th August 1867 the quiet little town of Alton, Hampshire, midway between Farnham and Winchester and two miles from the home of Jane Austen, was the scene of a child murder of appalling ferocity. Three small girls, Minnie Warner, 8, and two sisters, Lizzie Adams, 7, and Fanny, 8, were playing in a field known as Flood Meadow about 400 yards from their homes in Tan House Lane, when a respectable-looking young man approached them and said, "Ah my little children, here you are again". After helping them to pick blackberries for a little while he gave Minnie Warner three ha'pence and told her to take Lizzie away and spend it. He offered Fanny a halfpenny to come with him to a hollow in an old road leading to a nearby village called Shalden. Fanny took the halfpenny but declined the invitation. He then gave her an additional twopence, picked her up and carried her away. Lizzie and Minnie wandered around for a while and then went home. At four o'clock, when Fanny had still not returned, her mother and neighbours became alarmed and started to search for her. At 5.30 a young man was seen in the meadow, and Minnie recognized him. He was challenged by a Mrs Gardiner, who knew him as Frederick Baker, 29, a solicitor's clerk, and admitted giving the children money for sweets, but said Fanny had later left him to join the others. So impressive was his general air of respectability that Mrs Gardiner, after saying she had "a great mind to give you in charge of the police", did nothing further about the matter. Baker then joined a colleague for a drink in the Swan Inn, Alton, and told him he might join him when he left Alton the following day to take up another job.

While the two young men sat over their beer, horror was sweeping over the little town. At about seven o'clock a labourer stumbled into a pool of blood in a hopfield near Flood Meadow and a moment later saw in front of him the severed head of a child laid on two poles. The right ear had been severed and both eyes were missing. Close by were a leg and thigh, and a little further off the dismembered torso. This had been cut open and nearly all the organs removed. Five incisions had been made in the liver, the whole contents of the chest and pelvis were missing. He took the dreadful remnants to the police, who later came across the heart and then an arm. As a final ghastly climax two eyes were found floating in the river Wey close to the bridge.

Baker was taken into custody as being the last person known to have been with the child. At the inquest it was stated that blood had been found on his clothes and that he had in his possession two small knives, one clean, the other slightly blood-stained. A few days later a diary was discovered in which he had written under the date of 24th August, "Killed a young girl. It was fine and hot." Baker declared his innocence, saying that he had no motive, that the knife was too small to have inflicted such frightful mutilations, that Minnie's identification was unreliable, that the diary entry merely meant "a young girl was killed" on a fine, hot day. He admitted he had written the words after Mrs Gardiner had spoken to him, but said he was drunk at the time. It was revealed at the trial that up to the age of 26 Baker had never touched alcohol and was a regular attendant at church every Sunday—each visit being duly noted in the diary. Recently, however, he had been very depressed over a broken engagement, complaining that his work was too much for him and sometimes bursting into tears as he sat at his desk. He had "head pains" and frequent nose bleeds, and there was a family history of insanity. The picture in the minds of the jury of that terrible, hacking frenzy in the secluded hopfield under a blazing August sun blotted out all arguments in palliation, and they quickly found him guilty of murder. He was executed in Winchester prison.

What came to be known as the John Barleycorn Murder took place in Portsmouth in November 1943. For 40 years Mrs Rose Ada Robinson had lived at the beerhouse of that name in Commercial road, managing it on her own after the death of her husband. On the morning of the 29th a charwoman and a young sailor arrived together to find the back door open and Mrs Robinson lying on the floor of her bedroom, her clothing disarranged and her head covered with a blue cloth. She had been strangled by someone using their right hand—the establishment of this apparently unremarkable detail was to prove of vital importance. The motive was clearly theft. Mrs Robinson was reputed to keep large sums of money on the premises and the bedroom had been ransacked. It was ascertained later that over £400 had disappeared. After three weeks had passed a man named Harold

Loughans, who had a lengthy criminal record, was arrested in London on a minor offence, giving as his address the Winston Hotel, Jermyn Street. While under detention he declared that he had killed Mrs Robinson. He was charged, but at his trial in Winchester he retracted his confession and said that he had spent the night in question in Warren Street Tube Station with other shelterers from the blitz. Several witnesses confirmed this. The jury were unable to agree, and a second trial began at the Old Bailey on 27th March 1944. Sir Bernard Spilsbury now stated that Loughans could not possibly have exerted sufficient pressure on Mrs Robinson's throat to have killed her. Some years earlier, his right arm and hand had been injured in a machine and his fingers had no strength in them at all—they could in fact be bent in any direction. Loughans was acquitted, and it was revealed that he had once before confessed to a crime of which he was innocent. Twenty years later, in 1963, when he was dying of cancer, Loughans again claimed—in a newspaper article—that he had killed Mrs Robinson of the John Barleycorn.

What ex-Detective Chief Superintendent Walter Jones describes as the "most senseless murder" occurred in Gosport, near Portsmouth, in 1966. Mrs Phyllis Pearce, a 48-year-old widow employed as part-time waitress at the Lee Tower Inn, Lee-on-Solent, called at the Gosport Working Men's Trade Union Club at about 11 p.m. on 23rd February for her friend Mrs Seal, so that they could walk home together as they lived in adjoining roads. Both Mr and Mrs Seal worked at the Club, and on the night, as usual, Mr Seal stayed behind to lock up the premises. It was his habit to catch the women up on his bicycle and then go beyond his own home in San Diego Road to accompany Mrs Pearce to Beryton Road near by. On this particular night it happened that he was without his bicycle—it had in fact been stolen—so Mrs Pearce left Mrs Seal and went on alone. Mr and Mrs Seal had barely entered their house when they heard a scream, and Mrs Pearce staggered back towards them crying that she had been stabbed. She collapsed with six wounds in her neck, and died on the way to hospital. In a gargantuan enquiry Superintendent Jones and his team interviewed some 80,000 people, among them a 20-year-old shipwright apprentice named Arthur John Smith, who mentioned that he had been in the neighbourhood but knew nothing about the crime. It was discovered, however, by a question put to him in pure guesswork, that he owned a knife, and had been teased by his workmates, who called him Murder Smith. On being examined further he said he had got rid of the knife a fortnight before the murder, but when pressed he broke down and confessed. It was, in fact, his father who had disposed of the knife *after* Mrs Pearce was killed. In all innocence, because his son was afraid its presence might arouse the suspicions of the police, he had dropped it into Portsmouth harbour. On the night of the 23rd, Smith said, he had been drinking. As he was walking along the road Mrs Pearce asked him to get out of the way. He let her go ahead towards a bus stop, then ran after her and attacked her. "She bumped into me—and I lost my temper and stabbed her."

Smith was sentenced to imprisonment for life. "From all my experience," comments Superintendent Jones, "I cannot think of any murderer who had less reason to kill."*

In 1928 Mr Vivian Messiter, 57, was local agent in Southampton for the Wolf's Head Oil Company, and used a garage at 42 Grove Street as a store. On 1st November his landlord at 3 Carlton Road reported to the police that he had not seen his tenant for two days, when he left early in the morning to keep an appointment. Enquiries were made, and police called at the garage to find it padlocked, but at the time no further steps were taken. It was supposed that Messiter, a solitary and uncommunicative man, divorced and with no ties, might have suddenly decided to go to America, where he had a number of commercial connections. Ten weeks later a man named Passmore arrived to take over the oil company agency—business in Southampton appears to have been pretty slack. He forced the padlock, made his way among the oil drums—and stumbled over Vivian Messiter's decomposing body on the concrete floor. Blood was spattered across piles of wooden boxes near by, and there was a punctured wound in the dead man's head. The latter was thought at first to have been caused by a bullet, later it was discovered that the weapon used was a sharp-pointed hammer. A number of fictitious transactions in an order-book found in a car in the garage led the police along a tortuous and lengthy trail to a man named William Henry Podmore. Under the name of W. F. Thomas he had answered an advertisement inserted in the press by Messiter and had worked as his assistant for only a few

* *My Own Case* by ex-Detective Chief Superintendent Walter Jones (Angley Books, 1966).

days. During that brief time he had been swindling his employer by collecting commission on imaginary sales of oil. A receipt which had been torn from the orderbook had left an impression on the page below it and this, photographed at an angle under a bright light, confirmed police suspicions of Podmore's activities. It was not until 17th December 1929, however, that sufficient evidence was gathered in to warrant charging him with murder. At his trial in Winchester in March 1930 the prosecution suggested that Messiter had discovered the frauds and confronted Podmore, who had thereupon killed him with a handy weapon in the store. Declaring to the last that he was innocent, Podmore was hanged.

A more recent Southampton murder is that of George Newbery, a 60-year-old taxi driver living at 3 Northumberland Road. In October 1964 his body was found lying by a farm track near the Hursley–Chandler's Ford Road at Ampfield, about seven miles north of the city. His head had been battered by an iron pipe that bore no fingerprints. His car, a Ford Consul, turned up on some waste ground near Six Dials, not far from his home. Among the precautionary measures taken by the police was a warning sent to the General Post Office, for Newbery had an account at the Savings Bank and the book was missing. After eight days of disheartening tracking and waiting, it was reported that a £3 withdrawal form had turned up at Woolston, a Southampton district. On it was a greasy fingerprint that had no counterpart on police files. Here at last was something definite to go on. A vast enquiry was set on foot and continued until January 1965, when a man named John William Stoneley, an unemployed cable maker, was caught trying to force his way into a garage. His fingerprint matched—his lodgings were in Knighton Road, Woolston. But—and it was a big 'but'—if Stoneley simply admitted that he had found the book in the road and made use of it, there might be nothing to link him with the actual murder. He could be speaking the truth. Fortunately for justice, Stoneley lied, denying ever having had such a book in his possession, or ever having written out such a withdrawal form. Now on surer ground, the police pressed on. Stoneley said that on the night of the murder he had been with a friend named —of all names—Bill Sykes. This man was proved to exist: his real name was George Ernest Sykes, and he was a 23-year-old dairyman of St Mary's Road, Southampton. At first he too denied all knowledge of the murder, but in due course—following depressing precedent—each admitted planning to commit a robbery, each blamed the other for the killing. Despite such valiant efforts at self-defence both were convicted—Stoneley of capital, Sykes of non-capital murder.

Five cases claim our attention in and around the dignified seaside resort of Bournemouth. The first, in 1908, concerns the death of Emma Sherriff, a small, shy, fragile woman of 33, whose body was found by a schoolmaster on a walk with his boys near a footpath running along the cliffs at Southbourne, on the eastern outskirts. The month was February, and the spot was a very lonely one during the winter. She had died from shock and internal haemorrhage. Two handkerchiefs, a man's and a woman's, had been thrust down her throat, and her injuries suggested either a fall or some more deliberate form of physical attack. A trail of loose imitation pearls and a track along the lane indicated that the body had been dragged some distance before being deposited where it was found. The motive appeared to be robbery as nothing of value was left except one ring that fitted her finger too tightly to be easily drawn off.

For some years Emma Sherriff had been lodging with a Mrs Lane over a general shop at 80 Palmerston Road in neighbouring Boscombe. She had recently become friendly with a young man named John McGuire, who had set up in business as a picture-dealer after a spell in the army. On 19th February, the day before the body was found, McGuire left his room in Denbigh Street, Pimlico, London, and came to see Miss Sherriff, having telegraphed his arrival in advance. She was not at Palmerston Road when he called, and her bed had not been slept in, so he informed the police that she had disappeared. The day after her body was found McGuire was arrested and charged. It was known that he was very short of money, and the suggestion was that he had in fact journeyed to Boscombe a day earlier than he stated—i.e. the 18th—met Miss Sherriff by appointment at Southbourne, murdered and robbed her, then returned to London. His visit to the police and his anxiety as to her whereabouts the next day were, it was alleged, all an act to turn suspicion from himself. Witnesses identified him as having been near the scene of the crime. Against this, McGuire asserted that he was in London. The jury at his trial failed to agree. McGuire was detained awaiting a new trial, but this could not take place until the following November, and eventually a *nolle prosequi* was entered, and he was released. The killer of Emma Sherriff has never been found.

Thomas Henry Allaway, chauffeur, was executed on 19th August 1922 for the murder of Irene Wilkins, 31, in what was then the village of Tuckton, on the outskirts of Boscombe. Miss Wilkins, who lived at 21 Thirlmere Road, Streatham, had advertised in the *Morning Post* of 22nd December 1921 for a position of cook. The same day she received a wire asking her to meet a Mr Wood of Beech House (a fictitious address) whose chauffeur would pick her up at Bournemouth Central Station. She made the journey, and the following morning her body was found in a field bordering Iford Lane. She had been savagely killed by blows on the head, and there were indications of an attempt at rape that had not been completed. Allaway, who worked for a man named Sutton, was questioned quite early in the investigation, and was later recognized as having sent three telegrams to women asking for jobs. A Mr Frank Humphries recollected seeing Miss Wilkins on the train, and also noted that a chauffeur-driven car met her at Bournemouth. Her attaché case, forced open, was found near a house to which Allaway had driven his employer's wife, and waited one hour for her, the day after the murder. On 20th April Allaway fled. He forged Mr Sutton's name on cheques from a book he had stolen from him, and was arrested in Reading on 29th April. Among the most telling points of evidence against him were a number of misspellings in the telegrams he had sent—"immidiate" for immediate, "Bournmouth" for Bournemouth, "expences" for expenses. Asked to write out the messages again, Allaway painstakingly reproduced all his errors. They played a large part in sending him to the gallows for a crime that, obviously starting out as an elaborate means to achieve a rape, ended up as murder.

Bournemouth's best-known case is probably that of Alma Rattenbury, 38, and Percy Stoner, 19, tried in May 1935 for the murder of her husband Francis Rattenbury, 63, at the Villa Madeira, 5 Manor Road, the previous March. The Rattenburys had moved to Bournemouth from Canada in 1928, and despite the great difference in their ages (he was her third husband, she was his second wife), seemed to live together happily enough in their seaside villa. Mr Rattenbury had a grown-up son from his former marriage, and Mrs Rattenbury a boy of 13. In 1929 a son, John, was born to them, and he was the only one of their children in the house at the time of the murder. Tht family was looked after by a companion-cum-housekeeper, Miss Irene Riggs, who was devoted to her mistress.

In September 1934 Mrs Rattenbury brought into this tranquil if unexciting household young Percy Stoner, who had answered an advertisement for a "Daily willing lad, 14–18, for housework". At first he lived out, but after about three months was invited to take up residence at the Villa Madeira: he had also added the job of chauffeur to his other duties. Stoner seems to have been a well-meaning if rather lumpish youth—far from brilliant, but of excellent character. "One could not wish for a better boy," said his father. In a very short time Mrs Rattenbury had completely lost her head over him. She dressed him up in silk shirts, crêpe-de-chine pyjamas and other expensive clothing from Harrods, took him for a week-end glimpse of the High Life as exemplified at the Royal Palace Hotel, Kensington, provided him with board and bed in the fullest sense. What Francis Rattenbury thought of these goings-on is unknown—like most victims of callous murders he remains a shadowy figure. Mrs Rattenbury declared that he knew all about it and did not care —but having been killed he was of course unable to confirm this. Miss Riggs certainly had little affection for the new servant. The effect of all this embarrassment of riches on young Stoner, however, is easy to imagine. He seemed genuinely fond of Alma (and no wonder), but if she had lost her own head, she certainly turned his. Unfortunately, but inevitably, he became both violently jealous of Francis (though it appears with little reason) and very touchy about his own situation. On 24th March, very shortly after living it up in wildest Kensington with another man's wife who was twice his age, he was informed that he was to take his employers to Bridport for a visit. The old man had become a little depressed, it seemed and Mrs Rattenbury wanted to cheer him up. Stoner became highly indignant, even threatening to kill his benefactress with an air-pistol. Later that evening he went to his grandparents' house in Pine Vale Crescent, Ensbury Park, collected a large mallet, returned to the Villa Madeira, beat the inoffensive old Mr Rattenbury about the head as he sat in his armchair, hid the weapon in the garden, then went upstairs to Mrs Rattenbury's bedroom (and into her bed) and told her what he had done. Her shrieks aroused Irene Riggs, and the rest of the night turned into a sort of nightmarish black comedy. A doctor, then a surgeon, arrived, followed by police. Mrs. Rattenbury quickly became deliriously drunk, insisting on keeping the radiogram going full blast and feeding it with records, turning on every light in the house, following the distracted officials from place to place shouting incoherencies, and repeatedly trying to kiss one of the astonished policemen. Later on she insisted on confessing to the murder herself (and she was, of course, largely if not wholly responsible for the events that led to it), but it was not long before Stoner himself went to the police and told them the true story. They were charged together with murder, for Mr Rattenbury, alive but unconscious during that incredible night, died not long afterwards. Mrs Rattenbury eventually withdrew her confession and went into the witness-box to give evidence. Stoner, on the other hand, the uncouth, barely literate youth, steadfastly refused to allow it to be part of his defence that she bore any responsibility, and did not go into the box.

Mrs Rattenbury was acquitted. Stoner was sentenced to death and his appeal dismissed. The sentence was later commuted to imprisonment for life. By the time this was announced Mrs Rattenbury herself was dead. Three days after her acquittal she committed suicide, stabbing herself six times in the breast. Her body was found on the bank of a tributary of the River Avon by a railway bridge near Stoney Lane, Christchurch.

Much sympathy has been expended on Alma Rattenbury. Up to the time of her meeting with Stoner, and indeed afterwards, she appears to have been devoted to her children, and could always rely on staunch friends. She seemed to feel at least affection for her husband, 25 years older than herself. He, though a man of unpredictable temper by all accounts, appears to have suffered her extravagances without complaint. She was unmercifully hounded by the public after the trial, and showed remarkable physical courage in her death. But in truth the picture of this comfortably provided-for, well-cushioned woman of nearly forty dressing up her chauffeur-handyman in silk shirts and jewellery, trotting him around a fashionable hotel, bringing him into her bed at night—sometimes with her own son asleep in the room—cheating and deceiving her way through a furtive affair—is not a pretty one. She continually lied to get more money out of Rattenbury than the £600 a year he allowed her, which in 1933 was a reasonably generous sum even if she was expected to make it cover a wide range of items. Particularly mean was the story she made up of having to go to London for an operation—in order to obtain from him no less than £250 for the Kensington week-end. Warning the jury that they were not there to judge moral responsibility, her own counsel said, "if you are [judging of moral responsibility] your task might be a light one, for you cannot resist nausea and disgust at the way this middle-aged woman has ensnared and degraded this hapless youth". Dreadful her end may have been—she had in the last resort no-one to blame for it but herself.

Branksome Dene Chine, on the western side of Bournemouth, was the incongruously lovely setting for the second ghastly murder by the psychopathic George Neville Heath. On Monday 8th July 1946 the body of 21-year-old Doreen Marshall, appallingly mutilated and naked except for a single shoe, was found under some rhododendron bushes in a deserted part of the Chine. She had been staying at the Norfolk Hotel since her demobilization from the W.R.N.S. a fortnight earlier and was known to have spent the evening of the 3rd at the Tollard Royal Hotel with a self-styled ex-pilot calling himself Group-Captain Rupert Brooke. Heath, already wanted in connection with the murder of Margery Gardner in Notting Hill Gate (see *Murderers' London*) had been to Brighton and Worthing (where he stayed at the Ocean Hotel under his own name) before arriving in Bournemouth. When, on Friday 5th July, the Manager of the Norfolk rang up the Tollard Royal to say Miss Marshall had not returned from her dinner engagement (which she had mentioned to members of the staff and guests) Heath himself went to the police, on the suggestion of the Tollard Royal manager, to give an account of his meeting with her. He said he left her by the Pavilion at about midnight as she did not wish him to accompany her any further. He was recognized as the man wanted in respect of Mrs Gardner, and detained. Later he was identified as having pawned jewellery belonging to Miss Marshall. Meanwhile her body had been found and the police were convinced he was responsible for both murders. He was tried for that of Margery Gardner (references were made also to Doreen Marshall), found guilty, and executed at Pentonville. On the night of the 3rd Heath had not returned to his hotel by the main entrance, but had used a ladder to get in through his bedroom window. The night porter glanced into his room at about 4 a.m. and saw him fast asleep—he also noticed that his shoes, which were by his bed instead of out in the corridor for cleaning, were covered with mud. One of the mysteries was how he could have inflicted the frightful mutilations on Doreen Marshall's body (her breasts were slashed, her throat and stomach lacerated) without becoming covered with blood—the most likely theory was that he had stripped beforehand, and afterwards washed himself clean in the sea. He then dressed, went back to the Tollard Royal, and calmly fell asleep.

Murder by a Boy Scout may seem an unlikely hazard, but this was the fate suffered by 74-year-old Amy Lloyd of Richmond Park Avenue, Bournemouth, on 15th May 1954. She was found at the door of her home stabbed with a sheath knife no fewer than 9 times. Miss Lloyd had always taken a keen interest in the Scout movement. As Badge Secretary it was her duty to issue badges when presented by a Scout or Cub with a certificate indicating that a certain test had been passed. Shortly after her death Barry Musson, 17, of Frederica Road, Winton, a Scout with an excellent record, was seen to be wearing a badge to which he was not entitled. When questioned by his Scoutmaster, Robert Ellerton, he confessed to having forged the necessary certificate but denied all knowledge of the murder. Later he admitted having been to Miss Lloyd's house, and eventually, under police examination, confessed that he killed her. The jury took under half-an-hour to find him guilty: being below the age of 18 he was sentenced to be detained during the Queen's pleasure.

"From Postman's Knock to Murder" might be the title of our next case. Even the names of those involved, Goozee and Leakey, have a touch of TV comedy series ill-suited to a grim and sordid story. In January 1955 Albert Goozee, an ex-merchant seaman and fitter's mate, went to lodge with Mr and Mrs Leakey and their 14-year-old daughter Norma in Alexandra Road, Parkstone, Poole. A few weeks later, apparently as a result of kisses exchanged during a somewhat bibulous version of Postman's Knock called Spin the Bottle, intimacy developed between the landlady and her lodger. Thereafter, together with Norma, they appear to have formed a *ménage-à-trois* (though post-mortem examination confirmed Goozee's denial that he had ever had intercourse with the girl), from which Mr Leakey was virtually excluded. In fact he left home for a while, but at the beginning of June 1956 returned and ordered the interloper to leave. Goozee went to live in Sunnyhill Road, Parkstone. He was then working at the Tollard Royal Hotel. On 15th June he got into trouble for annoying a 14-year-old girl during a performance at the New Royal Theatre, Bournemouth, and was due to appear in court on the 20th. On the 17th he went with Mrs and Miss Leakey for a picnic in Bignell Wood near Cadnam, about four miles west of Southampton, and later that afternoon was found in his car on the road from Cadnam to Brook (B3078) suffering from a knife wound. In the wood, amid kettle-boiling preparations for the picnic, lay the bodies of Mrs Leakey and Norma, dead from blows from an axe and a knife. Goozee told a fantastic story of a furious outburst of jealousy in which everyone seems to have attacked everyone else with whatever weapons were available. Examination of the knife blade, however, showed that Goozee must have been the first to use it to inflict injury, afterwards in all probability faking superficial wounds on himself. He was found guilty of murdering Norma Leakey and sentenced to death. This was later commuted to life imprisonment. Not the least strange part of this strange affair was a letter Goozee had written to the Chief Constable of Bournemouth earlier that afternoon and which was found in his car. In it he wrote, ". . . Mrs Leakey still comes after me so I have come to the only possible way out before I go after another young girl". As Detective Chief Superintendent Walter Jones, who worked on the case, suggests, Goozee seemed to have a foreknowledge of what was to happen, a foreknowledge shared by Mrs Leakey and her daughter. Norma had once remarked that Albert would kill them one day. As far as can be gathered from his numerous confused statements, the unfortunate Goozee seems to have been driven frantic by a combination of Mrs Leakey's possessiveness (she was 53 years of age) and his own leanings towards young girls.

Coombe, Dorset, is a small isolated village about two miles from Sherborne (off the B3148). In a cottage isolated even from the village itself there lived in 1935 a farm labourer named Frederick Bryant and his wife Charlotte, aged 33. They had met in Londonderry during the Irish 'troubles' when he was in the army. He married her and brought her to England a year or two later. By all accounts he was an easygoing, inoffensive man, but what his own character lacked in nastiness was more than balanced by that of his wife. Charlotte Bryant was slatternly, ill-tempered, promiscuous and illiterate, neglecting her home (the cottage, when searched by the police, was indescribably filthy), and picking up what she could in the way of casual sexual encounters around the pubs in the district. Among her lovers was a gipsy named Leonard Parsons, who came to the already bulging cottage—there were several children—as a lodger, and sharing not only Mr Bryant's wife but his razor as well. Frederick himself, stupefied perhaps by the squalor in which he lived and the formidable temper of his wife, seems to have raised little protest against her activities, though it is impossible he could have been wholly ignorant of them. Parsons, after continuing for a while a sort of on-again-off-again relationship with Charlotte, eventually disappeared, despite the threats of his blowsy paramour who even grabbed his clothes from him in an effort to make him stay. When this was of no avail she set off on fruitless and frantic expeditions to find him and bring him back. Among the places she visited was a camp of gipsies near Weston-super-Mare. Here she came up against his 'wife' (by whom he had several children) and her mother, and for once met her match, retreating from the encampment under a stream of abuse and threats. Frustrated and furious, she proceeded to complete a job begun some time before—the slow, agonizing death of her husband. For no less than eight months she slowly deprived him of his life by poisoning him, showing an instinctive cunning in murder that did not depend on intelligence. The unfortunate man succumbed to her treatment on 22nd December 1935.

Charlotte was arrested the following February, having spent the intervening period with her children in Sturminster Newton Institution. That old stand-by, arsenic-impregnated weedkiller, had been found in a burnt tin on the premises, in the pocket of her coat, in the organs of Mr Bryant. Charlotte made a statement implicating a woman named Mrs Ostler, with whom she had become friendly a few months previously. According to Mr J. D. Casswell, who defended Mrs Bryant, arrangements had been made for Mrs Ostler—and her seven children—to share the cottage, but the long-suffering Mr Bryant had at last been moved to object. Both women, admittedly, were around him during the night before his painful death, but obviously Mrs Ostler was nowhere in the picture during the earlier attacks. She gave evidence for the prosecution that showed that Charlotte knew about the presence of the weedkiller, and the use to which it could be put. Mr Casswell relates that she even admitted to her solicitor that she had bought the weedkiller (which she denied at the trial), though this fact was not revealed until after her execution. Despite her blanket denials, Charlotte Bryant was found guilty and sentenced to death. After the trial was over it was said that an expert witness for the prosecution had made a serious error regarding the proportion of arsenic normally found in coal ash, but the Court of Criminal Appeal refused to hear the new evidence, concluding that whether or not such a mistake had been made, her guilt had been proved. Charlotte Bryant was hanged at Exeter Prison in July 1936.

The family had lived in dire poverty, and a possible reason for Bryant's acquiescence in his wife's extra-marital unions was the cash they brought in, and which she spent on such items as cream, salmon and car-hire. In return for his tolerance, according to the result of the trial, she inflicted on him, slowly and deliberately, an appallingly painful death—for no other reason, apparently, than sheer malice.

A mile or two off the A354, north of Wimborne Minster, is the village of Gussage St Michael (the place, according to its name, where 'water suddenly breaks forth'). In 1913, when it was a good deal more isolated than today, it was the tragic scene of the Murder of the Cook by the Rabbit-catcher. Both were employed at the Manor Farm, though the rabbit-catcher lived at the village post-office where his wife, a few years older than he was, fulfilled the positions of both post- and school-mistress. The cook, 24-year-old Winifred Mitchell had, unfortunately for herself, caught the fancy of the rabbit-catcher, William Burton, who was 29. In time she yielded to his blandishments and the scene was set for the old familiar story. Winifred soon became an encumbrance rather than an enjoyment, and William determined to free himself. Under the pretext of discussing plans to leave his wife and elope, he arranged to meet the cook on 31st March in a little wood known as the Sovel Plantation, near the

(*above*) The author visiting Maria Marten's cottage, Polstead. (*right*) George Joseph 'Brides-in-the-Bath' Smith. (*below*) The Blue Anchor Inn, Byfleet—scene of the Vaquier poisoning case.

The Eastbourne Crumbles Case: (*left*) the victim, Emily Kaye and (*right*) the murderer, Patrick Mahon.

(*below*) Norman Thorne in the train taking him to Brixton Prison.

Farm. There he shot and buried her, and then returned to his regular occupation of exterminating rabbits.

There followed a strange period of inactivity. A group of children had reported seeing a freshly dug grave just before the fatal night—later it was seen to have been freshly filled in: the day previous to her disappearance Winifred had visited her home and then ridden off, presumably back to Manor Farm, on her bicycle—the bicycle shortly afterwards mysteriously re-appeared without her: Burton had borrowed a gun with three cartridges "to shoot a cat" and returned it with two, saying he had done the deed—but the cat was subsequently seen alive and flourishing: the pretty young cook before she left had told a fellow-servant that if she was not back by a certain time some-thing would have "happened" to her—and that time had long passed. None of this interested anyone very much—it was merely concluded that Winifred had left the district for a better job. The most macabre touch of all was the finding by a dairyman of three false teeth in the little wood—but all he did was to keep them. Fortunately, however, news of this last discovery came to the ears of the rector's wife. Her curiosity was aroused and the police were called in. Two and two were belatedly put together. Poor Winifred's body was found early in May, and so were torn fragments of two letters she had kept at the Manor Farm. These were written by Burton and clearly indicated the relationship between them. It was ascertained that the false teeth had been blown from Winifred's head by the force of the shot.

Burton was tried and found guilty. He was executed at Dor-chester, the first murderer to be hanged there for some thirty years. Before he died he made a full confession, and also solved a minor mystery. A feather boa Winifred was known to have been wearing had never been found; Burton explained that he had hidden it in a rabbit bolt-hole half-a-mile from the scene of his crime.

A last glimpse of Dorset brings in once more the ubiquitous George Joseph Smith with his predilection for seaside resorts. It was at Weymouth Registry Office in August 1910 that he 'married' Beatrice Mundy, giving his name as Henry Williams, picture restorer. He took her to rooms at 14 Rodwell Avenue and, three months later, left her penniless in the Alexandra Gardens. As we have seen, however, they were fated to meet again.

N

We now cross briefly to the Isle of Wight for a pathetic tragedy that occurred at Brighstone near the south-west coast (on the B3399) in 1958. Fred Phillips lived at Grange Farm with his wife and two daughters, Christine, aged 14, and Freda, aged 6. Working under him was a labourer named Roy White, 25, a somewhat strange and unapproachable young man whose home was at Upper Houses, Chale, a village about six miles down the coast. Most of his attention was given to motor-bicycles, but he formed an attachment for young Christine—an attachment which, understandably, was not looked on with any great favour by her parents. When requested not to pay the girl any more attentions he seemed very upset, but agreed. On 16th March, however, Mrs Phillips had to tell her husband that the whole business had started up again, and White was instantly dismissed. He went off on his motor-bike, muttering threats. Later, when the family were indoors after the day's work in the fields, he returned with a shotgun. When Phillips went to the door White fired, wounding him. The farmer staggered back, gathered the children together and rushed them into the cellar, calling his wife to join them. She was dialling for the police, and White fired at her, fatally wounding her. Phillips ran back up from the cellar and grabbed the gun. White escaped through a window into the snow as the farmer collapsed. Appalling weather conditions made a search for him almost impossible, but the very next day he gave himself up. He was convicted of the murder of Mrs Phillips and the attempted murder of her husband, but found insane and committed to Broadmoor. He said he had always wanted a girl to love, but "they stopped me seeing her".

Another case of frustrated love leading to violence occurred at Parkside, Bouldnor, on the north-west side of the Isle, in 1961. John Neale, 35, ran a small market garden with Anthony Hitchcock, 30, as his partner. On 28th May Neale was found dead near the house, his head beaten in with a rock. It transpired that Hitchcock had for some time been deeply in love with Mrs Neale. At first he hid his feelings, and when eventually he told her he met with no response. He tried vainly to conquer his infatuation, and once decided to leave the farm. He actually reached the ferry to the mainland before turning back—the business had not been doing well, and it seemed unfair to desert his partner in such circumstances. On the day of the murder, he said, Neale openly accused him of being in love with his wife, and for the first (and last) time a fierce quarrel arose. From his appearance and bearing Hitchcock seemed the last man to lose his temper and commit so violent a crime. If he had left his partner in the lurch when things were going badly, instead of—with the best of intentions—returning to the farm, the tragic results for all three of them would in all probability have been averted.*

As a footnote to the crimes of the Isle we may mention a lady who, at Ventnor in 1940, killed a 65-year-old man named Frank Cave with a shotgun. Afforded only a couple of lines in Browne and Tullett's biography of Sir Bernard Spilsbury, she deserves remembrance for possessing perhaps the most incongruous name of any murderess—Mabel Lucy Attrill.

* Ex-Detective Chief Superintendent Walter Jones, who investigated both these Isle of Wight murders, writes more fully on them than is possible here, in his book *My Own Case.*

10

THE RABBIT-CATCHER WHO CAUGHT HIMSELF
The South-West: Somerset Devon, Cornwall

On 17th July 1839 a relieving officer named Samuel Norman was on his way from Wick St Lawrence to Worle, on the outskirts of Weston-super-Mare. His route took him past a place with the pleasing name of Snatch-Cratch. Suddenly he noticed a young man climbing out of a ditch with blood dripping from his hands. He was followed by a girl, dreadfully injured in the face, who staggered a few yards and then collapsed on the road. The young man stood over her as if dazed, and, as Norman came up, turned to him and sobbed, "Oh, I must die!"

His trial lifted the curtain on a pathetic bucolic tragedy. The two young people, Charles Wakely and Eliza Pain, were employed as farmhands near Worle. They were very good friends, and were in fact regarded as "going serious". At 5 p.m. on 17th July they both went a-milking, with never a cross word between them. A little later Eliza set off for Worle, driving the cows before her. Charles asked if she would collect a pair of boots for him from the village, but she doubted if she would be there in time. A few minutes after she had left he told another farm worker that he would go to fetch them himself. On the road he overtook Eliza—who had apparently deposited the cows, for they now disappear from the story. For a while they walked along—hand-in-hand, one may imagine, her face hidden in her sunbonnet—and chatted of this and that. But alas, as Snatch-Cratch was approached, passion reared its ugly head. Hand-holding led to embracing, until Charles's attentions grew all too pressing, and Eliza began to resist. This inflamed him the more

and, as he later confessed, in a fury of frustration he drew a knife
and cut her throat. The boots remained unclaimed—sad monu-
ments to a sorry tale—and their owner paid the penalty for his
lack of control.

Moving eastwards towards Bath we pass (on the B3130) the
village of Winford, scene of a taxicab murder in 1960. John
Rogers, 20, of Church Road, Bishopsworth, Bristol, who worked
as a clerk in a local brewery, was charged with shooting William
Tripp, 41, of Briar Way, Fishponds, Bristol, with a gun stolen
from a rifle club run by his firm. Tripp was found dead in his
overturned taxi on 29th July, at a crossroads between Winford
and Chew Magna. The rifle, which had been sawn short for
concealment, was in a bag on the back seat, and the meter
showed an amount due that corresponded exactly to the distance
from Bristol, about seven miles. The motive was obviously
robbery, but as it happened Tripp had handed in his takings to
his employer shortly before he was killed. The man who discovered the car (with its lights on and its horn blaring) was
able to give a good description of someone he had noticed running away, and it took the police only five days to trace him.
Rogers admitted the crime, saying—with the usual lack of
originality—that he had only meant to frighten and rob the
driver, but pulled the trigger by mistake in a sudden moment
of excitement. This did not impress the jury, who found him
guilty of capital murder—he was, however, reprieved and sentenced to imprisonment. After murdering the taxi driver, Rogers
spent the rest of the August Bank Holiday at the Beaulieu jazz
festival, and then went on to London.

And so to Bath: where, on 22nd August 1870 at No 1 Spencer's Bellevue, Lansdown Road, a schoolmaster named Prankard
in a wild outburt of insane jealousy killed his elder daughter,
wounded his younger, and poisoned himself. Mary Minnie, 22,
had found herself a job on the Continent (at what is not recorded); her father, seems to have been a widower, objected to
the idea with extreme violence. At three o'clock that afternoon,
the pupils being on holiday, she was packing her things together in the schoolroom helped by her 19-year-old sister Kate.
Prankard strode in and closed the door. A few moment later a
servant heard sounds of a furious quarrel and then two ex-
plosions. Prankard, it transpired, had concealed a revolver under

his handkerchief, and when Mary Minnie refused to stay at home, had shot her, then turned and fired at Kate. Though wounded, Kate managed to escape through the schoolroom window, whereupon the demented father ran upstairs and swallowed prussic acid. It was revealed at the trial that he had had several more daughters. Three were imbecile, others he had spirited away no-one seemed to know where. How much the young pupils (or their parents) were aware of the background to their school life was not disclosed. Spencer's Bellevue, a terrace of nine tall houses, still stands on the heights overlooking the city.

A case with strong claims on our compassion was that which occurred in a little Bath sweetshop in 1928. The accused was William Bartlett, formerly a shoemaker, a man with a tragic family history of tuberculosis. His father, mother and sister had all died from it—he himself had a wooden leg as a result of an operation necessitated by its ravages. In the spring of 1928 he met a cousin of the family at Weston-super-Mare, fell in love, and married her—all in the matter of a month or two. As a new beginning they put their entire joint savings, about £300, into the new venture which they called The Chocolate Shop, in a tiny building, 3 Monmouth Street. Unhappily neither William nor his wife had any head for business. He was, in truth, somewhat mentally retarded and also suffered from agonizing fits of depression. By the autumn all their assets had vanished. On 24th October his wife sold up the small stock for £11.

On 26th October William Bartlett limped into the police station at Paddington Green, London, and confessed to the murder of his wife. The morning after the sale, he said, he got up to make tea. Marjorie, probably entirely without intention, made some cutting remark. He felt as if his head "had suddenly split open", and then remembered nothing until he heard an iron bar crash to the ground at his feet, and saw the bed all covered in blood. Apart from the effects of tuberculosis no family history of mental or other abnormality was discovered, but after a most moving plea by his counsel, Mr J. D. Casswell, K.C., a verdict was returned of guilty but insane.

The little shop, situated in a preservation area of the city, still stands. After the murder it was converted, with rather grim irony, to a butcher's shop: today, after changing hands a couple of times, it provides beef and horsemeat for animal-feeding purveyors. It is a bright and cheerful spot now, still retaining its former character but with no sign of the tragedy that took place on its premises over forty years ago.

Much sympathy may be felt for the unhappy William Bartlett, his wife and their little sweet shop: none, surely, need be wasted on Mr Reginald Ivor Hinks, hanged in Bristol on 4th May 1934 for the wilful murder of his ancient father-in-law. The deed itself was only accomplished after much abortive labour that resulted in a series of hopelessly bungled attempts. It would be difficult to find any redeeming qualities in Reginald Ivor—but if one had to make a choice it must surely be his persistence. Slim, smooth and slippery, with his hair brushed up in a sort of coxcomb resembling (in Miss Tennyson Jesse's vivid phrase) a loofah on the top of his head, he was roughly as old as the century. By 1933 he had already won himself a reputation as a handbag snatcher, petty crook and general cheat. His professed occupation was that of an electrical engineer (more accurately, vacuum-cleaner salesman), and while working in that capacity he met and speedily married Mrs Constance Jeffries, née Pullen, a young woman, divorced from her first husband, who lived with a baby daughter and a somewhat rickety old father (over 80 years of age) at 43 Milton Avenue, Bath. Poor Mr Pullen was, to tell the truth, so far gone in years as to be totally unable to look after himself, and was cared for by a male nurse, Mr Strange. He had, though, one advantage that outweighed all disadvantages in Reginald Ivor's estimation—he owned a certain amount of money. In no time at all Hinks took up residence in, and took over control of 43 Milton Avenue. He started with small economies, cutting down on food (the old man's food, that is) and reducing Mr Strange's wages from £1 10s. to £1 a week. Mr Strange, not surprisingly, left shortly afterwards, saving Reginald Ivor the £1 as well. He swiftly turned his mind to larger financial matters, and had soon managed to buy, with £900 of Mr Pullen's savings, a small pseudo-Tudor villa called Wallasey, in Englishcombe Lane. Thither he transported himself and family —and waited, with increasing impatience, for the old man to pass on. Indeed, he soon began trying to expedite matters. His first attempts consisted in sending the alarmingly incapable octogenarian out into the busy traffic of the city streets, in the hope that he would wander off the pavement and end up in the grave. Bath, however, proved maddeningly full of helpful and kindly folk who continually took pity on the bewildered, trembling figure and led him gently home. It must have been an increasingly irate Mr Hinks who opened the door time after time and was forced to greet with grateful relief the return of his peripatetic parent-in-law. At the end of November 1933 his efforts took a more sinister turn. He raised a sudden alarm, saying he had found Mr Pullen unconscious in his bath. There might have been some truth in this, bath-night in the Hinks household being a strange, and it is to be hoped unusual, ceremony. The same water was used in succession by the little girl, by her mother, by Reginald Ivor, and lastly by old Pullen. By that time the mixture might have been enough to stupefy anyone. Hinks did the job properly, summoning not only the doctor, but the police and the fire brigade as well to revive the victim. The following night, however, he overdid it. Back came the fire brigade (Mrs Hinks was at local cinema) to find Mr Pullen at last beyond their aid, lying by the gas stove in the kitchen, dead from coal-gas poisoning.

Hinks's story was that he had gone to the kitchen for a drink of water—and there lay old Pullen with his head in the oven and the gas turned full on. Distraught with sorrow, he had done his best, dragging the body away and turning off the gas—but too late. Too late indeed: bath-nights and walks among the swarming traffic were remembered. In addition, Hinks made a fatal slip. Too clever by half, he carefully called attention to a bruise on the back of the old man's head, explaining it away by saying it happened as he was being dragged from the stove. When it was proved that the bruise had occurred *before* death, Hinks quickly thought up another one and said Pullen had fallen over recently and banged himself on the dining-room sideboard. After a gruelling ordeal at the inquest, Reginald Ivor Hinks was charged with murder, tried, found guilty, and executed.

Before moving south from Bath we may glance across at Bristol for one more glimpse—happily the last—of the inescapable G. J. Smith, who settled there with Miss Pegler (the one woman for whom he seems to have felt a genuine affection), when he was not roaming the country in search of less fortunate females to fleece. He met her first at her home, 368 Gloucester Road, when he himself was running a small shop at number 389 —a business bought, after his usual fashion, with money filched from a woman tactfully referred to in his records as Mrs F. W.

After 'marrying' Miss Pegler (bigamously, but in his own name)
on 30th July 1908 and travelling around for a while either with
her or on his own, he returned to Bristol in 1910. They stayed
first at a house in Ashley Down Road and then, in 1912, moved
to Bath Road in the Brislington district. In 1914 they were lodging at 10 Kennington Avenue, where he advised her to be careful when taking a bath—it could be dangerous. "Women often
lose their lives through weak hearts and fainting in a bath,"
he said, doubtless enjoying his private little joke. It was in Clifton that he originally met Beatrice Mundy, his first known victim, and from Dalkeith House, 4 Stanley Road, Bath, that he
left to marry Margaret Lofty, his last.

A grim assault and murder mystery, never solved, occurred
at a farm cottage in the small town of Frome on 24th September
1852. Mr Watts and his wife returned from market at 4 p.m. to
find their kitchen floor spattered with blood. In the adjoining
dairy the dog could be heard lapping something. They went in
to find their 14-year-old daughter Sarah lying on the floor, her
clothes torn and pulled up over her head. She had been violated
and then suffocated, and her face was covered with bruises. The
floor around her was wet with whey and milk. Butter, cheese
and bread had been stolen, and the cottage ransacked. A watch
was missing, but no money. When the whey tub was emptied
blood was found on the bottom: this, together with marks on
the wood, indicated that the girl had been hit on the head
then held face downwards in the tub. The crime had been committed in broad daylight, within 100 yards of the main road and
close to other cottages. Three men, William Sparrow, William
Maggs and William Hurd, had been seen together in a pub,
and later Sparrow and Maggs walked off towards the cottage.
All three were noticed later in the market-place wearing different
clothing, and one of them was saying to Hurd, "A watch, but no
tin". On 29th September, at a fair held in North Bradly, Sparrow
told a woman who questioned him that he had seen Sarah lying
by the whey tub with her clothes pulled up round her head, that
only one man had done it, and that he would never say his
name. Sparrow's hand was bandaged, he asserted that he had
been bitten in a fight on the previous day, the 28th. When the
wound was examined, however, it became clear that it was
several days old. Sparrow, Hurd and Maggs were arrested and
charged, but the evidence was not strong enough to secure a

conviction. They were acquitted after the jury had deliberated for 15 minutes.

The village of Shapwick, about five miles west of Glastonbury, was the sphere of activities of another of our arsenic-dispensing women. Sarah Freeman, executed at Taunton in April 1845, had already poisoned her husband and her illegitimate son in nearby Ashcott before returning to her native village to complete her quota with a couple more members of her unfortunate family. From an early age she had been promiscuous, and was known as a prostitute in the neighbouring town of Bridgwater before marrying a 24-year-old labourer, Henry Freeman and settling in Ashcott. Family life clearly irked her, and having rid herself of such encumbrances (these first two murders were not suspected until later), she returned to the streets—literally—of Bridgwater. When trade grew slack she wanted to return to her original home in Shapwick but found her family—two ageing parents and two brothers—anything but welcoming. However, by December 1844 she managed to prevail on them to let her in—having first supplied herself with arsenic ("to kill rats") from a shop in Bridgwater. There she poisoned first her mother, then her elder brother. The latter dose was administered because he was about to marry and bring his bride home—thus, as Sarah probably correctly suspected, providing himself with an excuse for turning his unwanted sister out. After his death she went back once more to Bridgwater, where she was arrested the following day. The bodies of her other deceased relatives were exhumed, and arsenic was found in each. She was indicted on all four counts, but tried only for the murder of her brother Charles. The evidence against her was incontrovertible—the result a foregone and speedy conclusion.

One afternoon in February a quarryman named Frederick Morse, a lumpish, loutish man of dim intelligence, was seen leaving the village of Curry Mallet (off the A376 about six miles from Taunton) accompanied by his 12-year-old 'niece', Dorothy Winifred Brewer. He had a bottle of rum with him, and the couple appeared cheerful and affectionate—a pretty picture of family unity. Later, in a heavy rainstorm, Morse returned alone. When asked what had happened to the girl he said he had left her by a stream while he went to inspect some rabbit traps. When he returned, she was gone. He added that she had recently been very depressed because her schoolfriends had been teasing

her. A frantic search had proved useless, so he returned home—
a bereaved and sorrowing uncle. In truth he was more than an
uncle bereaved, for Dorothy was not only pregnant by him, but
was herself the fruit of an incestuous relationship between
Frederick and his sister. The subject of the schoolgirls' tauntings
may well be surmised. After the police had found her body in
the stream (with a great deal of rum inside it), Morse told a
story of a suicide pact, then contradicted himself, then said he
had found her that afternoon, before helping the men in their
search. He was convicted of murder and hanged. This squalid
story of inbreeding, incest and child-murder would appear to
belong to the Dark Ages: in fact it occurred in 1933, and the
accused was defended—a hopeless task—by J. D. Casswell.

In the light of these dire events the origin of the place-name
Curry Mallet is not without interest. 'Curry' is in all probability
the original name of the stream running through the series of
villages. As for Mallet—around the time of Richard I the spot
belonged to William Malet—the surname being an old French
nickname signifying evil. The 'evil stream' seems an apt description in the circumstances of 1933.*

The following year Casswell again appeared for the defence
in a crime committed in a Somersetshire village, Milborne Port,
near Sherborne (on the A30). The case is another grim reminder
that not all stories about mothers-in-law are music-hall jokes.
Reginald Woolmington, farm labourer, was 21 when he married
Violet Smith, and she was no more than 17. For the first six
weeks they lived with his parents in cramped conditions, then
moved to a tiny cottage of their own. A week later Violet's child
was born. Very shortly Violet's mother began calling on them
in order—according to his story—to persuade her to leave him
and return to her old home, 24 Newtown. The reason appears to
have been mainly financial: Violet used to help her mother to
make gloves at home before her marriage, and her contribution
was now missed. This interference quickly sufficed to break down
the frail structure of the marriage, and at the end of November
Violet did as her mother wished, and left him. A few days later
he heard from her brother that she had been seen at a cinema
with an unknown man. The following day he took a shotgun
from the farm where he worked, and, after sawing down the

* *The Concise Oxford Dictionary of English Place-names*, by Eilert
Ekwall.

barrels, bicycled over to Mrs Smith's house. A neighbour heard a shot and hurried in to find Violet lying by the wash tub fatally wounded in the chest: she caught a glimpse of Woolmington riding away as quickly as he could.

He went to his parents, told them what he had done, and announced his intention of killing himself, but his father managed to talk to him until the police arrived. Casswell, who described his client as "somewhat lacking in intelligence" faced a formidable task. Woolmington's defence—such as it was after so many damaging admissions—was that he had not intended to kill Violet but only to frighten her, but as he took the gun from his pocket it went off. It was a story that could well have been true, but it was hardly original. Casswell fought tenaciously —one point in his client's favour was that he could not possibly have known that Mrs Smith would not be in the house with Violet when he called. The jury disagreed. He was tried again, and found guilty. His appeal was dismissed, but Casswell succeeded in taking the case to the House of Lords. For the first time in history they quashed the death sentence, and Reginald Woolmington was released.

In 1854 there lived near Bideford, Devon, a chimney sweep with the majestic name of Llewellin Garret Talmage Harvey. On 16th May, driven to desperation perhaps by the strain of trying to live up to such a title, he went out with the avowed intention, as he himself confessed, of killing someone. Anybody, it appeared, would suit his purpose. Near a place called Stibb Cross (to be found on the A388 some eight miles from Bideford) he sat on a bank and waited. A girl named Mary Allen went by on her way to Little Torrington (on the A386), and L. G. T Harvey suggested that he should walk along with her. Being an observant young woman she noticed something that looked like a knife or the handle of a hammer sticking out of his pocket, felt nervous, and hurried on. Thwarted, Llewellin Garret Talmage Harvey returned home. The following day a labourer passing Croft Hill, between Little Torrington and Langtree Wick (or Week) heard groans coming from a field. He peered through the hedge and saw 21-year-old Mary Richards, well known locally as a quiet and religious-minded girl, lying on the grass covered in blood. Her head had been savagely beaten, and she had been sexually assaulted. She died on 30th May, but not before Harvey had been stood in front of her and she had recognized him, despite the fact that he had since shaved off a pair of sandy whiskers. Suspicion had quickly fallen on the sweep; threats to "go out and murder someone" are not readily forgotten in small villages, and though his home was some distance from Little Torrington he had been seen hanging around there on 16th May. After conviction he confessed to the dastardly crime.

Llewellin Garret Talmage Harvey was the son of "a loose woman". He was said to have received an excellent education but to have taken quickly to the life of a vagabond. Had he been called simple "Joe", he might have peacefully swept chimneys to the close of a long and honourable life.

The most famous of our Devon cases is certainly that of Edmund Galley, a man who suffered under the shadow of a wrongful accusation for over half a lifetime, and lived to see his innocence proclaimed. On 16th July 1835 a prosperous farmer named Jonathan May was returning from Moreton Fair along the Exeter Road. He never reached his home, but was found unconscious by a spring called Jacob's Well, above Moretonhampstead. He had terrible head injuries and died shortly after being taken to the White Hart Inn, Moretonhampstead, without having recovered consciousness. He had been robbed of his gold watch and all his money. A man named George Avery, a wrestler who performed at country fairs, was arrested on suspicion, but his mistress, Elizabeth Harris, swore that she had seen two other men, nicknamed "Buckingham Joe" and "Dick Turpin" actually commit the murder, and that "Dick Turpin" was the one who used violence. Now "Dick Turpin" was jokingly applied by his friends to Edmund Galley, a brickmaker by trade who spent much of his time buying and selling horses, and playing the "pea-and-thimble" game at fairs and races. He was known, in fact, as an unreliable and shifty character. Months later, on 30th April 1836, he was charged with the murder of Jonathan May and arrested while at Coldbath Fields Prison, where he was already being held for begging. On Monday 9th May "Buckingham Joe" (real name Thomas Oliver), who had been detained in Dorchester gaol since September 1835, admitted that he had been involved in the crime—and with someone called "Dick Turpin". Galley, desperately protesting that he was innocent and had been attending fairs in other parts of the country at the time, was convicted and sentenced to death. However, certain doubts clouded the evidence against him, and the important witness Elizabeth Harris, though hotly denying perjury, undoubtedly had an interest in diverting suspicion from her lover. Galley was reprieved and transported to Australia as a member of a chain gang. He was 36 years of age.

The curtain now falls to denote a time-lapse of 40 years. When it rises again Galley, having completed his sentence and became a respected man of affairs in the district of Australia where he lived, wrote to the prosecuting solicitor reaffirming his innocence, as he had done many times before. On this occasion, however, he made a definite accusation against a man called John Longley, also known as "Kentish Hero". Galley's letter came to the attention of Thomas Latimer, proprietor of the *Western Times* and a senior magistrate in Exeter, and he was impressed by what he read. He determined to take a hand in the enquiry that followed, using his considerable influence to arrive at the truth. It was discovered that Longley had also been known as "Dick Turpin" and that Thomas Oliver (of whose guilt there was no doubt and who had been hanged long ago) had informed the judge of this at the trial. In addition, Oliver swore that he had never seen the man who stood beside him in the dock. The man who shared his crime was, in fact, the other "Dick Turpin". Oliver's word alone had not been regarded as reliable, and no notice was taken of what he said.

Now, as a result of the newly launched enquiries, and the energy with which Latimer and others pursued them, Galley, then working on an isolated sheep-station, had the somewhat tardy satisfaction of hearing his innocence declared, and of receiving an award of £1,000 for forty years out of his life. For some time he had been living with a widow to whom he shrank from offering marriage because of the shadow that overhung him. Now that his name was cleared, he did so, was accepted and—it is to be hoped—lived in peaceful happiness for his remaining days. Longley, who according to Galley was also in Australia, was never run to earth. Even if he had been found there was little chance that after so long a period any charge could have been brought against him.

William Maynard was a rabbit-trapper in a big way—he ran over a thousand traps and employed two assistants. He lived in a small Cornish village called Poundstock, just off the A39 between Bude and Boscastle. In February 1928 Dectective Inspector Prothero paid him a routine call in connection with the murder of 84-year-old Richard Francis Roadley. Reputed to be a miser and consequently surrounded by hidden wealth, Roadley lived alone in a shabby, dirty, desolate cottage at Titson, Marhamchurch, about three miles nearer to Bude than Maynard's home. On 18th February he was found dead in his living-room with a deep wound in the front part of his skull. The grimy cottage had been turned inside out, his briefcase was split open and the contents removed. War Bonds to the value of over £1,600 lay on the floor. Bedding had been placed against the window as if to conceal the interior from view.

The Inspector found the rabbit-catcher unexpectedly jumpy, almost over-eager to assure him that he would rather hang himself than do such a thing to an old man—all this before the subject of the murder had been brought up at all. Admittedly, by this time the event was being discussed by everyone in the district and not too much attention should be paid to such remarks. But Maynard went on, quite gratuitously, to attempt to provide himself with an alibi. At the time of the murder, he said, he had been sitting in his own bungalow with a Mr and Mrs Yeo. Here he overreached himself, for it happened that the police already knew that though Mr and Mrs Yeo had certainly been there, Maynard himself had not. On being detained he thought up yet another story—this time a little nearer the truth. He said he had arranged with a man named Harris to break into the miser's cottage for what they could find—but Harris had gone in first and killed him. Even this tale, however, merely threaded another strand into the rope that awaited him, for Harris—unlike his accuser—was able to produce an unassailable alibi. Maynard's crowning indiscretion was to provide information as to where some of the loot had been hidden. How did he know? His allegation that he was physically forced to write the statement he made was rejected by the jury, and Maynard, the rabbit-trapper who trapped himself by talking too much, was executed.

Another small Cornish village briefly bathed in the glare of publicity on account of a murder trial was Lewannick (off the A30 just south of Launceston), scene of what came to be known as the Salmon Sandwich case. At Trenhorne House in 1925 lived Mrs Sarah Ann Hearn—long separated from her husband

—and her sister Lydia Everard, struggling to make ends meet on a very short shoestring. Nearby, at Trenhorne Farm, lived Mr and Mrs Thomas, close friends as well as neighbours. In July 1930, when Mrs Hearn's sister—always of a delicate constitution —died, the Thomases did all they could to console the bereaved Mrs Hearn, taking her on outings and making her welcome at the Farm. On 18th October 1930 they all had tea at a café in Bellevue Hill, Bude. To the regular fare Mrs Hearn added a little delicacy in the form of a packet of tinned salmon sandwiches she had brought along in a basket. On the way home Mrs Thomas was suddenly taken ill with symptoms with which we are alarmingly familiar—vomiting and severe stomach pains. Mrs Hearn moved from lonely Trenhorne House to nurse her friend at the farm, but on 4th November Mrs Thomas died. A post-mortem was ordered, arsenic was discovered. Gossip grew and rumours ran riot. There was much talk in the neighbourhood about salmon sandwiches. The late Mrs Thomas's brother in particular made no attempt to conceal his suspicions of Mrs Hearn. Even Mr Thomas himself came under a slight cloud. Suddenly Mrs Hearn disappeared, leaving a note declaring her innocence and her inability to bear any longer the aspersions cast on her, and hinting vaguely at an intention to commit suicide.

The next step was the exhumation of Miss Everard's body. Again arsenic was discovered. Then somebody recognized Sarah Hearn working as a housekeeper in Hesketh Road, Torquay, under the name of Mrs Faithful. She was arrested, and later indicted at Bodmin Assizes. She was tried for the murder of Mrs Thomas only, but the evidence concerning Miss Everard's death was admitted. It was proved that Mrs Hearn had bought weedkiller containing arsenic (but as long ago as 1920), and it was hinted that there might have been some idea of a possible "match" between herself and Mr Thomas—a suggestion she most emphatically denied. Mrs Hearn was brilliantly defended by Norman Birkett. As Mr Justice Roche said in his summing-up, "the sandwiches are the very kernel of this case"—and Mr Birkett (as he then was) had already stated that if there had been any arsenic from the weedkiller in them the bread would have been stained blue. As regards Miss Everard, it was shown that, on account of local deposits of tin, the soil in Lewannick churchyard where she had been buried contained a proportion

(*left*) Thomas Allaway, the Bournemouth murderer.

(*right*) Constance Kent at about the time she confessed, and (*below*) Road-Hill House, now Langham House, scene of the Constance Kent tragedy—recent photograph.

(*above*) Mr and Mrs Rattenbury.

(*left*) Miles Giffard, matricide and parricide.

of arsenic more than sufficient to account for that found in her body. The jury took under an hour to find Mrs Hearn not guilty of the murder of Mrs Thomas. No evidence was offered by the Crown on the indictment in respect of Miss Everard, and the poor woman had at last reached the end of her ordeal.

The inevitable arsenic turns up once more, at Tregonissey Lane End (on the A391 just north of St Austell), but dispensed, for a change, by a man. On 29th October 1921 Edward Ernest Black, insurance agent and former Council schoolteacher, bought two ounces of the poison at Timothy White's store in St Austell—to kill, need it be said, rats. His wife, 18 years his senior, became ill and died. Two days before her death, on 8th November, he fled from his home, having up to that moment apparently taken the greatest care of her. He was traced to Liverpool and found hiding in Cashin's Temperance Hotel, Bell Street, with a wound—obviously self-inflicted—in his throat. He was brought back to Cornwall, charged with murder, and tried at Bodmin in February 1922. He had been in trouble financially and faced a charge of fraud, which may have been the real reason for his flight. There appeared to be no motive for killing his wife. However, when questioned about the purchase of arsenic he foolishly denied the whole transaction, swearing that the signature in the poison register was not his, and that the two shop assistants, both of whom recognized him, were mistaken.

These blatant lies clearly told against him, and he was found guilty. Black was hanged at Exeter in March 1922.

On 8th November 1952 Miles Giffard, 26, met his girl friend, Gabriel Vallance, and her mother at Leicester Square, London, and took them to the Odeon to see Charles Chaplin in *Limelight*. That evening he went with Miss Vallance alone to the Star public house in Chelsea and told her that he had murdered his father and mother. "It upset her," he said, later, in what must be the understatement of the year, "and we just moved on to further public houses, drinking." The scene of this appalling crime was Carlyon Bay, Porthpean, about two miles south of St Austell. Mr and Mrs Giffard lived in a large house called Carrickowl, built very close to the edge of the cliffs above the bay. Mr Giffard was a well-known solicitor and Clerk to the Magistrates at St Austell. Their son Miles, after being taken from Rugby school as unteachable, had for a long time been a source of worry to his parents. He made half-hearted attempts to study law and estate management, failed in both, inherited £750 when he was 25 and spent the lot in four months in Bournemouth, "scrounged around a bit" in his own words, sold Walls' Ice Cream for a few weeks, then returned to Porthpean and lived entirely off his parents. Not surprisingly, this feckless existence led to some differences between him and his long-suffering father. In August 1952 he took a room in London, and while there he was introduced to 19-year-old Gabriel Vallance who lived in Tite Street, Chelsea. He very quickly became infatuated with her. She seems to have made some attempt to persuade him to pull himself together, but without much effect. At the beginning of November he was back in Porthpean. During the early evening of 7th November he telephoned Gabriel to say he was coming up to London on some business for his father. At 7 p.m. he went into the garage at Carrickowl, where Mr Giffard was working on his car, and hit him over the head with an iron bar. He then went into the kitchen and attacked his mother in the same way. Returning to the garage, he found his father recovering consciousness and hit him again, killing him. He then put his mother, who was alive but unconscious, in a wheelbarrow, wheeled her to the edge of the cliff, and tipped her over. He then did the same with his father's body, throwing the wheelbarrow down after him. At some point during all this he telephoned Miss Vallance again to confirm that he would be arriving in his father's car, and asked if he could have a wash and shave at her house in the morning. He arrived in London about 5 a.m. (after giving two hitch-hikers a lift for part of the way), parked the car in Tite Street and slept in it for an hour or two, then sold some of his mother's jewellery for £50. In the evening, as we have seen, he took Mrs and Miss Vallance to the cinema.

Meanwhile the Giffards' maid, Barbara Orchard, returned home from her evening out at about 9.30, to find blood all over the garage and kitchen, and one of the cars missing. The Metropolitan police, on information from Cornwall, located the car—which had the noticeable registration number ERL 1—and arrested Giffard after he had brought Miss Vallance home in a taxi late on the night of the 8th. He was charged with stealing the car, and the following day Superintendent K. Julian arrived from Cornwall and told him the bodies of his father and mother had been found. Giffard immediately confessed and was taken back to Cornwall to be charged with the murder of Mr Giffard. The charge was made in the very court where his father had been Clerk for so long. The only possible defence was insanity, but the prosecution pointed out the careful planning of the crimes and the undoubted fact that Giffard well knew what he was doing, and knew that it was wrong. There was the usual conflict of views as to whether or not he was a 'schizophrenic'. A psychiatrist found many characteristic features, but the family doctor, who was a close friend of the family and had known Miles all his life, expressed a somewhat different opinion. When the question of his mental condition came up at the trial, and whether treatment might have been advisable earlier, the doctor replied, "The picture was more of just an idle little waster". Asked whether that was still his opinion, he replied sturdily, "As a non-expert, I'm afraid it is". After the jury had required only a very short time to find the accused guilty a panel of three psychiatrists examined him further and found him sane in law, and responsible for his actions. He was sentenced to death.

The interest in our final case lies more in the extraordinary life led by the victim than in the circumstances of the crime itself, which was a commonplace and sordid example of murder for gain. William Garfield Rowe, 64 years old in 1963, lived in a lonely house called Nanjarrow Farm, near Constantine, about six miles from Falmouth (off the B3291). He had, in fact, lived there without putting a foot out of doors in daylight for over 40 years. A deserter from the First World War, he had managed to hide out all that time in the secluded farmhouse, looked after by his family and coming out for exercise only after dark. Gradually, as the months and years passed, the family dwindled. His father and one brother died, another brother married and moved away. Finally, left alone with his mother, he nursed her through her last years and fatal illness, emerging for the first time—to the understandable astonishment of the villagers—at her funeral. Thereafter he lived alone in the most primitive conditions, working on the farm by day, sitting alone in the kitchen at night with a shotgun by his side, studying Spanish and other languages with the aid of self-instruction booklets. According to rumour he rarely if ever removed his clothes. Nevertheless, though existing in such squalor, he was regarded as an honest man and was well liked in the neighbourhood, eccentric or not.

He was one of the comparatively few people to draw up a will actually leaving his money to a cats' home (though he was killed before he could sign it), following a despairing joke by his solicitor who could suggest no-one and nothing that pleased his client.*

As so often with the recluse, it was popularly supposed that he had large sums of money about the house, and when, on 15th August 1963, a cattle-dealer named Henry Pascoe called in the way of business and found him lying behind the house beaten about the head and stabbed, it was quickly concluded that the motive was robbery. The movements of all local people with criminal records were checked. Among those interviewed was a man named Pascoe, no relation to the cattle-dealer who had found Mr Rowe's body. Russell Pascoe, 23, a builder's labourer, had left his wife and child and with living with three girls and another young man, Dennis Whitty, in a caravan near Truro. Cigarettes of the brand that Rowe smoked were found in the caravan, and skilful questioning of the girls elicited the fact that they knew the old man had been stabbed as well as bludgeoned—though this detail had not yet been released by the police. At first, perhaps from fear, the girls tried to shield their two companions, but eventually, when it became obvious the men were implicated, they provided the police with sufficient evidence to make an arrest. When charged, Pascoe and Whitty admitted having driven to the cottage on a motor-cycle, bringing with them offensive weapons and housebreaking tools, intending to force an entry and rob: they then followed precedent by each blaming the other for the actual murder. It was proved, however, that the attacks by knife and bludgeon were made simultaneously, and both murderers were executed in December 1963. Their haul from the brutal assault was, they told the girls, "a few quid and some matches". For once, had they but known, rumour was true. Sums of money were hidden all over the grounds: a document in the old man's self-taught Spanish contained clues leading to the discovery of about £3,000 in one-pound notes. Later, when a relative took up farming at Nanjarrow he was forced to put up barbed wire and Keep Out notices to discourage treasure seekers.

---

* For a detailed account of Rowe and his long-suffering solicitor see Gerald McKnight's book *The Murder Squad* (W. H. Allen, 1967).

EPILOGUE

We have travelled from northern Northumberland to southern Cornwall, from the fourteenth century to the present day, from cottage to castle. In every age, and every county, the murderers are amongst us. As Sir Richard Jackson, formerly Assistant Commissioner C.I.D. New Scotland Yard, comments in recounting a case on which he worked, ". . . perfectly ordinary people, going on their lawful occasions, taking the dog for an evening walk, may be only a hedge's thickness away from murder".* In the year 1971 the number of murders committed in England and Wales rose by 42 to a new peak of 177—a figure referred to by the Home Secretary as "a disturbing increase". A coroner opening an inquest on a 17-year-old girl killed in Preston, Lancashire, remarked that "a few years ago a murder made headlines—now it is commonplace, like careless driving".

Many such crimes are committed in the heat of the moment, by a man or a woman overcome by frustration, jealousy, revenge, a sudden spurt of anger—actions in general unlikely to be repeated. Others are the result of insanity or mental defection. Yet others are cold-blooded and deliberate killings undertaken to satisfy individual greed, or done in the furtherance of an organized crime. Against the latter in particular 'society' has a right, a duty, in fact an urgent need, to protect itself if it wishes to survive. And 'society' is no more, and no less, than all of us, and our children, and their children to come.

Ultimately it all depends on 'us'. The rule of law, slowly and painfully developed through the centuries (and of course still developing) is, with all its imperfections, all we have to hold together the frail fabric of our hard-won civilization. If we disdain it, if we try to bend it for our own private purposes, if—doubtless with the best of warm-hearted intentions—we attempt to draw its teeth, we have surely only ourselves to blame if the whole pattern disintegrates.

Three cardinal points stand out. The rule of law demands our

* *Occupied with Crime* (Harrap, 1967).

respect, our co-operation, our realization of its value to all of us, even when it inconveniences us personally or when some anomaly becomes glaringly apparent.

The consequences of flouting it need to be sufficiently unpleasant to discourage those who would consider doing so for their own advantage.

Last, and perhaps above all, those "ordinary and imperfect human beings" whom 'society' pays—far from munificently—to undertake the dirty work of protecting it, must be accorded the support, the encouragement and the appreciation due to them in the performance of an arduous and often thankless job.

SELECT BIBLIOGRAPHY

ADAM, HARGRAVE LEE. *Murder by Persons Unknown* (Collins, 1931)
—— *Murder Most Mysterious* (Sampson, Low, 1932)
ADAMSON, IAIN. *The Great Detective* (Muller, 1966)
Annual Register
BAILEY, GUY. *The Fatal Chance* (Peter Davies, 1969)
BIRMINGHAM, G. A. *Murder Most Foul* (Chatto & Windus, 1929)
BLOM-COOPER, LOUIS. *The A6 Murder* (Penguin Books, 1963)
BRIDGES, YSEULT. *Saint—with Red Hands?* (Arrow, 1958)
BROCK, ALAN. *A Casebook of Crime* (Rockliff, 1948)
BROPHY, JOHN. *The Meaning of Murder* (Corgi, 1967)
BROWNE, DOUGLAS G. *Sir Travers Humphreys* (Harrap, 1960)
BROWNE, D. G., and TULLETT, E. V. *Bernard Spilsbury, His Life and Cases* (Harrap, 1951)
CAPON, PAUL. *The Great Yarmouth Mystery* (Harrap, 1965)
CASSWELL, J. D. *A Lance for Liberty* (Harrap, 1961)
CHERRILL, EX-SUPT. FREDERICK. *Cherrill of the Yard* (Harrap, 1954)
DEANS, F. STORREY. *Notable Trials, Difficult Cases* (Chapman & Hall, 1932)
DEELEY, P., and WALKER, C. *Murder in the 4th Estate* (Gollancz, 1971)
Famous Trials Series (Geoffrey Bles)
FAY, E. S. *The Life of Mr Justice Swift* (Methuen, 1939)
FIRMIN, STANLEY. *Murderers in our Midst* (Hutchington, 1955)
FOOT, PAUL. *Who Killed Hanratty?* (Cape, 1971)
FRANKLIN, CHARLES. *Woman in the Case* (Corgi, 1964)
FRERE, BARTLE H. T. *Amy Robsart of Wymondham* (Jarrolds, 1937)
FURNEAUX, RUPERT. *Famous Criminal Cases*, 7 volumes (1954–62)
GRATUS, JACK. *The Victims* (Hutchinson, 1969)
Great Unsolved Crimes (Hutchingson, nd)
HASTINGS, MACDONALD. *The Other Mr Churchill* (Harrap, 1963)
HAWKES, HARRY. *Murder on the A34* (John Long, 1970)
HUGGETT, R., and BERRY, P. *Daughters of Cain* (Pan Books, 1961)
HUMPHREYS, CHRISTMAS. *Seven Murderers* (Heinemann, 1941)
HUMPHREYS, SIR TRAVERS. *A Book of Trials* (Heinemann, 1953)
HUSSEY, ROBERT F. *Murderer Scot-free* (David & Charles, 1972)
JACOBS, T. C. H. *Aspects of Murder* (Stanley Paul, 1956)
—— *Cavalcade of Murder* (Stanley Paul, 1955)
—— *Pageant of Murder* (Stanley Paul, 1956)

JESSE, F. TENNYSON *Comments on Cain* (Heinemann, 1948)
JOHNSON, PAMELA HANSFORD. *On Iniquity* (Macmillan, 1967)
JONES, EX-DET. CHIEF SUPT. W. *My Own Case* (Angley Books, 1966)
KEETON, GEORGE W. *Guilty but Insane* (Macdonald, 1961)
KNOWLES, LEONARD. *Court of Drama* (John Long, 1966)
LAMBERT, R. S. *The Innocence of Edward Galley* (Newnes, 1936)
LEFEBURE, MOLLY. *Evidence for the Crown* (Heinemann, 1955)
LUSTGARTEN, EDGAR. *Verdict in Dispute* (Wingate, 1949)
MCCORMICK, DONALD. *Murder by Witchcraft* (Arrow, 1969)
—— *The Red Barn Mystery* (John Long, 1967)
MCKNIGHT, GERALD. *The Murder Squad* (W. H. Allen, 1967)
MARCHBANKS, DAVID. *The Moor Murderers* (Leslie Frewin, 1966)
MARJORIBANKS, EDWARD. *The Life of Sir Edward Marshall Hall* (Gollancz, 1929)
NARBOROUGH, EX-SUPT. FRED. *Murder on my Mind* (Wingate, 1959)
Newgate Calendar, The
Notable British Trials Series (Hodge)
PARRIS, JOHN. *Most of my Murders* (Muller, 1960)
PELHAM, CAMDEN. *Chronicles of Crime* (London, 1841)
POTTER, J. D. *The Monsters of the Moors* (Elek, 1966)
ROWLAND, JOHN. *Murder Mistaken* (John Long, 1963)
—— *The Peasenhall Mystery* (John Long, 1962)
RUSSELL OF LIVERPOOL, LORD. *Deadman's Hill—Was Hanratty Guilty?* (Secker & Warburg, 1965)
SERENY, GITTA. *The Case of Mary Bell* (Eyre Methuen, 1972)
SHARPE, F. D. *Sharpe of the Flying Squad* (John Long, 1938)
SHEW, E. SPENCER. *A Companion to Murder* (Cassell, 1960)
—— *A Second Companion to Murder* (Cassell, 1961)
SIDNEY, PHILIP. *Who Killed Amy Robsart?* (Elliot Stock, 1901)
SMITH-HUGHES, JACK. *Nine Verdicts on Violence* (Cassell, 1956)
THOMPSON, C. J. S. *Poison Mysteries Unsolved* (Hutchinson, 1937)
TRAINI, ROBERT. *Murder for Sex* (Kimber, 1960)
WAKEFIELD, H. R. *The Green Bicycle Case* (Philip Allan, 1930)
WALBROOK, H. M. *Murders and Murder Trials, 1812–1912* (Constable, 1932)
WHITTINGDON-EGAN, RICHARD. *The Ordeal of Philip Yale Drew* (Harrap, 1972)
WILD, ROLAND. *Crimes and Cases of 1933* (Rich & Cowan, 1934)
WILSON, COLIN. *A Casebook of Murder* (Mayflower, 1971)
—— *Order of Assassins* (Rupert Hart-Davis, 1972)
—— and PITMAN, PATRICIA. *Encyclopedia of Murder* (Barker, 1961)
WILSON, PATRICK. *Murderess* (Michael Joseph, 1971)
WYNDHAM-BROWN, W. F. *The Trial of William Herbert Wallace* (Gollancz, 1933)

Index